Learning from World Class Companies

Edited by
Rosalie L. Tung

THOMSON

LEARNING Australia • Canada • Mexico • Singapore • Spain • United Kingdom • United States

Learning from World Class Companies

Copyright © Rosalie L. Tung, 2001

The Thomson Learning logo is a registered trademark used herein under licence.

For more information, contact Thomson Learning, Berkshire House, 168–173 High Holborn, London, WC1V 7AA or visit us on the World Wide Web at: http://www.thomsonlearning.co.uk

British Library Cataloguing-in-Publication Data
A catalogue record for this book is available from the British Library

ISBN 1–86152–609–1

First edition published Thomson Learning 2001

Typeset by Saxon Graphics Ltd, Derby
Printed in the UK by T.J. International

In memory of my mother who taught me well

Contents

Acknowledgements

The publishers would like to thank the copyright holders for granting permissions to use copyright material. A notice of permissions and copyright is credited to each article.

Every effort has been made to trace copyright holders of material reproduced in this book. Any rights not acknowledged here will be acknowledged in subsequent printings if notice is given to the publisher.

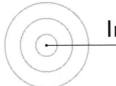

Introduction

To survive and indeed thrive in a global economy characterized by intense competition, exponential growth in information and rapid technological advances, an organization has to attain the rank of world-class, i.e., it must be able to compete with the best and the brightest anywhere in the world. To become world-class and to maintain this sought after status, the company has to possess superior technology and/or knowledge that sets it apart from its competitors, be able to formulate and implement strategies that will enable it to excel over time, and at the same time be responsive to the needs and demands of its various stakeholders.

The *Handbook of International Business* (1999), which grew out of the soon to be released second edition of the eight-volume *International Encyclopedia of Business and Management* (IEBM, in short), contained the short profiles of thirty-four world-class companies. These profiles were intended to illustrate and highlight the concepts, issues, challenges and opportunities that leading firms have to contend with in the international business arena. While the number of transnational companies that qualify as world-class run into the hundreds, the thirty-four organizations selected for inclusion in the *Handbook* all met one or more of the following criteria: (1) size as measured in terms of assets, annual revenues or number of employees worldwide; (2) global reach; (3) dominance in a given industry worldwide; and (4) significant contributions to the industry, including technological innovations and/or best management practices/systems.

As with all other lists, there are bound to be omissions due to space constraints. Every attempt, however, has been made to include companies from diverse countries and industries.

To enable practitioners and students of international business to benefit from the experiences and challenges faced by these world-class organizations, this book puts together in a single volume the short profiles of twenty-six of these companies and pairs each with a brief case highlighting a significant recent development in that organization. These brief cases are taken from the popular press and academic journals. As opposed to the lengthy cases developed by some institutions that are more appropriate for use in a 3- to 4-hour class devoted solely to the case method, an instructor can use the short corporate profile and its accompanying case presented in this book for class discussion within a 50- to 60-minute time frame. Thus, this book can be used as an independent or companion text for a variety of courses in strategic management and international business/management.

By focusing on a significant recent development in a company, students can devote their attention to a specific issue or set of issues without having to read a lot of material which may be peripherally related to the topic and thus channel their energies more fruitfully to analysing the situation at hand.

The profile on each international company begins with an overview of the company/group, followed by a brief history, a summary of major innovations and significant contributions, and concludes with an identification of major challenges and opportunities that lie ahead.

The cases selected for inclusion in this book are organized into five parts:

1. Turnaround strategies
2. Japanese multinationals
3. Knowledge management
4. Mergers and acquisitions
5. Corporate social responsibility

Part 1 focuses on the turnaround strategies in fourteen transnational corporations. The cases selected for inclusion show (a) how the chief executives of the respective organizations were able to turn their companies around; (b) how the chief executives plan to turn their firms around in the face of challenges, internal or external; or (c) threats and opportunities facing these established companies.

Part 2 examines the changes that are taking place in Japan and the corporate response at two leading Japanese multinationals in light of these challenges.

Part 3 revolves around knowledge management, the currency of the new economy. The cases selected for inclusion in this section highlight the important role knowledge management can play in helping firms gain a competitive advantage.

A distinguishing feature of the last two decades of the twentieth century was mergers and acquisitions. Part 4 looks at the impact such mergers and acquisitions have on three transnational corporations.

The final section, Part 5, is directed to corporate social responsibility. Besides profit maximization, stakeholders increasingly demand that global corporations undertake actions and activities that are socially responsible. In some cases, stakeholders even require that corporations redress misdeeds of the past.

I would like to thank all those who have contributed in different ways to the successful completion of this volume. Specifically, I would like to acknowledge the assistance of my co-author on the corporate profiles, Mohi Ahmed. I also want to applaud Professor Malcolm Warner and others who have the vision to embark on the IEBM project. As usual, I would also like to thank my husband, Byron, and daughter, Michele, for their understanding of why I spent weekdays, weeknights and weekends sifting through endless journals and magazines in search of the most appropriate articles for inclusion in this volume.

Rosalie L. Tung, Ph.D., FRSC
October 2000

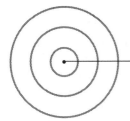

Part I
Turnaround Strategies

Sun Tzu (also spelt as Sun Zi), the legendary Chinese military strategist who lived some 2,500 years ago, summed up the importance of strategies to attaining a desired outcome as follows: 'To win one hundred victories in one hundred battles is not the acme of skill. To subdue the enemy without fighting (i.e., to use strategy) is the supreme excellence.' Sun Tzu's principles of warfare have influenced military leaders and business executives around the world down the ages.

The thirteen entries in this section examines the strategies adopted or planned at fourteen international companies to enable their companies to attain, retain or regain the rank of world-class. Since strategic vision is often attributed to an organization's CEO, in several of these entries, the cases focus on the strategies allegedly crafted by the leaders of these companies. The cases in this section also highlight that even though some strategies may be very effective in an earlier period of time, it may prove dysfunctional in light of changed environmental conditions. Hence the need for companies, even the most successful ones, to constantly re-evaluate their strategies in order to stay ahead.

The first entry focuses on General Electric (GE) and Jack Welch. Much of GE's successes could be attributed to Jack Welch who assumed leadership of the company in 1980. Jack Welch is credited with turning GE's lacklustre performance in 1980 (with market capitalization of $14 billion) to its current status as the one of the most admired and profitable companies in the world (with market capitalization of $40 billion). Welch plans to step down from the helm of GE when he turns 65 in April 2001 not because of age but to practise what he preaches, i.e., the need for organizations to renew themselves every now and then. Since he has occupied GE's top post for over two decades, Welch believes that it is time for someone else to step in with new perspectives. In end October, 2000, just months before his scheduled retirement, Welch stunned the business world by finessing the biggest acquisition in GE's 108-year history by purchasing Honeywell International for $45 billion. Welch will stay on till end 2001 to see the transaction through. Of course, it remains to be seen what strategic direction Welch's successor Jeffrey R. Immelt would take and whether he/she could enable GE to remain at the top.

The second entry examines how American Express, a long-time leader in the travel and financial businesses, seeks to maintain this competitive edge through initiatives in e-commerce and addressing the tastes of the younger generation of consumers.

While the demise of Caterpillar, the earth-moving equipment giant, has been penned by some in the 1980s when it encountered serious challenges from Komatsu, a Japanese competitor, Caterpillar was able to engineer a strategic turnaround. The third entry in this section seeks to examine whether Glen Barton, Caterpillar's CEO, could once again turn the company around in light of the latest challenges confronting the company.

Despite the fact that Coca-Cola remains the most valuable brand in the world at an estimated $72.5 billion (*The Economist*, 15–21 July pp.26–7 2000), the company is facing slow growth and declining profits. The fourth entry speculates that Douglas Daft, an Australian national and considered by many as an 'outsider' in a company steeped in tradition, is perhaps the ideal person to shake up the company, a symbol of US cultural dominance around the world.

The fifth entry looks at how consumer products' giant, Unilever, seeks to remain competitive through a drastic reduction of its 1,600 brands to 400 (*The Economist*, 26 February 2000), become more consumer-oriented, and adopt stratified marketing strategies throughout the globe.

The next case outlines the change in strategic orientation at Procter & Gamble (P&G), another leader in consumer products, from one of marketing to that of innovation. Superior marketing has traditionally been key to success for companies specializing in consumer products. It has been said, for example, that shampoo is nothing more than detergent, water and advertising. Effective marketing can often stimulate demand for a certain brand of shampoo and make consumers willing to spend more money on purchasing a particular brand. So P&G's decision to emphasize innovation makes for interesting study. The case studies of the two consumer products' giants (Unilever and P&G) can be used in conjunction to compare and contrast how two leaders in related industries seek to grow their respective companies.

The seventh entry examines how IBM, who has exhorted its customers to enter e-business, is taking the plunge itself. To survive and prosper in the new economy, virtually all companies have to contend with the e-business challenge.

The next entry continues along the same theme by highlighting the challenges created by technological innovations on the imaging industry giant, Kodak. To maintain its world-class rank, Kodak has to successfully bridge the old and new worlds of photography.

The ninth entry shows how the financial crises that erupted in Asia in 1997 had exposed the weaknesses inherent at Gillette which until then was 'a fat, happy company'. As the Chinese characters for 'crises' are made up of the two words 'danger, opportunity', if Gillette could take advantage of this crude awakening (danger) to create an opportunity for restructuring the underlying weaknesses in the organization, it could emerge from the situation a sounder and stronger company.

The tenth case, 'Eisner's mouse trap', highlights the troubles confronting Michael Eisner, the head of Disney. Less than a decade ago, Eisner was one of the most admired corporate executives in the United States and indeed around the world. Now, he has to contend with declining earnings. The case illustrates how strengths which were once admired in Eisner have now been cited as sources of Disney's weaknesses and problems.

The eleventh case examines the strategies at two aerospace industry giants, Boeing and Airbus. The European governments' sponsored aerospace consortium, Airbus, which was a money losing venture for many years, has turned the corner and has become a serious threat to Boeing's dominance in the industry. What must Boeing do to avert further problems?

The next case focuses on how AT&T continues to face growing challenges in the fast-changing world of telecommunications and growing competition both at home and abroad. In end October, 2000, ATT announced plans to split the company into four separate entities: broadband applications, wireless, consumer services, and business services. This move marks a complete reversal of its strategy of buying small companies over the three preceding years.

The final case in this section profiles the strategies that Christopher Galvin, grandson of the founder of Motorola, has taken to turn his company around from the near disaster in 1998. In that year, Nokia, a Finnish company which was relatively unknown outside of its home country until fairly recently, became the largest manufacturer of mobile phones in the world. Whether Motorola can continue to stay ahead of its competitors – Canadian-based Nortel, Finnish-based Nokia, and Swedish-based Ericsson – remains to be seen.

Company Profile 1
General Electric Company
(GE)

Company overview

General Electric (GE) is one of the world's largest diversified manufacturing, technology and services companies, with revenues of more than $79 billion (1996). The company operates in over 100 countries around the world, including 250 manufacturing plants in twenty-six different countries, and employs about 239,000 people worldwide. The company's major products and services include aircraft engines, appliances, capital services, electrical distribution and control, information services, lighting, medical systems, industrial control systems, broadcasting and communications services, plastics, power systems, transportation systems and support operations (including GE supply, investments and corporate R&D Center). The company has its corporate headquarters in Fairfield, Connecticut.

Brief history

In 1892, as a result of a merger of the Edison General Electric Company and the Thomas–Houston Electric Company, General Electric Company was established in New York. In 1895 GE built the world's largest electric locomotives (90 tons) and transformers (800 kw), and GE controlled 97 per cent of the lamp business in the United States in 1905. In 1919 GE organized the Radio Corporation of America (RCA). In 1932 RCA became an independent company, but it was re-acquired by GE in 1986.

During the early 1940s, to meet wartime needs, GE manufactured and tested the first US jet engines and 400 plastic aircraft parts. In 1946 it began to study power generation from nuclear energy. From the 1950s to the 1970s GE expanded the range of its products and services. The range covers automatic washing machines; the world's first jet engine, with which an aircraft can fly at twice the speed of sound; earth-oriented meteorological satellites, which can supply scientific data on atmospheric and environmental conditions; computer tomography (CT) scanners; and the world's largest nuclear power plant.

In 1919 International General Electric Company was formed, but foreign revenue accounted for only 10 per cent of its total revenues in 1953. In 1970 international revenue accounted for only 16 per cent of GE's total revenues, and the company had more than 100,000 employees outside the US. At that time the company had 129 affiliated companies, manufacturing products in twenty-three countries and serving markets in 150 countries through 350 distributors. Since the mid-1980s GE has increased the number of joint ventures with foreign firms to gain technical and/or marketing advantages around the world. In 1996 GE had 250 manufacturing plants and employed 131,000 people outside the US; it derived 40 per cent of its revenue from abroad.

Innovation and significant contributions

Prior to the merger of Thomas–Houston and Edison Electric Light Company to establish GE, Thomas A. Edison's vision was to establish a company that would light a nation by producing all components of electrical power stations and electric lamps. Since the beginning, the company had the vision of making continuous innovations. GE established a research laboratory in 1900, the first industrial R&D lab in the United States. Its corporate R&D Center is currently one of the world's largest and most diversified industrial laboratories, providing international trade support, market development, licensing and investment information to GE's various businesses around the world.

GE's contribution goes far beyond the innovation of new products and services – its business management concepts are well recognized around the world. At the company's Management Development Institute at Crotonville, New York – dubbed 'the Harvard of corporate America' – GE executives engage in a continuous debate on the management issues confronting the company in a changing business environment. GE was the first company to establish such an institute, in 1956. GE's CEO John F. Welch, Jr (Jack Welch), has established several examples of best practice in managing an organization in a changing global business environment. Welch pioneered the #1 or #2 strategy of 'fix/close/sell'. According to Tichy and Sherman (1993), 'Jack Welch divided GE businesses which met the requirements of being #1 or #2 globally into three strategic circles: core manufacturing; technology-intensive, and services, and any businesses outside these circles would have to be made more competitive or be closed or sold.' 'The human engine', 'shared values', 'boundaryless organization', 'reward systems' and 'walk the talk' are other significant business/management concepts that have been pioneered by GE and which have been emulated by companies around the world. In end October, 2000, just months before Welch's planned retirement, he engineered GE's acquisition of Honeywell International for $45 billion, outbidding rival suitor United Technologies Corporation. This is the largest acquisition in GE's 108-year history. Welch plans to postpone his retirement to complete the acquisition. GE has been selected by *Fortune* magazine as one of the ten most admired companies in the US and is the third most profitable company in the world, after Royal Dutch/Shell and Exxon.

Challenges and opportunities

Most of GE's products and services are known worldwide. The company competes with Siemens, Hitachi and ABB (Asea Brown Boveri) around the globe. The company seeks to expand its market share in India, China, Mexico and other emerging markets in the Asia-Pacific region. To meet the challenges of increasing business opportunities around the world, GE has focused on different products and services for each country to meet local demands. For example, GE focuses on jet engines and capital in China, medical systems in India and power systems in Mexico.

ROSALIE L. TUNG AND MOHI AHMED
SIMON FRASER UNIVERSITY

Further reading

(References cited in the text marked *)

Burton, J. (1997) 'The stars that make Jack shine', *Chief Executive*, September: 24–31. (Profiles twelve GE executives, including its CEO, Jack Welch.)

Curran, J. (1997) 'GE Capital: Jack Welch's secret weapon', *Fortune* 136(9), 10 November: 116–34. (Tells the inside story of GE Capital and its contribution to the success of GE.)

Fisher, A. (1997) 'The world's most admired companies', *Fortune* 136(8), 27 October: 220–8. (Gives an overview of several world-class companies.)

Hoover, G., Campbell, A. and Spain, P.J. (eds) (1995) 'General Electric Company', *Hoover's Handbook of American Business*, Austin: The Reference Press, Inc. (Gives a general overview of the company.)

Nash, J.C. (1989) *From Tank Town to High Tech: The Clash of Community and Industrial Cycles*, New York: State University of New York Press. (Provides a historical background of GE, with a special focus on the company's linkage to American society at large.)

Slater, R. (1993) *The New GE: How Jack Welch Revived an American Institution*, Homewood, IL: Business One Irwin. (An examination of how Jack Welch brought significant change to GE and created the new GE.)

Smart, T., Engardio, P. and Smith, G. (1993) 'GE's brave new world: Welch sees the future, it's China, India, Mexico', *Business Week*, 8 November: 64–70. (Outlines GE's efforts in expanding its businesses in the emerging marketplace.)

Stewart, T.A. (1998) 'America's most admired companies', *Fortune*, 2 March: 70–82.

* Tichy, N.M. and Sherman, S. (1993) *Control Your Destiny or Someone Else Will: How Jack Welch is Making General Electric the World's Most Competitive Corporation*, New York: Currency Doubleday. (Tells the inside story of the transformation of GE and gives the views of the company's CEO, Jack Welch.)

Further resources

GE website
http://www.ge.com

The ultimate manager

Fortune; New York; 22 November 1999; Geoffrey Colvin

Abstract:

In a time of hidebound, formulaic thinking, General Electric's CEO Jack Welch gave power to the worker and the shareholder. He built one heck of a company in the process. Welch transformed GE and multiplied its value beyond anyone's expectations: from a market capitalization of $14 billion to more than $400 billion today. Welch wins the title of manager of the century because in addition to his transformation of GE, he has made himself far and away the most influential manager of his generation. Welch has enriched not only GE's shareholders but also the shareholders of companies around the globe. His total economic impact is impossible to calculate but must be a staggering multiple of his GE performance.

"I want a revolution," Jack Welch told another General Electric executive just after the company revealed Welch would be its next CEO. He got what he wanted soon enough. Looking back from our high-tech, information-driven era, it may seem surprising that the chief of one of America's biggest, oldest companies emerged as the leading management revolutionary of the century. But it shouldn't be.

To see why Welch wanted – needed – a revolution, you have to remember the sorry state of the world when this driven, intense 45-year-old got his job: On the December day in 1980 when GE announced his promotion, the prime rate rose to 21.5%; the economy was coming out of one recession and was about to drop into another; and the Dow was at 937, a level it had first reached 15 years earlier. Stocks had just come through their worst decade since the '30s.

As for GE, its stock had done terribly. Adjusted for the merciless inflation of the time, it had lost half its value over the previous ten years. And this was considered an outstanding performance! As Welch settled into his new office at headquarters in Fairfield, Conn., FORTUNE published the results of a survey of the FORTUNE 500 CEOs. Who was the best CEO among them? Reg Jones, Welch's predecessor, his peers agreed by a wide margin. What was the best-managed company in the 500? Another landslide: GE.

Yet Welch proposed to blow up this paragon – its portfolio of businesses, its bureaucracy, many of its practices and traditions, its very culture. And though he acted with what seemed at the time like blitzkrieg aggressiveness, he regretted in later years that he hadn't moved even faster. Having been handed one of the treasures of American enterprise, he said, he was "afraid of breaking it."

Not only did Welch not break it, but he transformed it as well and multiplied its value beyond anyone's expectations: from a market capitalization of $14 billion to more than £400 billion today. GE is the second-most-valuable company on earth, behind Microsoft, and at times during the past few years has been No. 1.

That record is stunning but in itself may not be enough to make someone manager of the century. Welch wins the title because in addition to his transformation of GE, he has made himself far and away the most influential manager of his generation. (Indeed, his only competition would be Alfred P. Sloan, General Motors' chief from 1923 to 1946, who's in the running for a still higher honor; see "The Businessman of the Century.") As the most widely admired, studied, and imitated CEO of his time, Welch has enriched not only GE's shareholders but also the shareholders of companies around the globe, His total economic impact is impossible to calculate but must be a staggering multiple of his GE performance.

What Welch did is so sweeping that it begs for some kind of unifying idea. Think of it this way: He got his job at the moment when the ideas that governed late-19th and early-20th century business had finally lost their purchase, when an old world was giving way to a new one. That old world was based on manufacturing – made efficient through scientific management – and workers were programmed accordingly, with detailed procedures, manuals, hierarchies. This approach had met the century's first great business challenge in successfully controlling the massive new organizations that were multiplying globally. And through the military it had done even more: It had won World War II. Who could say it nay?

But by 1980 the central premise of Taylorism – that most workers did physical work – was long since invalid, and evidence was overwhelming that the old world was falling apart. A decade of stock market stagnation was screaming to CEOs that management was failing, though hardly anyone wanted to admit it. (Instead, conventional wisdom held that the stock market was "broken.") Total employees of the FORTUNE 500 had just peaked and would never again reach the level of 1979 (about 16 million), but few recognized the symptoms of corporate bloat. The economies of Germany and Japan, finally rebuilt from near-total destruction in the war, were threatening American markets and signaling the onset of global competition, but U.S. corporations like Xerox and the

carmakers dismissed the danger. A 1980 NBC documentary on quality guru W. Edwards Deming called "If Japan Can Do It, My Can't We?" brutally demonstrated the poor quality of U.S. products and processes, yet Deming was then virtually unknown in the U.S. The personal computer had just appeared, but IBM still wasn't interested.

Welch was hardly the first person to see the new world coming. His great achievement is that having seen it, he faced up to the huge, painful changes it demanded, and made them faster and more emphatically than anyone else in business. He led managers into this new world, which we still inhabit, and just as important, he showed business people everywhere a method of attacking change of any kind.

He began at the beginning, by changing GE's goal. The company was so big – then as now, sales equalled about 1% of America's GDP – that most people considered it a proxy for the economy as a whole, rising and falling by forces beyond its control. GE's ambition had long been simply to grow faster than the economy, an objective with at least two problems. First, it was hardly inspiring: If the economy was growing 2%, you could grow GE 2.2% and claim success – but no one would care. And second, it was wrongheaded: Shareholders pay managers to make their company not bigger but more valuable; over the previous decade, GE had grown steadily but wasn't worth any more than it had been in 1972.

Welch gave GE a new mission: to be the world's most valuable company. This profound shift in focus not only reoriented the company but also was so audacious – GE was then No. 10 – that it could actually stir people. As the centerpiece of his new plan, Welch declared that every GE business must be No. 1 or No. 2 in its industry, another radical change in self-assessment, and he reportedly wasn't crazy about any of them being No. 2.

As employees puzzled over what this might mean for them – many, used to decades of bureaucracy, figured it wouldn't mean much – Welch cleared the decks for transformation. He blenderized GE's portfolio of businesses, in his first two years getting into 118 new businesses, joint ventures, or acquisitions while selling 71 businesses. The theme was to make GE more of a service company and to get out of businesses in which the company had no competitive advantage. The biggest divestiture symbolically was Utah International, an Australian coal outfit that had been Reg Jones' largest acquisition. Under Welch, GE was not going to sell commodities.

He simultaneously dealt with other irritants and distractions. Corporate strategic planners were one of the most misguided fads of the 1970s, and Welch saw that effective planning had to come from the individual businesses – so he decimated the planning staff. Big-deal CEOs like him were also expected to spend lots of time in Washington as virtual statesmen of business; Welch refused. And startlingly for a man in his position, he declined all invitations to sit on other corporate boards, reasoning that he had a full-time job already.

Now Welch could concentrate on reforming the innards of GE, the practices and culture that determine day by day how the company performs. Too numerous to count, these changes were virtually all expressions of one big notion: that GE's competitive edge would come from individuals and ideas. That sounds soft and mushy and commonplace, but in fact it can legitimately be called epochal.

In the business world that Welch saw ending, a company's competitive advantage came from headquarters. GE had elevated this belief higher than any other company with its famous blue books, the five thick volumes of guidance for every GE manager. They were indeed an awesome achievement, written by America's best business thinkers, including Peter Drucker, but to a GE manager their message was clear and dispiriting: You don't have to think; the thinking has been done for you, by people who are probably smarter than you.

Welch burned the blue books. His message to GE's managers, preached since day one with remarkable consistency, is, You own these businesses. Take charge of them. Get headquarters out of your hair. Fight the bureaucracy. Hate it. Kick it. Break it.

If employees were surprised by the vehemence of the words, they were more surprised by the actions that followed. Welch wiped out entire layers of management, including one high-level layer Jones had installed. Eventually he launched the famous workout process, in which employees at all levels of an operation gather for "town meetings" with their bosses and ask questions or make proposals about how the place could run better – 80% of which must get some kind of response then and there. This was a true cultural revolution. As an electrician at a GE aircraft engine plant said to FORTUNE, "When you've been told to shut up for 20 years, and someone tells you to speak up – you're going to let them have it." The multiday workout sessions took huge chunks of wasted money and time out of GE's processes, but their more important effect was to teach people that they had a right to speak up and be taken seriously; those who advanced good ideas were rewarded, as were those who implemented them.

The next natural step was to spread those good ideas across the company. Logical, obvious – but it hadn't been done before. Then a more radical move: borrowing good ideas from other companies. Welch loudly advocated this one to show it was actually okay, and today he'll tell you what GE learned about asset management from Toyota or about quick market intelligence from Wal-Mart. Again, it was an obvious idea but a profound cultural change for GE. You've heard of not-invented-here? GE invented it. Welch killed it.

At least as important as these high-profile changes are his behind-the-scenes people practices, which he says take more of this time than anything else. When a manager meets with Welch, the exchange is candid, not scripted. There will be arguments. There may be shouting. The manager will almost certainly have to stretch his mind and do new thinking on the spot. Afterward Welch will dispatch a highly specific written summary of commitments the manager made, and when Welch follows up later – also in writing – he will refer to the previous summary. He does this with relentless consistency with scores of managers.

Of course managers then see how it's done and replicate the system down through the organization. One result is that all employees at GE are graded annually on a five-level scale and told where they stand. That's more honest than what most companies do, but then comes the really hard part: continually making sure the lowest level, the bottom 10%, move up or get moved out. Cruel? Far from it, says Welch. Falsely telling a manager he's doing fine for 20 years, then firing him at age 53 when he's got two kids in college – "that's the definition of cruelty." GE is just facing reality, says Welch, and of the many precepts he has made famous ("Control your destiny, or someone else will," "Change before you have to," "Be candid with everyone"), the most fundamental and important may be, "Face reality."

Some people are having trouble facing the reality of Welch's retirement, scheduled for Dec. 31, 2000, the date sticklers say is the century's true end. An audience member at the recent FORTUNE Global Forum in Shanghai challenged Welch: "You are 60-some years young. How can you make as great an impact on this world after you retire?" Then, with mock sternness: "What's wrong with you?"

The question drew laughter and an ovation, but Welch had a ready answer: "I'm not retiring because I'm old and tired. I'm retiring because an organization has had 20 years of me. My success will be determined by how well my successor grows it in the next 20 years. I've got a great management team, and they're ready to get the old goat out of there so they can do their thing.

"To be vital, an organization has to repot itself, start again, get new ideas, renew itself. And I shouldn't stay on the board. I should disappear from the company so my successor feels totally free to do whatever he wants to do. Now if I go to another company, I can do that to another company. But there I've done it enough."

Wait. "Go to another company"? What's that about? Welch may be the manager of the century, but apparently that doesn't mean he has to quit when the century does.

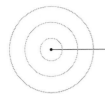

Company Profile 2
American Express Company

Company overview

American Express Company is one of the largest companies providing diversified financial, travel and business services. At present the major businesses of the company range from travel-related services (including credit card, traveller's cheques and travel planning) to financial services (including financial planning, property/casualty insurance and banking services). Established in 1850, the American Express Company now provides services in more than 130 countries and has regional management operations in more than fifteen countries. The company employs about 72,000 people (1997) worldwide and its revenues exceeded $17 billion in 1996. The corporate headquarters of the company is located in New York City.

Brief history

The history of the American Express Company dates back to the 1830s. During that period, along with the growth in population and migration to America's heartland, business expanded around the United States. There was a growing need to move goods faster and more safely over vast distances. At that time the company offered to transport goods with speed and safety, and assumed responsibility for damage and loss. In the early years the company carried all kinds of financial instruments for banks, including cash, securities and gold. Later this became a major part of the company's business. In that era rail was the primary means of transportation and communication for American commerce. In 1950 the American Express Company was formed by a merger of two competitors, Wells & Company and Butterfield, Wasson & Company. Soon thereafter it also merged with yet another competitor, Livingston, Fargo & Company. In the early years, even though the company went through battles in its management after the mergers, the company continued to expand.

In 1918 the US government wanted to nationalize express companies. Through negotiations with the government, however, American Express executives were able to keep the company in the private sector, but the company emerged with only 40 per cent of the stock, at a cost of about $11 million. In late 1918 the company began to expand its business. In the 1940s the company entered into international business. The company introduced the American Express credit card in 1958. The company continued to grow from 1960 through the 1980s and became one of the best-known financial services organizations in the world. As the overall business environment changed significantly in the early

1990s, the company needed an entirely new strategy. According to Peter Grossman, a long-time observer of American Express and its businesses, 'the history of the company was dependent not on structure or theory of management, but on its people.'

Innovation and significant contributions

The American Express Company itself was formed around the concept of service innovation. Since its beginning, the company has introduced innovative services for individual and corporate customers, and made significant contributions to the industry by providing high-quality services and gaining trust. The company seeks to provide the best services to its customers by making them easier to access while maintaining a high level of security. The company has developed several services for its card members, such as membership rewards and special offers. In addition, it has specially designed business services (e.g. small business services, merchant services and corporate purchasing card), individual and corporate travel services, and financial services (e.g., financial advisers, online investment, educational loan programme, etc.). American Express has set the standard in the travel service industry.

Significant advances in information and communication technologies (ICTs) have facilitated the growth of electronic commerce (e-commerce) throughout the world, thus enabling the buying and selling of products and services over the Internet and the World Wide Web. As a result, virtual global shopping has become a reality, enabling people to shop without leaving home. However, security remains a primary concern. American Express has now implemented state-of-the-art security systems such as SSL (Secure Socket Layer) and SET (Secure Electronic Transaction Protocol), developed in conjunction with partners such as Microsoft, IBM, Netscape and GTE.

Challenges and opportunities

Up to the 1980s the American Express Company was more focused on the quality of its services. As customers have become more cost-conscious and value-oriented, competition in the industry has become more intense. In addition, significant developments have been made in ICTs. In response to these developments the company has introduced new services, including the provision of high-quality, secure and timely services in the emerging e-commerce, and integrated marketing. This was done in partnership with other organizations, such as Microsoft, GTE, Hewlett Packard and Mercantec.

ROSALIE L. TUNG AND MOHI AHMED
SIMON FRASER UNIVERSITY

Further reading

Friedman, J. and Meehan, J. (1992) *House of Cards: Inside the Troubled Empire of American Express*, New York: G.P. Putnam's Sons. (Introduces the historical background and challenges of American Express.)

Grossman, P.Z. (1987) *American Express: The Unofficial History of the People Who Built the Great Financial Empire*, New York: Crown Publishers Inc. (Profiles the history of the company and people who contributed to building American Express.)

Hoover, G., Campbell, A. and Spain, P.J. (eds) (1995) 'American Express Company', *Hoover's Handbook of American Business*, Austin: The Reference Press Inc. (Gives a general overview of the company.)

Murphy, I.P. (1997) 'Amex looks beyond satisfaction, sees growth', *Marketing News* 31(10), 12 May 12: 6, 22. (Discusses customer satisfaction research and quality-control strategies at American Express (Amex).)

Nathans, L. and Landler, M. (1992) 'Less-than-fantastic plastic', *Business Week*, 9 November: 100–1. (Identifies challenges facing Amex.)

Nishimoto, L. (1996) 'American Express, Microsoft team up for travel', *InfoWorld* 18(32), 5 August: 40. (Discusses partnership between Microsoft and American Express.)

Further resources

American Express website
http://www.americanexpress.com

Plastic surgery at AmEx

Newsweek; New York; 4 October 1999; Adam Bryant

Abstract:

American Express recently rolled out a new high-tech face on their credit cards. This is the company's biggest product launch since Optima in 1994.

For years, credit cards were like Boy Scout badges that signaled the owner's financial status. But in an age when just about anybody can get a gold or platinum card, they no longer impress. So American Express has decided to try out a new color of money with its Blue credit card, its biggest product launch since Optima in 1994.

The card's biggest attraction is an initial teaser rate of zero percent for the six months. But AmEx is also hoping to win over the tech set with an "electronic wallet" feature that automatically fills in purchase forms at Web sites, sparing Internet shoppers from repeatedly filling in their addresses, credit-card numbers and the like. (That information is stored in AmEx's computers, and transmitted to e-commerce sites with a click of the mouse.) The Blue card also has a "smartchip" that adds another level of security. With a card reader that plugs into a PC (AmEx is giving away the hardware for several months), consumers will have to have the actual card and PIN to place online orders, thereby minimizing whatever worries they might have about online thievery of card data. More applications are in the works. "It's really kind of a novelty, but it does project a cutting-edge image," said Robert B. McKinley, CEO of CardWeb, an online newsletter.

It's an image that American Express needs to cultivate as it tries to court younger customers, many of whom view AmEx as the card used to help buy their father's Oldsmobile. The company has started regaining lost market share in recent years, in part by offering a slew of cards with rewards, such as Delta frequent-flier miles. Because consumers now view cards largely as commodities, the business has grown increasingly competitive. Visa and MasterCard are expected to come out with their own smart cards soon. "This lays the groundwork for the next battle," McKinley added.

American Express is spending heavily to make people want to spend heavily with its Blue card. The marketing campaign – $45 million by some estimates – includes everything from advertising on popcorn bags at movie theaters (its target customers like movies) to giving out water bottles with Blue advertising (its target customers also are into working out). The advertising copywriters have also been busy, turning phrases such as "Y3K compliant" and "Evolving Credit" to be used as marketing taglines. Earlier this month Blue from American Express sponsored a free concert in New York's Central Park featuring Sheryl Crow.

Why the color blue? American Express says it evokes a sense of excitement about the future. Remarkably, others share the opinion. Young & Rubicam's Brand Futures Group has deemed blue the color of the new millennium. Y&R's research found that a lot of people link blue with the future because they associate it with sky and water, "providing a sense of limitlessness and peace." Too bad the monthly charge statements don't inspire the same emotions.

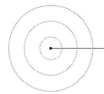

Company Profile 3
Caterpillar Inc.

Company overview

Caterpillar Inc. is one of the world's largest manufacturers of construction and mining equipment, natural gas engines and industrial gas turbines, and is a leading global supplier of diesel engines. Its major businesses include construction, mining and agricultural machinery, engines and financial services. The company's revenues exceeded $16 billion in 1996. With a network of 192 dealers, the company supplies its products and services to customers in nearly 200 countries and employs around 57,026 people worldwide (1996). The corporate headquarters of Caterpillar Inc. is located in Peoria, Illinois.

Brief history

The history of Caterpillar dates back to the late nineteenth century, when Daniel Best and Benjamin Holt tried to make steam tractors for framing. Prior to establishing Caterpillar in 1925, Best and Holt pioneered track-type tractors and petrol-powered tractor engines. After that they continued to make innovations in energy-efficient tractors. In 1931 the first Diesel Sixty Tractor was manufactured, and the company continued to expand its product line to include motor graders, blade graders, elevating graders, terracers and electric generator sets.

During World War II there was an increased demand for track-type tractors, motor graders, generator sets and a special engine for the M4 tanks. In 1950 the company established Caterpillar Tractor Co. Ltd in Great Britain. This was the company's first operation abroad and helped the company gain useful knowledge in managing foreign exchange, tariffs and import controls, and in providing better customer services around the world. The company continued to establish more manufacturing plants in strategic regions around the world, such as Great Britain, Belgium, Germany, Brazil and Australia. In 1963 Caterpillar and Mitsubishi Heavy Industries Ltd formed one of the first joint ventures, Caterpillar Mitsubishi Ltd, in Japan and two years later began manufacturing in their new plant in the Tokyo area. The joint venture was renamed Shin Caterpillar Mitsubishi Ltd in 1987, and became one of the most enduring and successful US–Japanese joint ventures.

Since the 1970s Caterpillar has continued to introduce a broad range of new products, and in 1981 the company established Caterpillar Financial Services Corporation to provide financing options to its customers around the world. In 1989 Caterpillar also established a Building Construction Products Division to serve its customers in the construction industry, and continued to improve its management and expand around the globe. Caterpillar currently has thirty-two manufacturing plants in the United States and a total of twenty-nine in Australia, Belgium, Brazil, China, France, Germany, Hungary, India, Indonesia, Italy, Japan, Mexico, Poland, Russia and the United Kingdom.

Caterpillar's growth between 1950 and 1980 can be attributed in large part to investments in infrastructure around the world. In 1981 the company reported its highest sales and profits ever. However, shortly after this record performance things began to unravel. Part of the problem was a 'sense of invulnerability . . . that sometimes bordered on arrogance' stemming from its 'virtually unchallenged success' in more than half a century. Management was overcentralized in corporate head offices which had an ethnocentric outlook (Bartlett and Ehrlich 1989).

This situation was further exacerbated by two major developments in the early 1980s. In 1982, during the global recession, the US dollar was close to its all-time high. This made US products very expensive in the global marketplace. Furthermore, Caterpillar had to contend with a 205-day strike by members of the United Auto Workers (UAW). Komatsu, a Japanese competitor, took advantage of the situation, rapidly expanding its share of the world market to 25 per cent by 1984, double its share six years earlier. Caterpillar responded successfully to Komatsu's challenge by closing plants, downsizing, sourcing for parts and components from around the world, and reducing inventory. Through massive restructuring, the company was able to accomplish a strategic turnaround, so much so that in the early 1990s Komatsu, which had posed such a formidable challenge to Caterpillar just a few years earlier, announced that it was quitting the earth-moving equipment market altogether.

Innovation and significant contributions

Caterpillar's continuous efforts in product and service innovation have made significant contributions to the industrial equipment industry throughout the world. Caterpillar construction machines are now used in building, maintaining and rebuilding much of the world's infrastructure – highways, dams, airports and commercial buildings. Caterpillar machines were used to build the Hoover Dam and the Chunnel under the English Channel, to put out fires in the oil fields of Kuwait and to tear down the Berlin Wall.

The company's famous brand engines are used to power ships and boats, locomotives, highway trucks, and construction, mining and agricultural machines. The engines are also used in offshore drilling rigs and huge mines in remote mountain ranges. Their engines are also used to supply power to hospitals, factories, airports and office buildings in case of emergencies. The company's financial services provide assistance to customers worldwide to buy its products. In addition, Caterpillar Insurance Services Inc. offers insurance coverage to its customers and dealers throughout the world.

Challenges and opportunities

The major challenges confronting Caterpillar are to make continuous innovations; to design, manufacture and supply quality products to its customers around the world; and to sustain growth in a slowing global market. The company seeks to build closer relationships with its customers worldwide so as to provide better products and services.

ROSALIE L. TUNG AND MOHI AHMED
SIMON FRASER UNIVERSITY

Further reading

(References cited in the text marked *)

* Bartlett, C.A. and Ehrlich, S. (1989) *Caterpillar Inc.: George Schaefer Takes Charge*, Boston, MA: Harvard Business School.

Elstrom, P. (1997) 'This cat keeps on purring: despite labor woes, Caterpillar's plans are paying off', *Business Week*, 20 January: 82–4. (Discusses product development at Caterpillar.)

Eric, S. (1994) 'Working to delight the internal customer', *Work Study* 43(6), September–October: 27–9. (Examines departmental support teams and their activities.)

Fites, D.V. (1996) 'Make your dealers your partners', *Harvard Business Review* 74(2), March–April: 84–90. (Examines Caterpillar's relationship with its dealers.)

Hendricks, J.A., Defreitas, D.G. and Walker, D.K. (1996) 'Changing performance measures at Caterpillar', *Management Accounting* 78(6), December: 18–24. (Discusses performance measurement at Caterpillar.)

Hoover, G., Campbell, A. and Spain, P.J. (eds) (1995) 'Caterpillar Inc.', *Hoover's Handbook of American Business*, Austin: The Reference Press, Inc. (Gives a general overview of the company.)

Weimer, D. (1998) 'A new cat on the hot seat', *Business Week*, 9 March: 56–61.

Further resources

Caterpillar website
http://www.caterpillar.com

Sharpening the claws

Forbes; New York; 26 July 1999; Bruce Upbin

Abstract:

Glen Barton, chief executive of Caterpillar, promised that profits in 1999 would be off no more than 15%. It was either a heroic gesture or a dumb one. Everyone is looking for a collapse after seven terrific years for the earthmoving equipment giant. Two-thirds of Cat's product line is for economic sectors already in recession. And yet, despite this wobbly world, Cat earned $1.5 billion last year, its second-best ever, on $21 billion in sales.

Glen Barton has guts. The 60-year-old farm boy from Alton, Mo. became chief executive of Caterpillar in February. A month later he stood up in front of 150 financial analysts at a Las Vegas trade show and promised that profits in 1999 would be off no more than 15%.

It was either a heroic gesture or a dumb one. Everyone is looking for a collapse after seven terrific years for the Peoria, Ill. earthmoving equipment giant. As proof, they point to Cat's first quarter, when earnings fell by 50% on a 2% sales increase. Memories go back to the last two troughs, in the early 1980s and early 1990s, when Cat lost a billion dollars, all told.

But consider this: Two-thirds of Cat's product line is for economic sectors already in recession, estimates machinery analyst John McGinty of cs First Boston. Count 'em up: Asia, Latin America, the Middle East, as well as industries like forestry, mining, agriculture and energy extraction.

And yet, despite this wobbly world, Cat earned $1.5 billion last year, its second-best ever, on $21 billion in sales, an alltime record.

Are we supposed to believe a 15% profit haircut is a worst-case scenario? FORBES heard the same pitch from Deere & Co. six months ago. Despite its great strides to diversify into construction equipment and lawn mowers, the farm machinery maker, hammered by weak grain prices, is facing a 60% drop in profits this year.

If something very different is going to happen to Cat, how will Barton pull it off? Barton, a quintessentially reserved midwesterner who joined Cat as a trainee fresh out of the University of Missouri, slouches a bit in his leather chair and struggles with a smile: "We have a big job in front of us, delivering on what we promised."

Cat is a vastly leaner company now than most people give it credit for. Under Barton's predecessor, Donald Fites, Cat squeezed its working capital in the machinery and engine businesses down to 10% of sales from 25% in 1991. That beats Deere's 16% and Case's 20%. Cat also doubled its sales in the same period while head count rose only 22%.

Barton isn't taking chances, though. He has pushed through two price increases since February, the greatest increases since 1996. And there will be the usual cost-cutting. But unlike the past, when Fites would have ordered his five group-vicepresidents to take 10% off the top, Barton is taking a page from Machiavelli.

In March he bypassed his direct reports and requested a personal letter from each of the 26 group bosses outlining potential cuts should volume drop 30%, as it did after the 1981 recession. All those managers are still Fites people. If they don't come through with good answers, there are 50 more managers behind them who will be more loyal to Barton.

Already he's seeing pet projects, like new mining shovels and motor graders, postponed until next year, and workers laid off in Brazil, at several Illinois plants and at the Solar engine division in San Diego. "You have to go through this process now, otherwise you sit around six months after the horse is out of the barn, wondering what to do," he says.

But cutting costs won't win Barton any prizes. He has to find ways for Cat to grow, to a targeted $30 billion within the next decade. Barton points to Cat's $6.5 billion business in diesels and gas turbines. With the purchases of Germany's MaK in 1996 and Britain's Perkins Engines for $1.3 billion last year, Caterpillar became the world's largest dieselmaker. Barton wants to double engine sales by 2005, implying a 12% growth rate and the distinct possibility that engines will eventually represent half of the company's business.

Perkins, which grosses about $1.5 billion, puts Cat squarely in a market it long ignored, smaller diesels for farm and light construction equipment. But Cat will earn most of its profit selling the 1,000hp to 30,000hp generators used by oil rigs and little Chinese villages.

Here Cat dominates rival Cummins. Through its Asia dealers, Cat could eventually become a private utility, leasing the engines and charging for hourly usage. Asia is soft now, but it won't be forever. Within five years, predicts Barton, the $5 billion world market for engines attached to medium-size generators will triple.

Big acquisitions won't get Cat far in its $13 billion construction-machinery business. There isn't much left to buy that would move the needle. Littler guys like Case and New Holland are merging just to stay competitive with Cat around the globe.

What Cat can do is add new products here and there, none of which are blockbusters but, when added up, make a difference. Fifteen years ago Cat had no mining trucks or front shovels, nor did it sell any paving equipment in North America. Now Cat either dominates or comes a close second in sales of all three products.

Barton badly wants to make up ground in the $4 billion forestry equipment business, where Cat trails Deere and Timberjack. Three years ago all it sold were log skidders to take trees out of the woods. Cat is adding seven new product lines by 2000, including handlers and knuckleboom loaders used in the Southeast U.S. The 1997 acquisition of Sweden's Skogsjan has led to the marvellous new 570 Harvester, a sixwheel beast that grabs a fallen tree, delimbs it and cuts it to 5-foot lengths for board – in ten seconds. Price: $460,000.

Cat also has its sights set on competing with Hertz' equipment arm and United Rentals. These are both billion-dollar companies growing 20% or more annually renting hydraulic lifts, compressors and other smallish equipment to general contractors. When times are good, renting is good for a 13% profit margin before interest and taxes. But Cat dealers don't rent many small machines since they're more motivated to sell the big iron.

So Barton is trying to convince dealers to open Cat-branded rental stores. So far Cat has 200 rental outlets. The target is 350. All these stores create an instant home for Cat's new line of compact machinery. Sales of mini-excavators and skid-steer loaders (four-wheeled machines that operate in tight places) were a paltry $15 million last year, but Barton expects $800 million by 2005.

Cat will always be cyclical. But even if U.S. markets weaken, things can't get much worse elsewhere. There are already signs of life. Asian dealers have begun restocking. Private-sector construction is on again in Brazil. Excavating western Canada's vast oil sands will require huge trucks and shovels. So maybe Barton can deliver on his promise to keep profits at 85% of last year's level.

Reprinted by permission of *Forbes Magazine* © 2000 Forbes 1999.

Company Profile 4
The Coca-Cola Company

Company overview

The Coca-Cola Company is one of the world's largest beverage companies. The company manufactures and sells syrups, concentrates and beverage bases for Coca-Cola and the company's flagship brand products worldwide. As a global leader in the soft drinks industry, the Coca-Cola Company operates in more than 195 countries and employs about 30,000 people worldwide. The company's operation consists of five geographical groups: the North American Group (the United States and Canada), the Latin American Group (Central and South America), the Middle and Far East Group (the Middle East, India, China, Japan and Australia), the Greater Europe Group (most parts of Western Europe and parts of Eastern and Central Europe) and the African Group (47 countries in sub-Saharan Africa). The corporate headquarters of the Coca-Cola Company is located in Atlanta, Georgia. The revenues of the company exceeded $18 billion in 1996.

Brief history

The Coca-Cola Company was established in 1892 in Atlanta, Georgia, but the history of the company began in 1886 with the invention of a syrup by John S. Pemberton, a pharmacist. The inventor's bookkeeper, Frank M. Robinson, named the syrup Coca-Cola. While the formula for the syrup remains one of the world's best kept secrets, it is believed that the formula contained cocaine in the early years. Later, cocaine was removed from its formulation. Coke was first bottled in 1894. Within a very short time the drink became very popular and captured a significant share of the soft drinks market in the United States. The product is now one of the world's most popular non-alcoholic beverages.

Since the beginning, the company's advertising slogans (e.g. 1905: 'Coca-Cola revives and sustains'; 1927: 'Around the corner from everywhere'; 1963: 'Things go better with Coke'; 1996: 'Always Coca-Cola') have been very popular around the world. The company changes its slogan every few years. Since the company became a sponsor of the 1928 Summer Olympic Games in Amsterdam it has continued to expand its presence around the world. According to Coca-Cola, 'the Company takes pride in being a worldwide business that is always local', i.e. it offers standardized global products which are adapted to local tastes.

With few exceptions, its bottling plants are locally owned and operated by independent local business people. Local bottling companies provide capital for facilities, machinery, bottles and the distribution of products. The Coca-Cola Company supplies the concentrates and beverage bases to the local bottling companies, and provides some management assistance to the local companies to facilitate growth in profits. In some cases the Coca-Cola Company also shares its expertise in plant design, manufacturing, quality control, marketing and training in some areas. The company's juice business unit, formerly known as Coca-Cola Foods, is now called The Minute Maid Company. The Minute Maid Company is located in Houston, Texas, and is the world's leading marketer of juice drinks. The company's key competitors are PepsiCo, Dr Pepper/7Up and Seagram.

Innovation and significant contributions

The company began with the invention of a syrup named Coca-Cola. In the first year the company sold about six drinks per day; now it sells 834 million drinks per day throughout the world. The company's effective advertising slogans, its region-based product development and marketing activities have made its products very popular worldwide. For example, the company has introduced a carbonated soft drink, Smart, specifically designed for young Chinese consumers. The product was the first carbonated beverage introduced into China by an international beverage company. It has been very well received in China. The company has introduced Ciel, a new 'brand' water, in Mexico and new packaging graphics for Fanta in Thailand. Now Fanta is one of the fastest-growing soft drinks in Thailand.

The Coca-Cola company's innovation in marketing, distribution, quality control, development of human resources and adaptability to change have made significant contributions to the beverage industry. The company and its bottling partners have made efforts to solve environmental problems for more than twenty years. To reduce solid waste, all of its packaging is recyclable.

Challenges and opportunities

Sustaining its products and businesses throughout the globe by encouraging creativity in its human resources, strategy and brands is the major challenge for the Coca-Cola Company. The company is now making efforts to meet the challenges by maintaining the quality and value of its products; introducing new products; and maintaining and improving effective and efficient distribution systems, customer satisfaction, human resources innovation and management of assets. In this way, the company hopes to maintain its global leadership in the beverage industry.

ROSALIE L. TUNG AND MOHI AHMED
SIMON FRASER UNIVERSITY

Further reading

Fisher, A. (1997) 'The world's most admired companies', *Fortune* 136(8), 27 October: 220–8. (Profiles the world's most admired companies, including Coca-Cola.)

Hoover, G., Campbell, A. and Spain, P.J. (eds) (1995) 'The Coca-Cola Company', *Hoover's Handbook of American Business*, Austin (Gives a general overview of the company.)

Kishi, M. and Russell, D. (1996) *Successful Gaijin in Japan: How Foreign Companies are Making it in Japan*, Lincolnwood: NTC Business Books. (Profiles several successful foreign companies in the Japanese market, including Coca-Cola.)

Lorge, S. (1997) 'Coca-Cola', *Sales & Marketing Management* 149(11), October: 62–3. (Discusses Coca-Cola's sales structure.)

O'Reilly, B. (1997) 'The Secrets of America's Most Admired Corporations: New Ideas, New Products' *Fortune* 135(4), 3 March: 60–4. (Presents the management style, innovation and corporate culture of several of the most innovative US firms, including Coca-Cola.)

Sfiligoj, E. (1998) 'The Pepsi challenge', *Beverage World* 117(1652), 15 January: 98–101. (Identifies the challenges facing Coca-Cola.)

Further resources

Coca-Cola website
http://www.cocacola.com

Debunking Coke

The Economist, 12 February 2000

Douglas Daft is Australian. That makes him the ideal man to revive the world's most American brand

One the day he is appointed, the boss of Coca-Cola is meant to visit the vault of the SunTrust Banks, in Atlanta, to kneel before the original recipe for Coke, a secret known to only a handful of people in the world. However, this is one trip that Douglas Daft is not going to bother with. Whereas his predecessor, Doug Ivester, learned it by heart, Mr Daft, who in April will become only the eleventh chairman in the group's 114-year history, says: "The Coke formula represents the wisdom of the past. We have to look forward."

Mr Daft has little time for company mythology. Although he has been at Coca-Cola for 30 years, he remains an outsider. He is an Australian and the first genuine foreigner to run this most American of firms. He has also spent most of his career outside America, in remote corners of the world. In contrast, Mr Ivester was a local boy from Georgia who was never far from the group's Atlanta headquarters. Even Roberto Goizueta, Coca-Cola's boss during much of the 1980s and 1990s, quickly shed his Cuban heritage in favour of a Yale education, an American passport, and a career at head office.

Nor does the self-deprecating, rumpled Mr Daft look the part of a humourless, buttoned-down American boss. Unlike Mr Ivester, who sought to control every aspect of Coca-Cola's business, Mr Daft finds it easy to delegate. He readily defers to those who know more then he does, and is fond of a good joke (the name must help). Sitting rather awkwardly on a comfy chair in his new office, watching his assistant dutifully pour a Coke, he looks as if he might prefer a chat nursing something stronger down the pub.

Mr Daft's non-conformity gives him the detachment he needs at a time when Coca-Cola is suffering from poor volume growth, declining profits and a miserable share price. To his credit, Mr Daft has started his work in Coca-Cola's Atlanta heartland. Thrust blinking into the spotlight after the sudden resignation of the embattled Mr Ivester on December 6th, Mr Daft quickly announced he was chopping a fifth of the 29,000-strong workforce, half from the group headquarters. The decision has shocked local folk. In Atlanta, Coca-Cola is church and state rolled into one. People quaff two servings a day, double the national average. Pepsi is a dirty word.

The lay-offs are part of Mr Daft's larger plan to decentralise Coca-Cola's management. He is moving the group's regional chieftains out of headquarters to place them closer to their local markets. Mr Daft remembers interference from Atlanta in his days in East Asia. As responsibility is devolved, the firm should become decisive and agile. Mr Daft points ruefully to Coca-Cola's launch of a new carbonated tea in north-east China last year, several months behind its rivals: "We had the formula, we had the flavour, we had done all the taste-testing, but Atlanta kept saying 'are you sure?'" Today, he claims, local managers would be free to take the decision – and the flack for any mistakes.

With local responsibility go local brands. Though old hands might call it sacrilege, Mr Daft recognises that Coca-Cola is not always "it". "People don't buy drinks globally," he says. "You can't pander to similarities between people:

you have to find the differences." He ran Japan in the 1980s. It is now the group's most profitable market and two-thirds of its sales are of such unfizzy things as canned tea. Although "brand Coke" has fallen from 70% to 64% of sales by volume since 1995, Mr Daft thinks that Coca-Cola is not yet the true multi-branded drinks company it should be.

Making it so will depend partly on boosting some of the 190 smaller brands Coca-Cola already owns. Tellingly, Mr Daft has appointed his number two in Tokyo as the group's new head of marketing. Having seen in Japan how quickly consumer tastes change, he thinks that the transformation will also depend on innovation. He is therefore opening four "innovation" centres worldwide.

A more urgent task for Mr Daft is to repair relations with Coca-Cola's affiliated bottlers. Mr Ivester offended the bottlers by frequently raising the price of syrup concentrate, despite the fact that this squeezed the bottlers' margins. Mr Daft, instead, talks of restoring health to the entire bottling system. He has made a start by letting bottlers reduce their stocks, even though that will hurt Coca-Cola's short-term earnings.

The ring-pull of truth

But for all the changes he is making, Mr Daft has yet to tackle Coca-Cola's central myth: that the "specialness" of the Coke brand guarantees growth. Mr Daft has warned that he will soon cut Coca-Cola's long-term growth targets of 7–8% for volume and 15–20% for earnings. But he is expected to trim them by only a point or two. Although he dismisses as "esoteric" Mr Goizueta's ambitions that Coke should one day replace tap water, he still asserts that Coke can return to its historic growth rates.

An executive is right to be ambitious for his firm, but some myths are dangerous. Coke has been a fantastic brand, but tastes change. In recent years a lot of Coca-Cola's growth has come from pumping syrup into the bottling system and raising prices. For a while this worked, but it has recently led to the lacklustre growth in volume that is the root of Coca-Cola's present difficulties. Moreover, the myth of Coke's invincibility risks frustrating Mr Daft's aims that the firm should adapt global brand marketing to local tastes and nurture its own smaller brands. Forcing Coca-Cola's managers to realise that Coke is no longer so special, and that they have to compete to thrive, will be Mr Daft's biggest challenge.

Company Profile 5
Unilever

Company overview

Unilever is one of the world's largest producers of personal care and food products. The company was formed by a merger of Dutch Margarine Union and British soap-makers Lever Brothers in 1929. The company has headquarters in both London, England, and Rotterdam, the Netherlands. Unilever now produces hundreds of items, ranging from cosmetics/perfume (Calvin Klein, Elizabeth Arden) to foods (Lipton, Country Crock), personal care products (Vaseline, Timotei) and soap/laundry products (Sunlight, Dove, Lux). The company operates all over the world and employs about 300,000 people worldwide. The revenues of Unilever exceeded $52 billion in 1996.

Brief history

The history of Unilever dates back to 1885. William Lever established a soap-manufacturing company in the UK with his brothers and named the company Lever Brothers in 1885. Their product, Sunlight, the world's first packaged soap, was very successful. Fifteen years after the product's launch in the UK Lever Brothers started selling the soap in Europe, Australia, South Africa and the United States. As the company needed a large quantity of vegetable oil to produce soap, it established plantations and trading companies throughout the world to source raw materials and to distribute its products.

Two butter-makers, Jurgens and Van den Berghs, formed Margarine Union in 1927. The Dutch Margarine Union merged with Lever Brothers of United Kingdom in 1929 to form Unilever. For tax purposes, two separate entities were established, one in London and another in Rotterdam. While Unilever lost out to Procter & Gamble in the United States, it continued to enjoy success with its products in the rest of the world. Unilever has continued to diversify its product line and acquire other companies around the world. In 1991 Unilever acquired twenty-seven businesses worldwide. These have contributed to the expansion of the company's products and services. Unilever is now a global leader in the area of deodorants, fragrances, personal care, margarine, tea-based beverages and ice-cream products.

Innovation and significant contributions

Unilever's success lies in its ability to understand local consumers and in the process come up with new product innovations and ways of marketing to meet their needs. The company has innovation centres in strategic locations around the world. These centres have created new opportunities for the company. For example, Unilever has innovation centres for hair care-related products in Japan, France, Argentina and India; and innovation centres for ice cream in France, Germany, India, the UK and the United States. Unilever considers sustainable development to be critical to the company's continued success. The company is engaged in continuous R&D to produce new products.

Unilever has made contributions to the industry by introducing high-quality products and through its management concepts (e.g. regional focus; giving priority to developing and emerging markets; focusing on competitive cost and innovative products to improve profitability). Many global companies are now learning from the experiences of Unilever in doing business in the changing marketplace. The company states: 'Unilever provides basic products which are the first purchases when economies start to develop; it provides low-unit-cost priced convenience products which are the most in demand when incomes begin to rise; and it provides more sophisticated products which satisfy growing aspirations. Providing the right product at the right time is the key to successful introductions.' A case in point is Unilever's operations in Mexico. Several years ago its deodorants business there was insignificant; now it leads the market.

Challenges and opportunities

According to Unilever, the company's long-term success 'requires a total commitment to exceptional standards of performance and productivity, to working together effectively and to a willingness to embrace new ideas and learn continuously'. The company's continuous efforts to do business with the right products at the right time in the right places will create more opportunities and bring continued success to the company.

ROSALIE L. TUNG AND MOHI AHMED
SIMON FRASER UNIVERSITY

Further reading

Dwyer P. (1994) 'Unilever's struggle for growth: under fierce pressure in Europe and the U.S., it's grabbing a bigger share in emerging markets', *Business Week*, 4 July: 54–6. (Discusses how Unilever is gaining an advantage in emerging markets.)

Reader, W.J. (1980) *Fifty Years of Unilever, 1930–80*, London: Heinemann. (Gives the history of the company during the period 1930–80.)

Spain, P.J. and Talbot, J.R. (eds) (1995) 'Unilever', *Hoover's Handbook of World Business 1995–96*, Austin: The Reference Press, Inc. (Gives a general overview of the company.)

Wilson, J.F. (1995) *British Business History, 1720–1994*, Manchester: Manchester University Press. (Gives a detailed historical background of businesses in Britain.)

Further resources

Unilever website
http://www.unilever.com

A giant reawakens

Forbes; New York; 25 January 1999;
Deborag Orr

Abstract:

Niall FitzGerald, cochairman of Unilever, has hacked off some limbs that the company has long held dear, raising $9.5 billion. He has imposed order on what remains: 300 operating companies producing over 1,000 brands and overseen by 12 regional business group presidents who now yield more autonomy. FitzGerald and his cochairman, Morris Tabaksblat, still have a lot of work ahead. This year they hope to sell off businesses that provide $2 billion of Unilever's $48 billion in annual revenue. Unilever hopes to appeal to a wider range of incomes, segmenting its businesses into products at multiple price points. In the developing world, Unilever is moving away from catering to a rising middle class to targeting the dirt poor.

Even Unilever, which sells $130 million in products a day, can lose sight of its customers. Niall FitzGerald is getting back in touch.

Niall FitzGerald's career bubble almost burst in the soap wars of 1994. He was chief of Unilever Plc.'s soap division when it rolled out Persil Power, a laundry powder that packed an extra scrubbing chemical. Persil Power scrubbed so hard that it ate right through some fabrics. The British press had a field day – "It's Official! Persil Can Rot Your Knickers." Archrival Procter & Gamble gleefully aired the dirty laundry in ads displaying shredded boxer shorts.

In the midst of the crisis FitzGerald met with 30 Unilever executives to plot a way out. "I asked how many people in the room did their own laundry. Not one person raised a hand," he says with amazement. "There we were, trying to figure out why customers wouldn't buy our soap and we didn't even know the first thing about how it was used." That taught FitzGerald a lesson he heeds to this day: Never lose touch with your customer. Embarrassed and beleaguered, he pulled the plug on Persil Power, letting a few hundred million dollars go down the drain. FitzGerald was ready to quit. Observers thought he would.

"But what kind of message would that have sent?" he says. "We were trying to become more entrepreneurial, take more risks. If I walked out after my first failure, everyone else at Unilever would say, 'This business doesn't tolerate risk-taking. Remember what happened to FitzGerald?'"

He survived the soap opera and rose to cochairman of Unilever in September 1996. In the two years since, he has put some spring into its step. He has hacked off limbs that Unilever had long held dear – everything from plant-breeding to a Caterpillar tractor franchise-raising $9.5 billion. He has imposed order on what remains: 300 operating companies producing a thousand brands, and overseen by 12 regional business group presidents who now wield more autonomy.

FitzGerald and his cochairman, Morris Tabaksblat, still have a lot of work ahead. This year they hope to sell off businesses that provide $2 billion of Unilever's $48 billion in annual revenue. They must slash an inefficient, country-by-country infrastructure in Europe to exploit the new common currency. Some Unilever brands lag in the U.S. – Pepsodent toothpaste, Pond's cold cream, Wisk detergent and a lot you wouldn't recognize – and rarely attain the rank of number one.

But FitzGerald seems up to the task. He has revived Unilever by cozying up to consumers. Now, when he travels to Unilever sites, he makes house calls on "real people," as well. "I usually ask them to show me how they clean their clothes. One woman in Thailand was kind enough to show me how she washed her hair," he says. "I always ask to look in the fridge – not so much looking for my products, but just to get a sense of what people are buying." Recruits at Hindustan Lever, the 51%-owned India subsidiary, are asked to spend six weeks living with a family in a remote Indian village "so that from the very beginning they understand who our consumers are," he says.

It isn't exactly the stuff of focus groups and two-way mirrors, but FitzGerald says the approach works. "Consumers aren't some great amorphous aggregate. They are individuals who live in 150 different countries."

Yet an amorphous aggregate is precisely what mass-marketers have targeted, historically. They aimed catch-all products with midrange prices at the vast middle class. A few head for the plush profits of high-ticket goods; others go south to discount brands.

Unilever hopes to appeal to a wider range of incomes, segmenting its businesses into products at multiple price points.

In the developing world Unilever is moving away from catering to a rising middle class to targeting the dirt-poor. FitzGerald and Tabaksblat hope to create new markets where none existed before, selling to some of the world's poorest consumers, who earn less than $200 a month and make up just under half the world's population.

The Everyman project, as it is now called, began in India five years ago. For women who wash their clothes in the Ganges, the company's laundry soap is sold as bars for a few cents. Now the tack is being tried in Brazil. For the poorest regions there, Unilever developed a special shampoo for long, wavy, mulatto hair. Africa and the rest of Latin America will be next.

Unilever doesn't advertise these low-end staples, and it distributes the products on a shoestring budget, yielding just enough profit to earn back a reasonable return.

This new attitude has turned marketing on its head at Unilever. "Now we are following a more stratified approach. Even in mature markets, we try to cater to different income levels," says Tabaksblat, who is based in Rotterdam in the Netherlands, while FitzGerald works out of London.

The poverty push plays to Unilever's strengths in emerging markets, where it went in early before even the most fearsome competitors. "In markets like India, Procter & Gamble doesn't even come in second in a two-horse race," says Charles Mills of Credit Suisse First Boston. The sheer breadth of Unilever's lines insulates it to some degree from things like regional depressions; if people can't afford the expensive detergent, the same factory can turn out more of the cheap detergent.

Whether Unilever can stay insulated if global economic turmoil worsens is uncertain. Still, Unilever has made impressive strides in the past two years. The net profit margin has perked up from 4.8% in 1996 to 6.5% (the Value Line estimate) last year. But it's still a long way from P&G's 10.5%.

Unilever's shares, which rose at only half the rate of its peers from 1990 to 1996, have more than doubled in price since FitzGerald became cochairman. FitzGerald, 53, a charming but hard-charging Irishman who has spent his entire career at Unilever, gets much of the credit for that rebound. Tabaksblat, another Unilever lifer, who landed the cochair title two years ahead of FitzGerald, retires later this year, and a successor is expected to be named.

That two-chair tandem is a remnant of the 1929 merger between the Dutch Margarine Unie and British soapmaker Lever Brothers. Another remnant: two holding companies through which investors own the company. (Both the Netherlands shares and an American Depositary Receipt, representing British shares, trade on the Big Board.)

As the rebuilding project continues, FitzGerald vows to keep an unflinching focus on return on invested capital. He will unload more beloved businesses that don't make the grade. "We have stopped sentimental management. The only justification for something is its ability to deliver value in the future," he says.

He has even managed a bit of vindication in the soap business he once ran. Last year Unilever rolled out a new, gentler version of Persil in tablet form. This time Unilever stole a march on rivals and increased its market share in Britain by three points. Analysts say it was the first such gain in four years–since that unpleasant episode with the knickers.

Reprinted by permission of *Forbes Magazine* © 2000 Forbes 1999.

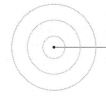

Company Profile 6
The Procter & Gamble
Company (P&G)

Company overview

Procter & Gamble (P&G) is one of the world's largest manufacturers of consumer products. In 1996 the total revenues of P&G exceeded $35 billion. Its major products are in personal care (soap and cosmetics), laundry and cleaning, and food and beverages. P&G was the first company in the world to hire full-time professionals to study consumer needs to facilitate new product development. P&G was established in 1837 as a result of a merger between a candle-maker (William Procter) and a soap manufacturer (James Gamble). With its head-quarters in Cincinnati, Ohio, the company employs 103,000 people and has operations in seventy countries. P&G products are sold in over 140 countries around the world.

Brief history

On 12 April 1837 William Procter and James Gamble produced and sold soap and candles. Twenty-two years later P&G sales reached $1 million and the company employed eighty people. In 1886 P&G started production at the Ivorydale factory, a facility recognized for its progressive approach towards creating a pleasant work environment for its employees.

In 1887 P&G established a profit-sharing programme for its employees. This policy has contributed, in part, to the success of the company. In 1915 P&G built its first manufacturing plant in Canada, the first of many manufacturing facilities to be established outside the United States. P&G established a market research department to analyse consumer preferences and buying habits, the first of its kind in the world.

In 1930 P&G established its first overseas subsidiary, in England, and it built a manufacturing company in the Philippines in 1935. In 1937 P&G celebrated its 100th birthday with revenues of $230 million. In the late 1940s P&G set up an overseas division to manage its growing international business activities. In 1973 P&G began operations in Japan. In the early 1990s P&G introduced its new corporate logo and expanded to Eastern Europe (Hungary, Poland and Russia).

In 1993, for the first time in the company's history, more than 50 per cent of the company's revenue was derived from outside the United States. Since 1995 P&G has managed its business under two broad divisions: the US and international. All regional reports are directed to a single chief operating officer, however. This strategic coordination at the very top has contributed to the company's global competitiveness.

Innovation and significant contribution

P&G is well regarded in the industry for its innovations and efforts to analyse consumer needs. P&G has done a good job in meeting the needs of consumers around the world, including adaptation to the needs of individual markets. Every year the company spends about $1.5 billion in R&D and files about 20,000 patent applications. According to P&G, 'innovation is a global network of insight and discovery' and 'innovation is the ability to combine fresh consumer insights with deep technology understanding'. Over the years P&G has made many innovations, including the creation of a pleasant work environment and a profit-sharing programme, the establishment of one of the earliest product research laboratories in the manufacturing industry, the establishment of a market research department for studying consumer preferences and buying habits, the discovery of detergent technology, and development of the first detergent shampoo and the first fluoride toothpaste.

In 1990 P&G won the International DuPont Packaging Awards for being the first manufacturer to package with 100 per cent recyclable plastics. P&G has also received the World Environment Center Gold Medal for International Corporate Environmental Achievement. In 1994 the US Department of Labor presented P&G with the Opportunity 2000 Award in recognition of its commitment to equal employment opportunities and creating a diverse workforce. P&G values diversity among its employees as the company makes products for diverse consumers around the world. In 1995 P&G received the National Medal of Technology, the highest award in the United States for achievement in technological innovation.

Challenges and opportunities

A major challenge for P&G is to maintain its market share in a fast-changing environment by delivering the highest-quality products at the most affordable price to its consumers worldwide. Localized operations and continuous study of consumer needs around the world have helped the company to sustain its global competitiveness. In 1993 the company started an initiative to improve organizational effectiveness and cost competitiveness in the global marketplace. This initiative has contributed to the company's continuing success.

ROSALIE L. TUNG AND MOHI AHMED
SIMON FRAZER UNIVERSITY

Further reading

Galuszka P. (1997) 'Where P&G's brawn doesn't help much', *Business Week*, 10 November: 112–14. (Presents the challenges facing P&G's pharmaceuticals business.)

Hoover, G., Campbell, A. and Spain, P.J. (eds) (1995) 'The Procter & Gamble Company', *Hoover's Handbook of American Business*, Austin: The Reference Press, Inc. (Gives a general overview of the company.)

Kishi M. and Russell D. (1996) 'Becoming a household name: Procter & Gamble', *Successful Gaijin in Japan: How Foreign Companies are Making it in Japan*, Lincolnwood: NTC Business Books. (Details the success story of P&G in Japan.)

O'Reilly, B. (1997) 'The secrets of America's most admired corporations: new ideas, new products', *Fortune* 135(4), 4 March: 60–4. (Discusses P&G's innovative capabilities.)

Schisgall, O. (1981) *Eyes on Tomorrow: The Evolution of Procter & Gamble*, Chicago, IL: J.G. Ferguson Publishing. (Provides the historical background of the company and its many innovations.)

Further resources

P&G website
http://www.pg.com

Jager's gamble

The Economist, 30 October 1999,
Cincinatti, Ohio

*Durk Jager, Procter & Gamble's new chief
executive, wants to turn it into an innovative company. Easier said than done*

A FEW years back, scientists at Procter
& Gamble hit upon a big idea.
Combining know-how in absorbent
paper with a new "dry-weave" polyethylene mesh, they came up with a thin,
highly absorbent sanitary towel, the
first breakthrough in feminine hygiene
in 50 years. Today, P&G's "Always"
pads, now jazzed up with wings and
even thinner, are sold in 80 countries,
and are the mainstay of a product
family that generates around $1.6
billion in annual sales.

This is just the kind of innovation
that Durk Jager, who took over at P&G
in January, sees as essential to rekindling growth at the world's largest
consumer-products group. As its latest
move, P&G announced on October
26th that it is prepared to give away or
license any of its 25,000 patents,
including those used in established
brands. Chuck Hong, the firm's
director of R&D for corporate innovations, thinks this will "force us to
continually invent".

But why must P&G be forced to
invent? Surely a firm with £38 billion
in sales, more than 300 brands and
110,000 employees in 70 countries,
with patents spanning fats and oils,
plant fibres, surfactants and calcium,
with vast marketing and financial
resources, ought to be churning out
exciting new products all the time?
The trouble is, the new sanitary towel,
which Mr Jager himself admits was the
company's last big innovation, was
launched away back in 1983. The story

at P&G is not so much "Always" as
"almost never".

Mr Jager blames the consumer-product industry's problems on its
failure to innovate. It has, he told this
month's annual meeting in Cincinnati,
"led to commodity products and
pricing pressure." P&G has done worse
than most. It has lost some 10% of its
global market share in the past five
years. Volumes this year will grow by
2% at best.

Turning a marketer into an innovator requires money, ideas and a
nimble culture. P&G's problem has
never been a lack of money or even
ideas. Last year it was America's 21st-largest investor in research and
development, spending $1.7 billion. Its
R&D budget has grown from 2.9% to
4.5% of net sales over the past decade –
still well below the 15% typical in the
pharmaceuticals industry, but double
that of Gillette. That spending has,
however, yielded little. Less than 10%
of P&G's thousands of patents are used
in its hundreds of brands.

The fault lies with the culture. The
firm has stifled innovation and
prevented new ideas from getting to
market quickly. Years after P&G
developed its tissue-towel products,
they have only just started to be rolled
out globally. "We're slower than my
great-grandma," says one executive.

Mr Jager is trying to change all
that. In June he announced a big
internal shake-up, sacking 13% of the
workforce to streamline management
and speed up decision-making. He is
tying strategy and global profit targets
to the performance of brands, rather
than countries, and handing responsibility for new ideas to new business
managers, not ones steeped in existing
businesses. He has set up innovation
teams to shoot promising ideas rapidly
around the company and rush the best

to market. And P&G plans to take more risks, cutting pre-market laboratory testing and putting products on sale earlier.

Spiffy Swiffer

P&G has had some success with the recent launch of products, including Swiffer, a dry mop that traps dust, Febreze spray to eliminate smells in fabric and Dryel, a home dry-cleaning kit, all of which he says are "new-to-the-world" products, not just variants of old ones. Febreze, which was introduced in June last year, is already America's fifth-most successful new packaged product, with sales of $230m in its first year. And whereas Febreze took forever to be launched, Mr Jager boasts that Swiffer went from test marketing to global roll-out in a record 18 months.

P&G has even started looking outside for new ideas. To develop "NutriDelight", a fortified orange powdered drink unveiled at the annual meeting, P&G worked with Unicef and licensed in the technology that lets iron exist with iodine and vitamin A in a stable form, helping undernourished children put on weight. And the group recently bought Iams Petfoods, admired for a scientific approach to pet health that includes low-calcium nosh for big dogs prone to overgrown bones, and oil and mineral formulas for "senior" pets with bad joints.

Mr Jager is getting on the Internet, too. In November P&G will launch its majority-owned venture, reflect.com, an Internet-only range of 50,000 beauty products sold direct to consumers. Nathan Estruth, who helps run reflect.com, calls the venture "heresy" for a mass-market company that has always sold through retailers.

Yet turning a marketing giant into a nippy innovator will be hard. P&G's line managers and country chiefs are trained to squeeze the last drop of sales out of existing products, not back risky new ones. Sam Stern, a professor at Oregon State University who has written a book on creativity in consumer-goods companies, points out that new ideas threaten the status quo.

However esoteric they sound, most consumer-goods technologies are unlikely to fend off imitators for long. A drug's effect is tied closely to its complex technology. Having gone through rigorous approval and lengthy clinical trials, patent challenges on drugs are rare. By contrast, Gillette's patent on a new toothbrush may specify with utmost precision how bristles are laid out; but there are lots of different "technologies" that can clean teeth just as well. Lynn Domblaser, director of the Global New Products Database, estimates that only 10% of the 55,000 brand new products that were launched globally last year are really innovative.

Even when consumer-products companies do come up with something novel, competitors catch up fast. "Always" went unchallenged for ten years. Now, only one year after the launch of Febreze, Johnson & Johnson, Clorox and others have launched their own improved versions – mainly because Febreze was in pre-market testing for two years. Similarly, Gillette took ten years and spent $1 billion developing its Mach3 triple-blade razor, launched last year. Within a few months, Asda, a British supermarket, rushed in with its own product, Tri-Flex, claiming that it was just as good and 40% cheaper.

What is more, packaged-goods companies not only have to develop the product, but also try to get jaded consumers to think they need it. That sometimes works. Upbeat marketing turned a very ordinary orange drink, Sunny Delight, into one of P&G's best brands.

But few new products are so successful. Information Resources, which researches packaged goods in America, finds that less than 1% of products launched in 1998 achieved $100m of sales in their first year. More than two-thirds flop in their first year. Hence, many managers in consumer-goods firms associate innovation with failure. Mr Jager has to persuade them that it is a condition for success.

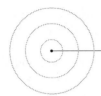

Company Profile 7
International Business
Machines Corporation (IBM)

Company overview

IBM is one of the world's leading providers of information technology and services. The company's two primary missions are to lead in the creation, development and manufacturing of the most advanced information technologies, and to translate those technologies into value for its customers. IBM designs, develops and manufactures computer systems, including software, networking systems, storage devices and microelectronics. In 1996 the revenues of the company exceeded $79.9 billion. The company operates in most countries around the globe and employed about 222,000 people worldwide in 1994. IBM has its headquarters in Armonk, New York.

Brief history

In 1911 IBM was first incorporated in New York as the Computing-Tabulating-Recording Company. The company's history, however, can be traced back to 1890, when the United States was receiving waves of immigrants. To meet the needs of measuring population the US Census Bureau sponsored a contest to find the most efficient means of tabulating census data. The contest was won by German immigrant and Census Bureau statistician, Herman Hollerith. Hollerith formed the Punch Card Tabulating Machine Co. in 1896. In 1911 Hollerith's company merged with Computing Scale Co. of America and International Time Recording Co. to form the Computing-Tabulating-Recording (C-T-R) Co. The company manufactured and sold products ranging from commercial scales and industrial time recorders to meat and cheese slicers, tabulators and punch cards.

In the beginning the company operated in New York City only. Within a short period of time, however, it quickly expanded its offices and plants to other parts of New York State, Washington, DC, Ohio, Michigan and Toronto, Canada. In 1914 Thomas J. Watson joined the company and became the president of the company within eleven months. Under his leadership the company continued to expand its products and services. At that time the company focused on producing large-scale custom-built tabulating solutions for businesses. Within ten years Watson had expanded the company's business operations to Europe, South America, Asia and Australia, and in 1924 the company was renamed International Business Machines Corporation (IBM) to reflect the firm's worldwide expansion.

IBM refers to the decades between 1939 and 1963 as the 'Era of Innovation'. During this period the company's product line expanded significantly. During World War II IBM made its first steps towards the development of computers. In

1944 IBM developed the automatic-sequence-controlled calculator, the first machine that could automatically execute long computations. In 1952 the company introduced the IBM 701, its first large computer based on the vacuum tube. This machine was used in business for billing, payroll and inventory control. Between 1960 and the 1980s IBM introduced the system/360 computer, which used interchangeable software and equipment. In 1969 IBM changed its way of selling products; instead of selling hardware, software and services in packages, the company began to sell the components separately, while remaining as the world's leader in the hardware and software industries.

In 1981 IBM introduced personal computers (PCs) for small businesses, schools and homes. For the first time, IBM collaborated with Intel and Microsoft to produce PCs. In 1985 IBM introduced local area networks (LANs), which permitted PC users to exchange information and share printers and files within a building or complex. IBM established a foundation for network computing and numerous applications of PCs. In 1993 Louis V. Gerstner, Jr, a former executive at American Express, Nabisco and McKinsey & Co., joined IBM as CEO. Gerstner emphasized the need to provide integrated solutions for the company's customers. He also decided to keep the company together instead of splitting it into separate independent companies. Today IBM's strength lies in its combined expertise in solutions, services, products and technologies.

Innovation and significant contribution

IBM has changed the way people work, live and interact today, and has made significant contributions to the industry by revolutionizing the way in which business is conducted. IBM's recent innovations range from the DRAM memory chip, semiconductors, display technology, storage technology, design automation, computer architecture and software to computer networks, user interfaces and multimedia. Five IBM researchers have received Nobel prizes for their contributions to science and technology. The company's research division headquarters is located in New York, and the company has several other key sites in San Jose, California; Austin, Texas; Beijing, China; Haifa, Israel; Yorktown Heights, New York; Tokyo, Japan; and Zurich, Switzerland.

IBM has received the first edition of worldwide ISO 14001 registration, which covers all the company's global manufacturing and hardware development operations across all its business units. IBM has received the Best of the Best Award from the US Environmental Protection Agency (EPA) for its contributions to stratospheric ozone protection, and the Environmental Excellence Award from the US and Japan for contributions to environmental protection and product design.

Challenges and opportunities

To respond to challenges in the rapidly changing computer industry, IBM has expanded its collaboration with other firms around the world. For example, IBM has begun collaboration with Netscape, Oracle and Sun Microsystems to promote a standards-based approach in the information-communication industry. IBM's leadership in the area of electronic commerce will likely give it a competitive edge in the future.

The goal to bring integrated solutions to its global customers may bring further benefits for IBM. The company's continuous and coordinated efforts in innovation and marketing to provide information and communication technologies, products and services at the right time in the right markets may further contribute to the company's success in the future.

ROSALIE L. TUNG AND MOHI AHMED
SIMON FRASER UNIVERSITY

Further reading

Arnst, C., Verity, J.W. and Rebello, K. (1993) 'Rethinking IBM', *Business Week*, 2 October: 86–97. (Presents the major challenges to IBM.)

Cortese, A. (1995) 'The View From IBM', *Business Week*, 30 October: 142–8. (Provides an inside look at the network-centric computing at IBM.)

Hoover, G., Campbell, A. and Spain, P.J. (eds) (1995) 'International Business Machines', *Hoover's Handbook of American Business*, Austin: The Reference Press, Inc. (Gives a general overview of the company.)

Jones, P. and Kahaner, L. (1995) *Say It & Live It*, New York: Currency Doubleday. (Presents the mission statements of fifty corporations.)

Kanter, R.M. (1989) *When Giants Learn to Dance*, New York: Simon & Schuster. (Offers guidelines on how large companies can collaborate effectively with other entities.)

Kanter, R.M. (1995) *World Class: Thriving Locally in the Global Economy*, New York: Touchtone. (Discusses how companies can become globally competitive in their respective industries.)

Mills, D.Q. and Friesen, G.B. (1996) *Broken Promises: An Unconventional View of What Went Wrong at IBM*, Boston, MA: Harvard Business School Press. (Provides an historical background of the challenges confronting IBM.)

Further resources

IBM website
http://www.ibm.com

IBM follows its own advice

Informationweek; Manhasset;
13 December 1999; Rick Whiting

Two years ago, IBM began spending millions of dollars for advertising to exhort its customers to transform themselves into E-businesses. And then management had a revelation. "We had to expect our customers to turn around and ask us what IBM was doing to transform itself into an E-business," says Dick Anderson, general manager of Enterprise Web Management.

So IBM – which ranked No. 2 on the InformationWeek E-Business 100 list – followed its own advice and began a number of initiatives to adopt E-business practices. The goal was not just to sell products, although sales to customers through the "Shop IBM" Web site and to resellers through E-commerce channels may reach $15 billion this year. IBM employed Internet technology to improve processes across a number of its operations, including procurement, customer service, business-partner relations, and employee support.

"We had different audiences that we thought we could focus on with this," Anderson says. "It's establishing new linkages and new ways of doing business." But the executive is quick to dismiss any idea that IBM's transformation is complete. "Everyone is in a 10- or 15-year transformation," he says. "So I don't want to suggest that we're there!"

Though it may not be there yet, IBM certainly can point to a number of early successes from its E-business efforts. Take customer support, for example, for which IBM has moved more of its call-center functions to the Internet. Last year, 14 million such transactions were conducted over the Web, and IBM expects that number to reach 35 million this year – about 58% of all customer service requests. That cuts the cost of such transactions by 70% to 90% – an estimated total cost avoidance of some $600 million this year – even while providing customers with more comprehensive and timely support, according to Anderson.

IBM is taking the same approach toward servicing its business partners, who will account for $5 billion to $7 billion of the vendor's E-commerce revenue this year. Resellers and other partners can use the Web to place and track orders and access product-marketing information. Arranging financing terms, which used to take up to 10 days to process, is now completed in as little as 20 seconds. On the procurement side, IBM purchased $3 billion in goods and services over the Internet from some 10,000 suppliers, saving $110 million in the process.

IBM's E-business efforts are directed inward as well. The company's intranet, which gets some 65 million hits a week, is used for everything from collaborative product development to online distributed learning programs – the latter saving IBM an estimated $80 million in the first half of this year alone.

But Anderson is the first to acknowledge that transforming a business into an E-business isn't easy. Some of the biggest challenges have nothing to do with technology. For example, IBM – as do all technology companies – prices its products differently around the world, based on such variables as local business factors and regional competition. But that becomes difficult with the Web, "where the world can see one price," Anderson says.

And E-business doesn't negate the need for old-fashioned business practices such as building relationships with suppliers. For example, IBM uses Internet links to help its subassembly contract manufacturers lower their costs by finding suppliers of cheaper components – and then passing some of those savings along to IBM. "But to do that, we had to convince our subassembly manufacturers to upload their bills of materials to us," Anderson says. Getting suppliers to divulge that kind of information requires the kind of trust that has been the foundation of vendor–customer relationships since commerce began.

© CMP Media Inc. 13 December 1999.

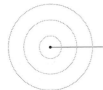

Company Profile 8
Eastman Kodak Company
(Kodak)

Company overview

Eastman Kodak is one of the world's largest manufacturers of imaging products and services. Kodak had revenues in excess of $15 billion in 1996 and in the same year employed 94,800 people worldwide, including 53,400 in the US. Kodak has nine business units: Business Imaging Systems, Consumer Imaging, Commercial and Government Systems, Global Customer Service and Support, Digital and Applied Imaging, Health Imaging, Professional Motion Imaging, Office Imaging and Kodak Professional. The company's products and services are now available in more than 150 countries. The corporate headquarters of the company is located in Rochester, New York.

Brief history

The history of Kodak dates back to the 1880s. George Eastman established the Eastman Dry Plate and Film Company in 1884. Eastman espoused four basic business principles (mass production at low cost, international distribution, extensive advertising and a focus on customers) and adopted three major policies ('foster growth and development through continuing research; reinvest profits to build and extend the business; and treat employees in a fair, and self-respecting way'). The company's success is closely linked to these principles and policies. Since the early years, Eastman has made efforts to mass produce at low cost.

In 1888 the name Kodak was first registered as a trademark. According to Eastman Kodak, K was George Eastman's favourite letter. Eastman tried to make words that began and ended with K and the word Kodak came out. The first Kodak camera was sold to the market with the slogan 'You push the button – we do the rest'. That marked the beginning of snapshot photography. By 1896 Kodak had manufactured its 100,000th camera, and the company continued to innovate and develop imaging systems.

To sell abroad, Eastman established a sales office in London only five years after the establishment of the Eastman Dry Plate and Film Company in New York. In 1889 the Eastman Photographic Materials Company Ltd was established in London, England, to distribute Kodak products in overseas markets. In 1892 the company became the Eastman Kodak Company of New York, and in the early 1900s several other distribution outlets were established in France, Germany, Italy and other European countries. Now the company has manufacturing operations in Canada, Mexico, Brazil, France, Germany, Australia, the UK and the US, but its products are marketed by subsidiary companies in more than 150 countries.

Innovation and significant contributions

Kodak's innovation started with the photographic dry plates for photographers invented by George Eastman. He also became one of the first American industrialists to employ a full-time research scientist to support the commercialization of a flexible, transparent film base. Since its beginning in the late 1880s, Kodak has continued to innovate in the area of imaging products.

The company's breakthrough development of Kodak T-Grain technology has contributed to the further improvement of its major imaging products. Hybrid Imaging, Kodak photo CD and Digital Imaging some of the company's other recent major innovations. In 1995 the US Environmental Protection Agency (EPA) gave Kodak an Environmental Champion award for voluntary efforts to reduce air emissions of seventeen targeted chemicals. Kodak has undertaken R&D efforts to reduce the emission of ozone-depleting chlorofluorocarbons (CFCs) as well.

Kodak has succeeded in making photography a popular leisure activity for millions of people around the world. According to Kodak, 'in 1996, people [would] take some 65 billion pictures, most with cameras that owe their basic design to Eastman's first roll-film models'. Kodak is also the world leader in medical laser imaging.

Challenges and opportunities

Eastman Kodak has led the imaging market for more than a century. Its major challenge now is to remain competitive in the emerging digital era. The new digital technology also poses tremendous opportunities for Kodak. To compete in the changing global marketplace, Kodak is now making efforts to improve its customer focus, reduce costs and increase collaboration with other organizations. Some of the collaborative ventures include its efforts with IBM to develop digital imaging, with Microsoft to develop co-brand software to market digital images and with Kinko's to market photo CDs. Through continuous innovation and collaboration with other organizations, Kodak expects to remain in the forefront of the world's imaging business.

ROSALIE L. TUNG AND MOHI AHMED
SIMON FRASER UNIVERSITY

Further reading

Champy, J. (1997) 'What makes you so special', *Sales and Marketing Management* 149(12), November: 24–6. (Identifies the marketing strategies of some innovative firms, including Kodak.)

Hoover, G., Campbell, A. and Spain, P.J. (eds) (1995) 'Eastman Kodak Company', *Hoover's Handbook of American Business*, Austin: The Reference Press, Inc. (Gives a general overview of the company.)

Maremont, M. (1995) 'Kodak's new focus: an inside look at George Fisher's strategy', *Business Week*, 30 January: 62–8. (Presents the perspectives on strategy of George Fisher, Kodak's CEO.)

Smith, G. (1997) 'What Kodak is developing in digital photography', *Business Week*, 7 July: 108–9. (Discusses Kodak's strategy for the digital era.)

Swasy, A. (1997) *Changing Focus: Kodak and the Battle to Save a Great American Company*, New York: Times Books. (Identifies the challenges confronting Kodak.)

Further resources

Kodak website
http://www.kodak.com

Film Vs. Digital: Can Kodak Build a Bridge?

Business Week; New York; 2 August 1999; Geoffrey Smith in Rochester, NY

Abstract:

George M. C. Fisher spent his entire 5½ years as chairman of Eastman Kodak Co. struggling to move the world-famous photography giant into the Digital Age. He recently announced that he will step down as CEO on January 1, declaring that Kodak's digital strategy is finally poised to reignite the company's sluggish sales. However, success in the digital world requires constant innovation and change – things Kodak is not known for. Moreover, the projects Kodak has unveiled so far are unlikely to provide the short-term sales jolt the company badly needs.

George M. C. Fisher spent his entire five-and-a-half years as chairman of Eastman Kodak Co. struggling to move the world-famous photography giant into the Digital Age. The once-idolized ex-Motorola Inc. chief recently announced that he will step down as CEO on Jan. 1, declaring that Kodak's digital strategy is finally poised to reignite the company's sluggish sales. Fisher cites an array of digital initiatives that will help boost overall sales by 8% to 12% a year in five years. "We've finally turned the corner," Fisher says, "even though we don't have the results to prove it yet."

Those results aren't a lock. For one thing, success in the digital world requires constant innovation and change – things Kodak is not known for. Moreover, the projects Kodak has unveiled so far are unlikely to provide

the short-term sales jolt the company badly needs. And the job won't get any easier as digital technology comes down in price, opening the door to new competitors. "Kodak's digital-imaging initiatives appear to be aimed at brand building, not revenue generation," says Donald Strickland, a former Kodak executive who is now CEO of digital-imaging software maker PictureWorks Technology Inc.

Indeed, building its brand may be Kodak's best move. It's critical that the company extend its name to digital since the technology represents a long-term threat to its core franchise in 35mm film. Although experts disagree over how long it will take for digital imaging to start shrinking the worldwide film market, that day is surely coming. Kodak sees just 5% growth in its film market over the next decade and even that may be optimistic. Market researcher Lyra Research estimates that worldwide film sales will grow only 1% annually through 2003 and slowly shrink after that. Rapid growth in markets such as China will be tempered by a shift toward digital cameras, especially in the U.S. and other developed markets.

That's where Fisher's heir, Daniel A. Carp, comes in. A 29-year Kodak vet, Carp made his name as a brand builder rather than a techie. His challenge: build the consumer trust in digital that Kodak already has in film. That way, as the technology spreads, Kodak will be set to profit. "We see digitization creating a film and a photo-finishing aftermarket that should fuel an explosion of pictures and use" of digital and 35mm technology, Carp says.

At its core, Kodak's digital strategy is to create a profitable bridge between the old and new worlds of photography. Even as it hopes to jump-start sales of digital cameras, the company wants to transfer as many of its customers' traditional snapshots as possible to digital form. It figures there's big money to be made uploading traditional pictures onto the Internet and in expanding its share of the market for reprints, inkjet paper, and photo-editing software.

Such changes can't happen soon enough. Amid the long-term shift in its market, Kodak has been struggling. A debilitating price war with Fuji Photo Film Co. has crimped sales in its core business, which accounts for just over half of total revenues. Meanwhile, Kodak has been pouring money into new ideas for digital imaging that have yet to pay off. At a recent $74 a share, Kodak stock has barely budged since 1997. A $1.2 billion cost-cutting program launched in 1997 that will trim 20% of its workforce by yearend has buoyed profits. But revenues dropped 5% in 1998 and are expected to be up just 3% this year, to $13.8 billion, with about $1.5 billion coming from digital. Second-quarter earnings were flat on a 2% rise in revenues.

Net identity

The company's long-suffering investors don't sound convinced that Carp has the right angle to get Kodak in focus again. "Kodak is going to be controversial until they can do something right on a consistent basis," says one money manager whose fund has 5 million shares.

The centerpiece of Kodak's digital strategy is a joint venture with America Online Inc. called You've Got Pictures, which could give the photo company a strong Internet identity. When it is rolled out this fall, consumers will be able to drop 35mm film off at the drugstore and for about $6 have a roll of 24 pictures digitally scanned and uploaded into their AOL accounts. From there, consumers will be able to E-mail the images to friends, order reprints or gifts, or download high-resolution copies that can be edited on a PC. They'll be able to store 50 pictures on the site for free.

Even under the brightest scenario, You've Got Pictures won't translate into big revenues quickly. Analysts estimate that Kodak will get 40% of the upload charge. Even if each of AOL's 17 million subscribers uploads one roll of film by yearend, Kodak's take will amount to only about $41 million, plus merchandising and storage fees. Still, Barry Schuler, president of AOLInteractive Services, says the long-term potential is huge: "Over time, this could be as big as E-mail."

To expose even more consumers to digital photography, Kodak since June has offered a service nationwide called Picture CD. For $10 a roll, consumers can get images from 35mm film loaded onto a compact disk. But it won't be a big revenue producer anytime soon, either. The CDs simplify the process of getting high-resolution images into a PC and come with a wide assortment of image-editing software. Fisher forecasts that Picture CD will generate up to $100 million in revenue in its first year, and analysts say Kodak may get 40% of that total, after retailers and partner Intel Corp. get their share; that's barely $10 million a quarter. Still, Kodak plans to broaden the market for Picture CD by tailoring it to professional markets. Realtors, for example, might give customers Picture CDs with 3-D images of homes for sale.

High-end edge

Kodak also has high hopes for the fast-growing digital-camera market, even though it is currently losing money there. Its 17% share of digital-camera sales in the U.S. badly trails Sony Corp.'s 52%. However, analysts say most future market growth will come from the higher-end photo-quality digital cameras. Kodak leads in that segment, though Sony is preparing a new assault. International Data Corp. predicts that the worldwide digital-camera market will grow 25% annually, to $6.5 billion, in 2003. If Kodak keeps a 20% share, cameras could become a $1.3 billion business for the company.

The fourth leg of Kodak's digital strategy is already paying off. Over the past two years, the company has installed some 19,000 Picture Maker kiosks at retail stores worldwide that print pictures from both digital and traditional film. These devices accept negatives, CDs, or digital-camera memory cards and let users edit images and make prints. At about $15,000 each, Carp says they are highly profitable and account for about $200 million in sales. And with 95% of customers who use them coming back repeatedly, they produce steady photo paper sales.

For all their promise, however, each of Kodak's new products will be under intense competitive pressure every step of the way. Upstarts such as Photoloft.com Inc. are offering to store photos on the Web for free and make money selling trinkets like mugs and greeting cards. Seattle FilmWorks Inc. includes Internet uploads free with its $10 film-processing charge, and many analysts think upload prices will fall rapidly. It's a similar story with picture CDs. Some retailers sell Fuji-made picture CDs – without the software Kodak adds – for about 30% less than Kodak.

Fisher understands all too well the power of rivals to undercut his prices. And he acknowledges the uncertainty around Kodak's digital strategy and ability to nimbly create a bridge between the old and new technologies. Kodak has "to come up with at least one or two big ideas every year" to add to its digital arsenal, he says. Kodak may have a few already, but in the digital world, even the best ideas can fade fast.

The hand Kodak is playing

Kodak's new leader, Daniel Carp, is unrolling a host of digital products

Picture maker kiosks

These do-it-yourself printers are Kodak's biggest digital success. Available in 19,000 stores worldwide.

Digital cameras

Kodak is No. 2 behind Sony in U.S. market share but has yet to turn a profit on them.

You've got pictures

A service set to launch this fall lets film labs deliver pictures to a customer's AOL account. Competitors offer similar products for free.

Picture CD

A new joint venture with Intel lets consumers put their pictures on compact disks. Rivals offer similar services for less.

Data: *Business Week*

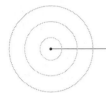

Company Profile 9
The Gillette Company
(Gillette)

Company overview

Gillette is the world leader in the blades and razors business. The company is also a major producer of toiletries, writing instruments and alkaline batteries. The company manufactures its products in sixty-four facilities in over twenty-seven countries and sells its products throughout the globe. In 1996 Gillette's revenues exceeded $9 billion. The company employs 31,000 people worldwide, with more than 75 per cent of them working outside the United States. The corporate headquarters of Gillette is located in Boston, Massachusetts.

Brief history

The history of Gillette dates back to 1895, when King C. Gillette developed the idea of disposable razor blades while shaving at home with a conventional razor. In 1901 William Nickerson of the Massachusetts Institute of Technology (MIT) joined Gillette to develop safety razors and formed the American Safety Razor Company in Boston. It first marketed the safety razor in 1903, and sold only fifty-one sets in the first year. By 1904, however, more than 90,844 sets had been sold. The company established its first overseas operation in London in 1905 and within thirteen years of the formation of the American Safety Razor Company its products were sold in eight countries. The company continued expansion through new product innovation and effective marketing of its products.

In the late 1940s the company started to diversify its business. In the 1950s Gillette adopted its current name. During the 1960s and 1970s Gillette further diversified its products lines. In 1967 Gillette acquired Braun, manufacturer of electric shavers and appliances. In 1984 Gillette expanded into dental products by acquiring Oral-B. In the early 1990s the company introduced the Gillette series, a line of men's shaving and skin products. In 1993 the Oral-B unit established a joint venture in Shanghai, China. At present the major business areas of Gillette are personal care products (blades, razors, oral care products and toiletries), stationery products (writing instruments and correction products) and small electrical appliances (small household appliances and batteries).

Innovation and significant contribution

Since the beginning, Gillette has made important innovations and expanded its business around the world. The company's strategically integrated international manufacturing, R&D, marketing and distribution systems have made significant contributions to the industry by establishing best management practices for global companies. Gillette's efforts to standardize products and services for the world market, its strategies on production, worldwide sourcing and management from any location, and coordinated international business activities have established the company as a leading world-class corporation.

Besides being the world leader in blades and razors, Gillette has many other products which are very successful around the world. For example, Braun is the number one marketer of electric shavers in Germany, other parts of Europe, North America and Japan. Oral-B is one of the major brand toothbrushes in the world. Duracell alkaline batteries are among the most popular batteries in the world. Each of Gillette's businesses has its own R&D facility. The company also has three corporate research laboratories, in Boston, Washington, DC, and Reading (in the UK).

Challenges and opportunities

Continuous product innovation and improvement of existing products, reduction of manufacturing costs and expansion to international markets (including the emerging markets in Asia, Eastern Europe and Latin America) are some of the major challenges confronting Gillette. To further increase its presence in the global marketplace Gillette must launch all its major products simultaneously in its markets around the world. To increase productivity of its global business activities it must implement state-of-the-art information and communication technologies (ICTs).

ROSALIE L. TUNG AND MOHI AHMED
SIMON FRASER UNIVERSITY

Further reading

Chakravarty, S.N. (1991) 'We had to change the playing fields', *Forbes* 147(3), 4 February: 82–4. (Discusses how Gillette manages change and integrates its marketing and product development.)

Higgins, R.B. (1996) *The Search for Corporate Strategic Credibility: Concepts and Cases in Global Strategy Communication*, London: Quorum Books. (Examines how Gillette manages stockholder communications.)

Hoover, G., Campbell, A. and Spain, P.J. (eds) (1995) 'The Gillette Company', *Hoover's Handbook of American Business*, Austin: The Reference Press, Inc. (Gives a general overview of the company.)

Kanter, R.M. (1995) *World Class: Thriving Locally in the Global Economy*, New York: Simon & Schuster. (Examines how companies can become competitive globally in their respective industries.)

Symonds, W. (1998) 'Gillette's edge: the secret of a great innovation machine? Never relax', *Business Week*, 19 January: 70–7. (Provides the historical background of Gillette's innovations and a discussion of the company's future plans as well as challenges.)

Gillette loses face

Fortune; New York; 8 November 1999;
Jeremy Khan

Abstract:

Until 2 years ago, Gillette was a fat, happy company; cushioned by years of double-digit growth, it was able to ignore a nasty snarl of problems just below the surface. The Asian crisis may have been painful in the immediate sense, but there are companies with greater exposure to international markets that have been making the estimates, like Colgate. The real damage inflicted on Gillette was to expose the company's underlying weakness: a culture plagued by inertia, inefficiency, and nostalgia; mismanaged inventories and receivables; a Goldbergian corporate structure cobbled together over years of acquisitions; and, most important, 3 decades-old divisions that have consistently – and badly – underperformed.

Gillette blames Asia – and a few organizational lapses – for its stock's slide. But the biggest problems are right under its nose.

Lab animals

At Gillette's shaving lab, new products get a test drive. The company could use a few more of them.

Nicked. Cut. Creamed. Over the past two years, headline writers have left no pun unturned in describing Gillette's performance. And if things keep going like this, the images are only going to get bloodier.

Anyone who watches the market knows the general contours of the story: A stalwart American stock – a company that since 1990 had pulled off not one but two of the greatest product launches ever, the Sensor and Mach 3 razors – suddenly finds itself tanking on an epic scale. By mid-1997, as the Asian economic crisis swept west, Gillette's earnings started to plunge (some 62% of its sales and 60% of its profits come from outside the U.S.). Compounding the shortfall was the company's recent $1 billion development and rollout of the triple-blade Mach 3, the most expensive launch in its history. By the end of the year, earnings growth had ceased completely; by the end of 1998, Gillette lagged its peer group – including Procter & Gamble and Unilever – in five year total return to shareholders. And on Sept. 28 of this year (1999), Gillette announced it would miss its quarterly sales targets – the fourth time in five quarters that it has fallen short of revenue or profit estimates, or both. The next day the company's stock dropped another 9%, to $33; that's 48% below its high for the year. In fact, the stock hasn't been this low since October 1996, when the Dow was at 6000.

True, Gillette, which is based in Boston, still owns the $7 billion worldwide razor and blade industry The Mach 3 is its most successful new product ever, hitting $1 billion in sales in just 18 months, something it took Sensor six years to do. Gillette is also the world leader in ten other product categories including alkaline batteries (Duracell), epilators (Braun), pens (Papermate), and toothbrushes (Oral B). And the company still has at least one well placed friend in Warren Buffett (see box), who for now hasn't moved to sell any of Berkshire Hathaway's 96 million shares. Obviously, the issue for Buffett – and for Gillette – is whether this is just a (big) dip or the beginning of a long slide.

Until two years ago, Gillette was a fat, happy company; cushioned by years of double digit growth, it was able to ignore a nasty snarl of problems just below the surface. The Asian crisis may have been painful in the immediate sense, but as Constance Maneaty, an analyst at Bear Stearns, points out, "There are companies with greater exposure [to international markets] that have been making the estimates, like Colgate."

The real damage Asia inflicted on Gillette was to expose the company's underlying weaknesses: a culture plagued by inertia, inefficiency, and nostalgia; mismanaged inventories and receivables; a Goldbergian corporate structure cobbled together over years of acquisitions; and, most important, three decades-old divisions that have consistently – and badly – underperformed.

Some of the company's logistical glitches have already been addressed. At the mundane level, for example, Gillette has been criticized for not moving inventory or collecting on credit sales as quickly as other makers of consumer goods – tying up capital that could be put to better use elsewhere. (Last year it overestimated demand for its razorblades and got stuck with hundreds of thousands in warehouses in December.) Now the company is finally installing software to help avoid the routine invoicing and delivery problems that have prevented it from collecting money on time.

Gillette has also begun rehabbing its structure. A new $535 million reorganization will shutter 14 factories and 12 distribution centers worldwide, consolidate 30 offices, cut 4,700 jobs (11% of Gillette's work force), and save $200 million a year. It will also try to streamline what has been a complex sales process. Until early this year, each of its product divisions operated autonomously: A given retailer was subjected to a seemingly endless stream of Gillette salespeople – one representing Braun, another peddling toothbrushes, a third pushing razors – none of whom knew much about what the others were doing. And this scene would be repeated in every market around the world. The new scheme should allow the sales staff to present "one face" to each customer.

All of that helps. In the end, though, those fixes skirt Gillette's real problem: It has been years since this company was more than just half great. Of Gillette's six businesses, three – razors and blades, Duracell batteries, and Oral B toothbrushes – are superstars. But Braun's profits fell 4% last year, dropping below 1996 levels. Gillette's toiletries such as shaving cream and Right Guard deodorant are down (earnings are 40% below their 1988 level, and profit margins are just 4%, compared with almost 40% for blades). And its stationery products group, which includes Papermate, Parker, and Waterman brand pens, has also flagged (profits fell 31% last year). Back when Gillette's overall earnings were leaping forward 15% to 20% a year, it was easy, convenient even, to ignore that these divisions were sucking wind. Now it's impossible. (Certainly, Henry Kravis isn't ignoring it. He recently filed to sell KKR's 51 million Gillette shares, which the firm received when it sold Duracell to Gillette in 1996, but hasn't done so because of their falling price.)

To analysts the solution is simple: Amputate. Gillette's three weak businesses account for 40% of its $10.1 billion in annual sales but less than 20% of profits, and that figure is dropping every quarter. There's no doubt that investors would like to see the company leaner. "Wall Street is wondering if the new CEO is going to roll up his sleeves and decide that some of the poor divisions are not as strategic as they were seen to be three to five years ago," says Mark Godfrey, an analyst at Invesco, which owns about 33,000 shares.

That new CEO is Michael Hawley, who took over in February. Hawley has worked practically his entire career – 38 years for Gillette, all but 14 of them away from company headquarters, mostly on international assignments in Hong Kong, Britain, Colombia, and Australia. Compared with his predecessor, Alfred Zeien, an extroverted salesman who relished proselytizing for Gillette on Wall Street, Hawley is affable but reserved. Still, he shares Zeien's vision of Gillette as a company driven by technological innovation and superior products – exactly the sort of R&D intensive strategy that produced Sensor in 1990. At that time, Gillette's razor business was threatened by disposables, which commanded more than 50% of the market and were moving it quickly toward commoditization. Gillette countered with a lavish campaign aimed at reestablishing brand loyalty (its "Best a man can get" ads). Then it backed up those ads with a demonstrably superior product – one that segmented the market and commanded a hefty premium from consumers. The result was that Sensor actually reversed the ascent of the disposable razor.

That formula – the use of superior technology and savvy advertising to segment markets and prevent commoditization – came to be known informally as "the Gillette way." And it's a model the company has returned to again and again, from Duracell's Ultra batteries to Oral B's $5 CrossAction toothbrush. But Gillette's efforts to apply this formula to its weaker divisions have been unconvincing.

While analysts urge Gillette to offload those divisions, Hawley plans to rescue them. But what if they're not worth saving? Gillette brass bristles at this kind of talk. It tends to engender long, quixotic speeches about Braun's leading market share in hand blenders. Almost to a man, these guys are company lifers. They've done tours of duty in every part of Gillette and feel a nostalgic affection for those hand blenders and aftershaves and Parker pens. They like to talk about "permanence." During the 1980s, Gillette fought off two hostile takeover attempts by corporate raiders that wanted to split it up; that they might have saved the company only to break it apart themselves a decade later is anathema to them.

This rather sentimental (or if you prefer, paternalistic) mindset means Gillette risks throwing good money after bad. Take Braun: Gillette bought the company in 1968, at a time when it feared electric shavers would doom the company's blade and razor business. That hasn't happened, in part because of the success of Gillette's own wet razors. But now Gillette is left with a business that doesn't fit so well with the rest of the company. Braun isn't even the clear leader in electric shavers, a market that has been in decline for the past four years. And while Braun is about to unveil a self-cleaning electric shaver in Japan that Gillette thinks will eventually be a hit worldwide, it isn't clear that this will be a Sensor-type breakthrough that can revolutionize the industry.

Moreover, holding onto Braun as is means that Gillette is also stuck manufacturing coffeemakers, kettles, and depilatory devices. And even if those products have great market share, they have lousy profit margins. Archie Livis, the executive vice president in charge of Gillette's diversified group (Braun, Oral B, and stationery) notes that those small appliances represent only 33% of Braun's sales, but "what happens is the Street equates Braun with small appliances." That's why Braun is cutting back spending on this part of its business. But why not sell it altogether? The best answer Livis can supply is, "At this point in time we wouldn't want to toss the baby out with the bathwater."

The only part of Braun worth keeping at the moment is its $550 million electric toothbrush business. Already run as a joint venture between Braun and Oral B, it is the fastest-growing category in the entire Gillette product line, with a 65% market share, profit margins that exceed the company average, and a $200 million to $300 million refill business. This part of Braun could easily be merged with Oral B completely, creating a $1.2 billion tooth-care unit. "If they would carve out the electric toothbrushes, they could sell the rest of Braun," says Bear Stearns' Maneaty.

Gillette's toiletries are also a drag on the overall operation, with the lowest profit margins at the company. And although Gillette leads the market in shaving cream, that's not the case with deodorant or shampoo. Last year, Gillette finally decided to bite the bullet and pare back some of its holdings. It sold Jafra cosmetics, and it's now looking to offload the White Rain hair-care line.

But if toiletries is a loser, you'd never know it from listening to Gillette executives. Peter Hoffman, Gillette's senior vice president in charge of grooming and batteries, insists that Gillette's shave-preparation business dovetails well with its razor business.

Fair enough. As for deodorants: "All our experience has taught us it is the next logical step in the grooming process," he says. "So when men and women get ready for the day, those functional toiletries they use, that have some cosmetic overtone, you would define as the shaving process and the deodorant process."

But this logic could be extended infinitely. Why doesn't Gillette make clothing? Or shoes? After all, once people shave and deodorize, most of them engage in what we would define as the dressing process. Edward DeGraan, Hoffman's boss, has a slightly better explanation. "Gillette does best in products that can demonstrate functional improvements," he says. "In products that move away from that kind of core premise, we do less well." But while the company has tried to apply the Gillette way to its toiletries, the basic problem remains: There's not much difference between Gillette's stuff and everybody else's, except that Gillette's costs more. That means toiletries become a kind of loss leader for Gillette's shaving business. But would retailers refuse to stock Gillette's blades – the bestselling blades in the world – just because they aren't getting Right Guard too?

Of Gillette's three weaker divisions, stationery may best lend itself to improvement through the Gillette way. Parker sold the same damn pens for 20, in one case 40, years. John Darman, the mastermind behind the Mach 3 launch and now senior vice president in charge of the stationery group, is looking to change that. He has introduced new advertising, which has already reversed Papermate's sliding market share during the all-important back-to-school season; a redesigned model line is set to launch early next year; and an R&D crew is working on a breakthrough – new inks, redesigned grips – that will do for writing what Sensor did for shaving. "We are not going to be a problem for this company starting next year," Darman says.

Darman is persuasive, but his plan will work only so long as Gillette doesn't have to spend too heavily to implement it. Even Hawley is cautious. "The danger is to make a big capital investment on something that doesn't have the type of margin and volume that a Mach 3 does," he says.

It has to be hard for Gillette, after so many years as a stock market stud, to find itself down and out. Indeed, simple denial may explain why, rather than facing the facts and sharply lowering earnings estimates for the year, the company has continued to set aggressive targets – and miss them. That in turn has created a credibility problem with Wall Street. "I think the stock reflects all this frustration that investors have felt for the past two years and skepticism about the timing of a recovery," says Wendy Nicholson, an analyst at Salomon Smith Barney, who recently lowered her fourth-quarter estimates for Gillette. "At its current price, any credible good news ought to be good for shareholders."

With Asia on the rebound and Hawley's restructuring well under way, good news isn't impossible. But without a few sharp cuts, Gillette may never be the growth stock it used to be.

Down, but hardly out

Ouch! No one has been hurt more by the precipitous drop in Gillette's stock than Berkshire Hathaway CEO Warren Buffett. According to Buffett's most recent letter to shareholders, Berkshire owned 96 million shares of "G" – 8.7% of Gillette's outstanding stock – as of Dec. 31, 1998. At Gillette's high in March that trove was worth more than $6.1 billion; today the value has shrunk to less than $3.7 billion (assuming Buffett has done no buying or selling since December).

To make matters worse, Buffett's 200-million-share position in Coke, worth as much as $17 billion in 1998, is now down to $10.5 billion. Thanks to Gillette and Coke alone, Buffett's stock holdings are down nearly $9 billion from their highs. Hardly the stuff of a rounding error! The reinsurance business has also been in the dumps lately, which has hurt Berkshire's General Re, and negative news in the car-insurance business is casting a shadow on Berkshire's Geico (though that subsidiary is in fine shape). No wonder that Berkshire A was recently trading around $57,500, down some 30% from its high of $81,000.

Still, you can't get too weepy for Warren. He got into Gillette by buying $600 million of preferred stock in 1989; he then exchanged it for 12 million shares of common in 1991. (Since then the stock has split three times, so it appears he's done no buying or selling.) As far as his investment in Gillette goes, he's up $3.1 billion. Coke? Up $9.2 billion. And there's been some pop in his portfolio this year too. His 50.5-million-share stake in American Express has climbed $2.4 billion since Jan. 1. Not only that, but lately Coke and Gillette have moved up a bit as investors nibble on those stocks, now at more than 30% off their highs. Not surprisingly, Berkshire has climbed a bit lately too. Andrew Serwer

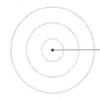

Company Profile 10
The Walt Disney Company

Company overview

The Walt Disney Company, together with its subsidiaries (Disney, in short), is one of the world's most diversified entertainment business organizations. Disney's major business segments consist of 'Creative Contents (consumer products operations, filmed entertainment activities not related to broadcasting, etc.)', 'Broadcasting (ABC television and radio networks, etc.)', and 'Theme Parks & Resorts (Disneyland Parks, Walt Disney World Resort in Florida, etc.)'. The company produces animated motion pictures, books and magazines, videos, computer-game software and live animation. The company distributes its products primarily through its own sales and marketing channels around the world. The company employs about 85,000 people worldwide and had annual revenues in excess of $18 billion in 1996. The corporate headquarters of the company is located in Burbank, California.

Brief history

The history of the Walt Disney Company dates back to 1919, when Walter E. Disney met Ub Iwerk while they were working together at a small studio that created animated commercials for use in local theatres in Kansas City. After learning about animation, Walt began creating his own cartoons and made short films called 'Laugh-O-Grams'. In 1922 Walt incorporated Laugh-O-Grams, but the company went bankrupt within a year of establishment. Walt moved to California in 1923 and began a short-film production business. The studio started to produce animated films and continued to expand. In 1955 Disney Land was opened at Anaheim, California. After Walt Disney's death in 1966 his brother Roy became the chairman of the company. In 1971 Disney World was opened in Florida.

Since 1984, under the leadership of Michael D. Eisner, Disney has continued to expand its business significantly. According to the company, the expansion includes international film distribution; television and radio broadcasting; ownership of cable systems and television stations, newspapers, magazines and book publishing; Disney stores; live theatrical entertainment; home-video production; interactive computer programs and games; online computer programs; ownership of professional sports teams; partnership with a telephone company; Disney regional entertainment; and Disney Cruise Line.

Innovation and significant contributions

The founder of the company, Walt Disney, established a standard for innovation and creativity throughout the entertainment industry. The company has made significant contributions to the entertainment industry by fostering creative talent. Since creativity is crucial to success in the industry, the company runs a professional development programme at its Disney Institute. The programme trains participants in how a world-class organization deals with real-world issues, in providing ideas for new strategies, and teaches knowledge and skills for new ways of doing business in the rapidly changing global marketplace. The company has shown that creativity is key to success in the entertainment business. Its leadership in this area has contributed to the development of the entertainment business. Disney was selected by *Fortune* magazine as one of the ten most admired companies in the US in 1998.

Challenges and opportunities

A major challenge for the Disney company is to maintain its leadership in the entertainment business in a world characterized by the globalization of the news media, products and services, extended deregulation of international telecommunication services, rapid technological change and increasing competition in the entertainment business. To compete with its emerging rivals (e.g. Universal Studios and Sony) and to increase opportunities in the global marketplace, the company has continued to diversify its businesses and make investments in new projects, such as building new theme parks and hotels.

ROSALIE L. TUNG AND MOHI AHMED
SIMON FRASER UNIVERSITY

Further reading

Flower, J. (1991) *Prince of the Magic Kingdom: Michael Eisner and the Re-making of Disney*, New York: J. Wiley. (Gives an overview of Disney's CEO, Michael D. Eisner, and a history of the Walt Disney Company, its productions as well as its reorganization.)

Grover, R. and DeGeorge, G. (1998) 'Theme-park shootout: a host of new competitors has Disney building like crazy', *Business Week*, 6 April: 66–7. (Explains how competition is shaping the business of Disney.)

Hoover, G., Campbell, A. and Spain, P.J. (eds) (1995) 'The Walt Disney Company', *Hoover's Handbook of American Business*, Austin: The Reference Press, Inc. (Gives a general overview of the company.)

O'Neal, M., Baker, S. and Grover, R. (1995) 'Disney's kingdom: as seismic shifts shake the media biz, Eisner lands on top – for now', *Business Week*, August 14: 30–4. (Discusses Disney's takeover of the ABC network.)

Stewart, T.A. (1998) 'America's most admired companies', *Fortune*, 2 March: 70–82.

Further resources

Disney website
http://www.disney.com

Eisner's mouse trap

FORTUNE; New York; 6 September 1999; Marc Gunther

Abstract:

Michael Eisner oversees the world's most troubled entertainment rodent giant. As Eisner sweats the details, earnings are dropping, top executives are defecting and Disney stock is plunging like a ride down Splash Mountain. Eisner, however, does not consider this a crisis. He does not believe that the company's problems are in the fabric of the organization. But shareholders do have reason to feel grumpy, with the stock trading at about 37% below last year's high, and there is no quick fix in sight. Home-video earnings have tumbled, and revenues from licensing and merchandising are down. Eisner presides over an insular – some say arrogant – corporate culture where decision making is hierarchical, centralized and slow. Eisner is cutting costs and reengineering, and he is making overseas growth a top priority. He also wants Disney to be an Internet giant, taking on Yahoo and America Online.

Disney's CEO says the company has a lot of varied problems he can fix. But what is the real issue is something he can't face?

Michael Eisner, the famously hands-on CEO of Walt Disney, is up to his old tricks. Last night he screened a rough cut of Dinosaurs, Disney's big animated movie for next summer; he loved the story but complained that some jokes were stale. Today he's holding a four hour brainstorming session about Mickey Mouse, looking for ways to keep the 71-year-old rodent relevant. (One idea: a skateboarding Mickey.) Later, he'll watch Peter Jennings' newscast on Disney owned ABC and surf the Internet to see how the company's Websites stack up. Is this any way to run the world's most troubled entertainment giant?

After all, as Eisner sweats the details, earnings are dropping, top executives are defecting, and Disney stock is plunging like a ride down Splash Mountain.

"Maybe I'm crazy," Eisner says, "but I don't consider this a crisis. I don't think our problems are in the fabric of our company. And I don't have my head in the sand." Sitting down for a two-hour interview, he admits mistakes. He says, for instance, that he should have settled former studio chief Jeffrey Katzenberg's suit against the company earlier to avoid a "parade of horrors" (see box). And he concedes that the company has sustained real damage: "It's like a train wreck, only nobody got killed." But Eisner denies that he has lost his touch. "The criticisms of me and Disney today," says the 57-year-old chief executive, "are as shortsighted as were the praises of me and Disney in the high economic times."

Sunday nights on ABC, Michael Eisner-celebrated CEO, business magazine cover boy, and author of his own life story – still hosts The Wonderful World of Disney. The rest of the week, life is not so sweet in the Magic Kingdom. Certainly shareholders have reason to feel grumpy, with the stock trading at about 37% below last year's high. There's no quick fix in sight either. Tarzan, the $160 million summer blockbuster, won't have much impact on earnings; the movie cost too much to make and isn't selling enough T-shirts and toys because the market's glutted with Star Wars stuff. That's one of the scary things about today's Disney: The company has grown so big and its problems are so far-reaching – ranging from the phenomenon of "age compression" to the explosion of media choices – that they can't be fixed by a couple of hit movies or TV shows or more Disney stores. The other scary thing is this: Disney seems less able than ever to cope with adversity. That's because Eisner, for all his creativity and charisma and grand plans, presides over an insular – some say arrogant – corporate culture where decision-making is hierarchical, centralized, and slow. It's an utter mismatch for the Internet age. "This isn't Mickey's house anymore," says a former Disney insider. "It's a multibillion-dollar company."

Eisner does have a plan. He is cutting costs and reengineering a company that got bloated with success. He's making overseas growth a top priority. He wants Disney to be an Internet giant, taking on Yahoo and America Online. And, yes, he'll keep on tweaking theme park rides and screening ABC pilots and driving subordinates up the wall with his meddling, because he fervently believes that if you demand high quality and develop synergy, financial results will follow.

"The interesting thing about our company," Eisner says, "which I think is extremely flattering, is that everybody takes for granted that we make good products. They think, Oh, the Disney cruise ship, they take a wand and a little pixie dust and all of a sudden you revolutionize the cruise industry from floating Vegas hotels to romantic ocean liners. There are zoos all over the world, and up comes the Animal Kingdom. Or Tarzan, or The Lion King on Broadway – people say, 'They have no trouble with the creative thing.' Well, it's the creative thing that turns the company around."

Besides, he declares, a bit impatiently: "We are the most profitable media company in the world. We're being buried a little prematurely here."

He's right about the bottom line. Last year Disney reported revenue of $23 billion, operating income of $4 billion, and net income of $1.9 billion – its net was far more than that of Time Warner (owner of FORTUNE's parent), News Corp., and Viacom combined. For the current fiscal year, which ends Sept. 30, Disney's revenue is expected to reach $24 billion. But all other key indicators are down, some shockingly so. For the first nine months of fiscal 1999, excluding a one-time gain from an asset sale, Disney reported declines in operating income of 17%, net income of 26%, and earnings per share of 27%.

Some Wall Street analysts have cut their fiscal 1999 earnings estimates as many as five times since last summer, and 13 of 25 analysts have a "hold" on the stock, according to Zacks Investment Research. The company has simply stopped growing, and it isn't a momentary dip either: Operating income fell slightly last year too, and Disney isn't expected to match its fiscal 1997 earnings until 2001 at the earliest – a startling comedown for a company that, for a decade after Eisner took over in 1984, delivered annual profit increases of 20% and a return on equity of 20%. Return on equity, a key benchmark that has been sliding ever since Disney's 1996 merger with Capital Cities/ABC, has slipped below 10%, estimates analyst Laura Martin of Credit Suisse First Boston. "Some people have the impression that Disney still is what it was – an animation company that generated great returns on capital," Martin says. "But that may be over."

Until recently Disney was propelled by a handful of big ideas that were executed almost flawlessly. First, Disney released its library of beloved animated films on video just as VCRs took off; nine of the ten bestselling titles of all time are Disney movies, and most, like Snow White and Cinderella, were paid for long ago. Second, Eisner and Katzenberg revived Disney animation with instant classics like Aladdin and The Lion King, which made big profits at the box office and on video and spawned even bigger ancillary revenues from licensing and merchandising. Third, Disney built more than 700 retail stores in the U.S., Europe, and Asia. Finally, the company embarked on a vast expansion of Walt Disney World, creating and updating dozens of attractions and building an astonishing 15,000 hotel rooms since 1988. (They called the strategy "Put the heads in the beds.") Disney's market capitalization soared from about $2 billion before the Eisner era to $85 billion at its peak in April 1998. Thanks to the rising stock price, Eisner got fabulously rich too, exercising accumulated stock options that gave him pretax gains of more than $500 million since 1992. He still holds 12.7 million shares, according to Disney's latest SEC filings, worth about $330 million at today's prices.

So what's gone wrong? Start with the fact that all the businesses that powered Disney, with the exception of the theme parks, are slumping. Home-video earnings have tumbled, partly because consumers now have shelves filled with Disney animation. Revenues from licensing and merchandising are down, partly because of the economic downturn in Asia, and sales and profits from the Disney Stores have declined because product lines have grown stale. "How many Mickey Mouse T-shirts can you sell?" asks Christopher Dixon, entertainment industry analyst for Paine Webber. Altogether, Disney's all-important Creative Content segment, which includes movie and TV production, home video, licensing, merchandising, and the stores, saw its operating income fall from $1.7 billion in 1997 to $1.4 billion in 1998; it decreased by another 42% during the first nine months of fiscal 1999. If that were a movie, they'd call it Honey, I Shrunk the Earnings.

In Eisner's view, the problems are unrelated. "A lot of things happened together to make our earnings slide," he says. Disney is attacking each concern, slashing costly production deals in the movie business, releasing fewer live-action movies, resting its classic video titles longer between releases to rekindle demand, and merging overseas distribution forces for film and video. To boost demand for consumer goods, the company will try to coordinate marketing in big retailers such as Wal-Mart. "We'd like to have a Disney boutique to sell the T-shirt, the lunchbox, the sheets and towels," says Peter Murphy, Disney's self-assured 36-year-old head of strategic planning.

Suppose, though, that the declining sales of videos and merchandise reflect a more fundamental issue-weakness in the Disney brand. This notion is such heresy inside Disney that everyone, including Eisner, dismisses it out of hand. "We have research on our brand in 20 or 30 countries, and we are almost without exception the No. 1 or No. 2 brand," Eisner says. Disney executives say that if the brand were in trouble, Disney's theme parks would be suffering along with the rest of the company; as it is, they're thriving – even the one in France. In the theme parks and resorts segment, revenues and operating income grew by 10% and 13%, respectively, in 1998, and they've grown by 14% and 13% so far this year. "We have as many kids lining up to see Mickey

Mouse as ever," says Paul Pressler, 43, the president of Walt Disney Attractions. "And our merchandise has done great." Disney World has reached beyond its core audience of young families to beckon conventiongoers, older people, and "pre-families," which is Disney-speak for single people. And it's capturing more money from visitors who stay in all those new hotels.

Sure, Disney's theme parks rule – it's parents who decide on family vacations – but the brand isn't holding up as well in crowded arenas like videogames and cable TV, where kids are more autonomous. Disney's interactive unit is an also-ran in the booming videogame business. On cable, the Disney Channel ranks a poor third in viewing among kids ages 2 to 11, behind market leader Nickelodeon and the Cartoon Network. Both Nick and Cartoon, relative newcomers to the kids' business, exploited Disney's vulnerabilities. "The Nickelodeon opportunity was to get inside the lives of today's kids," says Nickelodeon President Herb Scannell. "We've been contemporary. They've been traditional." While Disney characters are drawn from myths, history, and storybooks – just about every big Disney animated feature could begin with the phrase "long ago and far away" – Nickelodeon's TV shows and movies tell stories about real kids. Today the Viacom unit captures more than 50% of the audience of all children's TV programming.

When Disney tries to exude a hipper aura – think of the bestselling Phil Collins soundtrack from Tarzan – the company is more likely to speak to baby-boomer parents than to their offspring. Here's where that idea of "age compression" comes into play. Kids grow up faster these days, the experts say, and start emulating teenage behaviour when they're 9 or 10. They rebel against their parents and shy away from a "good for you" brand like Disney. Ten-year-old boys who watch wrestling or South Park on cable and 9-year-old girls who love Ricky Martin think Disney is for little kids. "They've never gotten past the problem that their core audience is girls 2 to 8 and their moms," says a former Disney executive. And even among young kids, the hot properties lately are Nickelodeon's Blues Clues, PBS's Teletubbies and Nintendo's Pokemon, now a hit TV show on the kids' WB, yet another new kid-vid network.

The cluttered kids' marketplace points to another fundamental problem facing Disney competition on a scale the company hasn't faced before, across all its businesses. Warner, DreamWorks, and Fox do feature animation. Universal just opened a second Florida theme park. Fox Sports is taking on ESPN. Can you begin to see why managing Disney today is harder than it was a decade ago?

What changed everything, of course, was Eisner's boldest stroke as CEO: his $19 billion merger with Cap Cities. That deal, cheered at the time, still appears strategically sound – the idea was to marry Disney content with ABC's broadcast and cable distribution. The problem has been execution. While ESPN and other cable properties have grown, no unit of the company is as besieged as ABC. It will lose money this year for the first time in a decade, despite a fantastic advertising marketplace, because audiences are splintering and programming costs keep climbing. (Disney agreed under competitive pressure to spend $9.2 billion-that's right, billion – for NFL rights for ABC and ESPN through 2008.) Operating income for the company's broadcasting segment, which includes ABC, its TV stations, 80% of ESPN, the Disney Channel, ABC Radio, and stakes in Lifetime, A&E, the History Channel, and E! Entertainment, grew by just 3% last year; it's down 18% so far this year, mostly because of ABC. "I'd be the first to say the results of the ABC television network, particularly in prime time, have been disappointing since the merger," says Robert A. Iger, 48, the lifelong ABC executive who is chairman of ABC Inc. While Iger's bailiwick extends way beyond the network, he keeps a close watch on programming and told FORTUNE in 1997, "Prime time is my No. 1 priority." Since then, ABC's ratings for its 18- to 49-year-old target demographic have fallen by another 13%, leaving the network No. 3, behind NBC and Fox. Oops.

Wait, it gets worse. Remember how the merger was supposed to marry content and distribution? That's not working well either. Owning and broadcasting a hit, then selling the reruns, is the best way to make big money today in television. Just ask Rupert Murdoch, whose Twentieth Century Fox TV studio not only owns the biggest hits on Fox – The Simpsons, The X-Files, and Ally McBeal – but also produces The Practice and Dharma & Greg for ABC, as well as key shows for NBC, CBS, and the WB. By contrast, Disney's Touchstone Television production studio has failed to develop a prime-time hit for ABC or anyone else since creating Home Improvement in 1991. Out of sheer frustration, Eisner last month merged the Touchstone studio into ABC; the idea is to save money and force the two units to cooperate. "It's a fantastic opportunity to reengineer the way television is done," says Lloyd Braun, the studio president who cochairs the merged unit with ABC's

Stu Bloomberg. Like a movie studio, ABC Entertainment now will develop, own, finance, and distribute more of its own content.

The trouble is, the new model could seal ABC off from the rest of the television world. While ABC executives say they'll still buy shows from studios like Warner Bros. and Fox, the studios worry about doing business with the new, vertically integrated ABC. "You're going to have to demonstrate to me in tangible ways that I'm going to get a fair shake," says Sandy Grushow, president of Fox's Twentieth Century Television. The other networks, meanwhile, suspect that any show they get pitched by a Disney entity will be an ABC reject. Beyond that, the merger adds another layer and the prospect of infighting at ABC Entertainment, now run by a posse that includes newcomer Braun, programmers Bloomberg and Jamie Tarses, network President Pat Fili-Krushel, ABC Inc. President Steve Bornstein, and Bob Iger, who still reads scripts of key ABC shows on weekends. Nor is Eisner shy about weighing in; he helped shape the fall lineup and ordered ABC to negotiate tougher deals with its affiliates and program suppliers, which are not happy. This management by committee has never worked in television, and it's not working at Disney-ABC.

There is much more at stake here than the unwieldy operation of the TV unit. The new ABC structure is emblematic of what may be Eisner's thorniest problem, if only because he doesn't seem to recognize it: It's Disney's corporate culture. Under Capital Cities, ABC was run in a determinedly decentralized way; executives were given authority and responsibility as long as they exercised fiscal discipline, and the company was generally well run. The Disney approach reflects different values: centralized control, an obsession with synergy at the expense of individual business units, a suspicion of outsiders, and a muddying of responsibility. The results speak for themselves.

Writing about the Disney culture is tricky because knowledgeable critics are unwilling to speak on the record; the company's just too powerful. But talk to enough people and you hear similar complaints. One persistent theme: Eisner insists on making too many decisions himself, which clogs the decision-making process. So do the roomfuls of strategic planners who analyze everything. A second complaint: Eisner's too tough. Working with Disney is notoriously difficult, so much so that a group of partners, including Coca-Cola, AT&T, Delta, and Kodak, used to meet informally to trade tips on how to cope.

A related point about Eisner: In spite of his affability, he doesn't really value other people. That's one reason the death of his longtime second-in-command, Frank Wells, in 1994, was a seminal event. Wells commanded Eisner's respect like no one else, told him when he was off-base, and deftly softened his edges. They were a great team. Eisner tried to replace him with Michael Ovitz, a crucial error at just the wrong moment. Ovitz's management got the ABC merger off to a dismal start, and his 16-month tenure scarred the company. Since then, strong executives have left, among them former CFOs Stephen Bollenbach and Richard Nanula, Internet guru Jake Winebaum, and former ABC executives Geraldine Laybourne and Steve Burke.

Finally, the critics say, the company has simply grown too big to be run from the top down. Eisner's approach worked for the old Disney, where the focus was on a single brand; he could gather a cadre of executives at his Monday lunches and get things done. Now Disney must manage multiple brands in a world where speed counts and partnerships are vital. A respected ex-Disney executive told me, "The company has changed and the world has changed, but Michael hasn't changed. Now he's got to change."

Eisner and his lieutenants bristle at the criticism from unnamed sources, and you can't blame them. Yes, they say, Disney is tough, but so are GE and Microsoft – which, by the way, lose lots of executives, too, because they have an abundance of talent. To the charge that he meddles, Eisner pleads guilty with an explanation: He wants Disney to excel. (Even his detractors say he has great instincts.) When he heard from a friend that the cast members at Disneyland Paris weren't as helpful as those at Walt Disney World, he recommended better training. "Is that meddling or is that insisting on a high standard of excellence?" Eisner asks. "If there's an area where I think I can add value, I dive in. Yes, at certain times I paralyze people. I'm never satisfied. It gets people crazy, I know that." But Eisner also says he leaves his best executives, like theme park chief Pressler, alone. "There's no brain drain," he says. "We have unbelievably strong management."

Eisner's turnaround strategy focuses not on Disney's culture but on operations, fiscal engineering, and growth. Consolidation and cost cutting are already under way across the board, with the movie division leading the way. Studio chief Joe Roth has already cut spending by about $550 million annually, by making fewer movies. "It focuses everyone much more closely on the films at hand," Roth says, "and ironically, I am quite sure that – for the fifth time in six years – we will be No. 1 in market share again this year.

Disney is also looking to sell Fairchild Publications, a magazine company. Sources say Disney also expects to write off a big chunk of the $9.2 billion NFL deal. In a move that should please Wall Street, CFO Thomas O. Staggs is reworking Disney's compensation system so that executives will be evaluated on cash flow and return on equity as well as on reported earnings; that's designed to encourage business units to use capital more efficiently. The theme park segment, in particular, has been a huge consumer of capital, but it will use less after new parks open near Disneyland and Tokyo Disneyland in 2001.

Disney's best growth opportunity probably lies overseas. Right now, the company gets about 21% of its revenues from abroad, less than other global brands like Coca-Cola (63%) or McDonald's (61%). That's why Bob Iger's recent promotion to president of Walt Disney International puts him in a crucial role, spearheading what Eisner calls "a monumental change in the way the company is structured." Iger has begun to overhaul all of Disney's operations outside the U.S., which grew up haphazardly as each business – film, TV, the stores, cable, or theme parks – built foreign outposts that reported back to the home office. Now those businesses will also report to regional executives in charge of continents or key countries; each territory will also get its own CFO and brand manager.

That may sound like more Disney layering, but Iger says it offers major advantages. First, the company will save money through consolidation, whether in renting office space or buying advertising. Disney also expects to do a better job of tapping into local trends. Iger cites a revealing example: "It's having someone in Japan who would see the Pokemon phenomenon at an early stage and have the clout, really, through me, someone who has a

seat at Michael's table, to be able to raise the consciousness level of the company about that potential quickly and effectively." Interestingly, the idea is not to delegate authority but to shorten the distance between the rest of the world and Eisner.

Eisner's other major focus is the Internet. Here, too, centralization is the watchword. Last month Disney agreed to combine its Internet assets with Infoseek, a search engine and portal company that it is buying outright; the properties, including the Go portal, ABCNews.com, ESPN.com, Disney.com, Family.com, and others scattered in five locations on both coasts, will operate as a single unit under a CEO to be named later. "This is to consolidate the Internet assets so that we can have them under common management with one agenda and one vision," says CFO Staggs, the 38-year-old architect of Disney's Internet strategy. The company will then issue a tracking stock called go.com that can be used as acquisition currency and a way to compensate talent.

Disney's assets should make it a force online. Its ESPN.com and Disney family sites are category leaders, and the company has unparalleled promotional platforms in ABC and ESPN. In a matter of months, they helped make Go the fifth ranked portal, behind AOL, Yahoo, Microsoft, and Lycos. And all the Disney Websites should sing when high-speed access makes it easier to watch video online. "As bandwidth expands," Eisner says, "content becomes more important. You must have sports and news and entertainment, or you are going to be a Western Union messenger in a fax world." He envisions a universe in which ABC News clips, ESPN game highlights, and movies like Aladdin are distributed online, cutting out middlemen like cable operators or Blockbuster Video. "I believe the entire company's product will mostly be distributed through the Internet," Eisner says. He's a passionate Internet user too, peppering his Web guys with suggestions. Says Staggs: "The only person I get more e-mail from than Michael is my mom."

The strategy sounds smart. Of course, buying ABC sounded smart too. Once again, it'll come down to execution. Patrick Keane, a Jupiter Communications analyst, likes Disney's Web assets but worries that "diversified media companies move at glacial speed when it comes to the Internet." Disney can't be as focused on new media as people at AOL and Yahoo are every day. And the straitlaced Mouseketeers will have to learn to live in an unbuttoned Internet culture, says new-media consultant Gary Arlen of Bethesda, Md. "Have you ever been to Disney World?" he asks. "You walk out of a ride and land in a place that sells souvenirs. They'd like to manage the Internet that way." Even with perfect execution, Disney's Internet investments need time to pay off; in the meantime, they'll dilute earnings.

Time is what Eisner needs too. Time for the cable and phone companies to help make his broadband Internet vision a reality. Time to build overseas. Time for DVD to take hold and provide another chance to resell the library. Time to create the next Tarzan and a hit for ABC, time for new theme parks to open, time to reinvent Mickey once more. Time, perhaps, to appoint a strong second-in-command with clout, whether it's Bob Iger or Paul Pressler or a dark horse who has yet to emerge.

Because he enjoys the support of the Disney board, Eisner can be patient. "We're in a transition period," he says. "I would rather have every quarter be up. It was for 13 years.

Everybody loves you. [But] you can't manage a company like ours quarter to quarter, maniacally, so that the media will write good things about you." He likes to quote Warren Buffett, whose Berkshire Hathaway, at last count, owned 51 million Disney shares: "I close my eyes and think about what a company's going to look like in ten years before I invest." Paine Webber's Chris Dixon says Disney's assets are top-notch: "It may take time, but we believe the values are there."

Other investors won't wait. They note that despite the earnings downturn, Disney is still priced as a growth stock; it trades at about 35 times this year's projected earnings, a 25% premium to the S&P 500. The Capital Research & Management Group, whose entertainment industry investments are managed by respected media analyst Gordon Crawford, used to be Disney's largest institutional shareholder, with 41 million shares as recently as last year. Crawford has sold them all.

So be it, says Eisner. "You can always tell your friends through the rough times," he says. He still gets to go to the movies, test-drive theme park rides, surf the Net, and call it work. And maybe it's just his turn to suffer in the media doghouse. After all, CEOs Gerald Levin of Time Warner and Sumner Redstone of Viacom fell out of favor when they struggled to get their arms around companies engorged by big acquisitions. Such mergers aren't easy. The challenge for Eisner is to learn from experience, show a little humility, seize the opportunity to shake up his company, and, perhaps, change his own stripes and let go a little. That's a lot to ask of anyone who's been as successful as he has for so long. But this isn't the old Disney. And the old Disney magic just isn't working anymore.

No hard feelings for Katzenberg

Here's a happy ending to a sad saga. Michael Eisner says that Jeffrey Katzenberg, the former Disney studio chief he derided as "that little midget" nano after they bitterly parted ways, deserved the payout he got for settling his three-year-old lawsuit against Disney.

"Frankly, he did a good job," Eisner says. Isn't that nice?

Eisner hesitates not at all when asked if Disney should have settled sooner. "Definitely. Definitely," he says. "We're not dumb. It was a parade of horrors." But, he says, contrary to the general presumption in Hollywood, it wasn't his personal animus toward Katzenberg that prolonged the litigation. The problem was that, at first, Eisner just could not believe the claim that Katzenberg had negotiated a lucrative private deal with the late Frank Wells entitling Katzenberg to a percentage, in perpetuity, of the profits made by certain Disney movies. Only as Wells' handwritten notes emerged at the trial did Eisner come to accept that Katzenberg had a legitimate claim.

While Disney and Katzenberg pledged not to disclose the settlement, published reports say it was worth about $200 million. Katzenberg had sought $250 million.

Says Eisner: "I'm glad it's over."

Company Profile 11
Airbus Industrie

Company overview

Airbus Industrie (Airbus) is one of the leading aircraft manufacturers in the world. Airbus was established in 1970 and has annual revenues of $9.6 billion (1997). Airbus shares its production with many partners around the world. Around 100,000 people worldwide are engaged in Airbus Industrie's operations, 32,000 of whom are directly involved in the manufacture of Airbus aircraft. Airbus Industrie is a consortium of four European aerospace companies: Aérospatiale of France (37.9 per cent), Daimler-Benz Aerospace Airbus of Germany (37.9 per cent), British Aerospace (20 per cent) and CASA of Spain (4.2 per cent). Its headquarters is located near the city of Toulouse in southwest France and has a staff of 2,700 of thirty-three different nationalities.

Brief history

In 1970 Airbus Industrie was established to build a twin-engine short-range wide-body aircraft. While European aircraft manufacturers had made a number of innovations in aircraft manufacturing – including the development of the turbojet engine, the first commercial jet aircraft, and the first supersonic airliner – they had less than a 10 per cent share of the world's aircraft market. Individual aircraft manufacturers in Europe were unable to compete against the size and resources of established aircraft manufacturers in the United States. To compete, a multina-tional consortium, Airbus Industrie, was formed. Airbus Industrie was established as a *groupement d'intérêt économique*, the French term for a grouping of economic interests. Under French law, the legal entity enabled its member firms to focus efficiently on a group project within a consortium framework. By 1995 Airbus had captured approximately 35 per cent of the world's aircraft market, and it hopes to increase its share to 50 per cent in the future.

Innovation and significant contribution

The consortium is one of the first major multinational collaborative arrangements in the world. It provides an outstanding example of how entities from different nations can set aside cultural differences to work together to accomplish a common objective, namely to develop an aircraft industry that could compete effectively against major US commercial aircraft manufacturers. The Airbus family comprises three different groups: 124–185-seat single-aisle A319/A320/A321; 220–266-seat wide-body A300/A310; and 263–350-seat wide-body A330/A340. From its inception, Airbus has followed one basic philosophy, namely to 'develop aircraft that fill market needs, design them with the requirements of airline users in mind, and apply the best technology to produce the most comfortable and economic airplanes available'. According to the company, these factors have contributed enormously to the consortium's success.

Airbus has one of the most efficient and flexible production systems in the world. Approximately 96 per cent of the aircraft are made in plants operated by its partner firms. Aircraft parts are manufactured throughout Europe, with final assembly in France and Germany. The consortium has been cited as an outstanding example of cooperative production in the manufacturing industry.

Challenges and opportunities

Airbus was formed to help increase the market share of European aircraft manufacturers through the sharing of development costs and cooperative efforts. At the beginning, each participating company had to meet the challenges of setting aside national pride and working hard to overcome difficulties posed by different languages, cultures, and systems of weights and measures. The founders saw a need to fill a market niche overlooked by the major US aircraft manufacturers, namely short- to medium-range aircraft with a capacity of 250–300 seats and which can operate economically. To expand its market share further in the decades ahead, the consortium must lower production costs and solve other management challenges, such as establishing a higher profile in industry and transforming itself from a joint venture to a single company.

Airbus has more than 1,500 suppliers in twenty-seven countries. It has also entered into cooperative agreements with other aerospace industries in nineteen countries. Its major suppliers in the world include General Electric, Honeywell, Westinghouse, and Allied Signal in the United States; Kawasaki Heavy Industry and Sumitomo Precision Products in Japan; Korean Air Aerospace Division in South Korea; and Hindustan Aeronautics in India. The challenge is how to work effectively with these various suppliers. Since many of these suppliers are leaders in their respective industries, there are tremendous opportunities for Airbus to grow and diversify further.

ROSALIE L. TUNG AND MOHI AHMED
SIMON FRASER UNIVERSITY

Further reading

Guyon, J. (1998) 'Airbus: the sole competitor', *Fortune* 137, 12 January: 102. (Discusses the transformation of Airbus management.)

McGuire, S. (1997) *Airbus Industrie: Conflict and Cooperation in US–EC Trade Relations*, New York: St Martin's Press. (Presents US–EC economic relationship, with special emphasis on Airbus.)

Spain, P.J. and Talbot, J.R. (eds) (1995) 'Airbus Industrie', *Hoover's Handbook of World Business 1995–1996*. Austin: The Reference Press, Inc. (Gives a general overview of the company.)

Thorton, D.W. (1995) *Airbus Industrie: The Politics of an International Industrial Collaboration*, New York: St Martin's Press. (Gives an overview of the consortium.)

Further resources

Airbus Industrie website
http://www.airbus.com

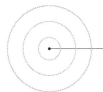

Company Profile 12
The Boeing Company

Company overview

The Boeing Company, McDonnell Douglas and North American, as one company, constitute the world's largest manufacturer of commercial aircraft. In 1997 the company received orders totalling $42.8 billion. These orders came from fifty-two customers around the world and constitutes almost two-thirds of the global market share. Boeing has its headquarters in Seattle, Washington, USA. The company's three major business segments are commercial aircraft, space systems and defence systems. Boeing is now the largest builder of military aircraft in the world, as well as the principal supplier of goods and services to the Pentagon and the National and Aeronautics and Space Administration (NASA). The corporate vision of the group is 'people working together as one global company for aerospace leadership'.

Brief history

Shortly after the Wright brothers' famous flight, William Boeing assembled his first seaplane and established the Boeing B&W Seaplane Company in 1916. In the 1930s and 1940s Boeing manufactured bombers and aircraft for commercial transport. In 1954 the company developed the first prototype of 707, which ultimately revolutionized air travel around the world. In 1967 McDonnell Douglas was formed by a merger of two separate companies, McDonnell and Douglas. The merged company continued to manufacture commercial aircraft, combat aircraft and space vehicles. McDonnell Douglas introduced the DC-3, which became so popular that 90 per cent of the world's air travellers flew on them. North American Aviation Inc. was first established in 1928. In the beginning the company focused its business primarily on small, single-engine aircraft to avoid competing with the manufacturers of large, multi-engine aircraft. During the late 1930s the company also began to make military aircraft. According to the company, between the years 1939–67 the company built more military aircraft than any other aircraft manufacturer in the United States.

McDonnell Douglas developed Mercury and Gemini, the manned space flights in the early 1960s. In 1968 Boeing introduced its jumbo jet, the 747, to meet the growing demand for air travel, and McDonnell Douglas developed the F-4 Phantom II fighter aircraft. The business interests of Boeing, McDonnell Douglas and North American began to intersect in the 1960s when they became partners in the NASA Apollo Program, followed by the International Space Station. The three companies finally merged in December 1996 to become the new Boeing. A prime motive for the merger was to compete more effectively with rivals.

Innovation and significant contributions

Boeing has made significant efforts toward system integration, customer satisfaction and continuous quality improvement and innovation. Boeing's knowledge and skills in designing, building, marketing and servicing of aircraft for decades has made it a truly global company. To reduce cost and to spread the commercial and economic risks associated with the design and manufacture of new aircraft, in the 1980s Boeing entered into co-production programmes with other entities around the world, including Alitalia of Italy and the Civil Transport Development Corporation of Japan. These collaborative efforts, particularly the one with Japan, have been decried by some in the United States as 'Faustian deals'. Some believe that, while Boeing may derive short-term economic benefits associated with such cooperative endeavours, in the long term, it may compromise the US's superiority in the aerospace industry.

According to Boeing, the development of the new Boeing 737 family and the new 767–400ER in response to customer demand was key to the company's position as market leader in 1997. In that year Boeing delivered 375 jetliners compared with Airbus's 182. Customer demand has also led to the expansion of the 767 family and the development of Boeing 777. The latter is the first aircraft to be designed from start to finish using computers.

Challenges and opportunities

Two major challenges lie ahead for Boeing. These include competition from Airbus and the financial crisis in Asia. Airbus, a European consortium which is heavily subsidized by the governments of France, Germany, Spain and the UK, has made significant inroads into the commercial aeroplane market around the world. Boeing has to deal effectively with this growing competition. Because of the economic growth in the Asia-Pacific region between 1960 and the mid-1990s, Asian countries have emerged as major purchasers of commercial aircraft. However, the financial crisis that began in late 1997 may lead to the cancellation of some orders.

According to the company, the long-term challenge for Boeing is to build a large-scale system that can integrate aeroplanes, space stations and launch vehicles. Success in such integration will create new opportunities for Boeing in the future. To maintain its competitive edge and to increase opportunities, Boeing must continue to integrate its systems, increase productivity in its manufacturing plants, reduce costs and respond effectively to the needs of its customers all over the world.

ROSALIE L. TUNG AND MOHI AHMED
SIMON FRASER UNIVERSITY

Further reading

Henkoff, R. (1998) 'Boeing's big problem', *Fortune* 137(1), 12 January: 96–103. (Discusses the challenges confronting Boeing's manufacturing systems.)

Rodgers, E. (1996) *Flying High: The Story of Boeing and the Rise of the Jetliner Industry*, New York: Atlantic Monthly Press. (Gives a historical account of Boeing and the jetliner industry.)

Further resources

Boeing Company website
http://www.boeing.com

Fearful Boeing

The Economist, 27 February 1999

It may come as a shock, but even Boeing's bosses admit that the firm is vulnerable to predators

THIS week Boeing's bosses swapped the mists of Seattle for the sunshine of Florida as they tried to reassure investment analysts and fund managers that the world's biggest aerospace company can pull its shares out of the descent that began when it announced its merger with McDonnell Douglas two years ago. Over that period, despite a few short rallies, the shares have lost a third of their value and Boeing has been the dunce of the Dow. At present levels, Boeing's capitalisation on some days dips below the value of its assets ($36.7 billion at the end of last year). That makes it vulnerable.

Indeed, last month Phil Condit, the firm's chairman, tried to shake the complacency out of 280 top Boeing executives by telling them that the company was a takeover target. He said that if they did not fix things soon, somebody else would come in and do it for them.

The idea that a predator could swoop on America's pre-eminent national champion might seem outlandish. Here, after all, is a company that still makes two-thirds of the big airliners in the sky, and is America's biggest exporter and its second-biggest defence contractor. But Boeing's new chief financial officer, Deborah Hopkins, reckons that, although the chances of a hostile bid are small, the company cannot be complacent until its shares are back nearer $60. Whether it likes it or not, Boeing is in play.

Boeing was vulnerable before, when T. Boone Pickens, a corporate raider, suddenly bought 15% of the company back in 1987. He soon melted away, but in the early 1990s there was speculation about a bid by General Electric (GE). It never happened. Instead Boeing has since turned predator, buying two defence groups, Rockwell Aerospace and McDonnell Douglas.

Boeing made a meagre profit last year of $1.1 billion on sales of $56 billion, after a loss the previous year. According to Ms Hopkins, only a quarter of its products – mostly military projects – are making decent returns. Most of its problems are in the civil-jet business. Boeing embarked on an expensive price war with its only rival, Europe's Airbus Industrie consortium, but Airbus still grabbed about half the orders last year. Because Boeing failed to make the 25% improvements in productivity that it sought, price-cutting led to losses on hundreds of deals. Worse, higher volume brought production lines to a halt, necessitating expensive overtime to unclog them and triggering penalty payments for late deliveries.

In the last quarter of 1998, Boeing, with its commercial-aircraft side under new management, started to recover, turning in a net profit of $465m. Around 50,000 workers are being shed. Unfortunately, the aviation cycle is now turning down; and Boeing is heavily exposed to the depressed Asian market. Mr Condit declared in early December that this year's profits might be as much as 25% short of the $2 billion that the market expected.

Boeing also has a couple of awkward products in its locker. Its smallest jet, the 717, is unlikely to sell any better under that label than it did when it was called the MD-95. It looks an early candidate for the chop. And its long-serving jumbo jet is coming to the end of its life. Boeing needs soon to replace it with an ultra-long-range version of its successful 777 aircraft. Otherwise it might have to spend more than $10 billion to develop a totally new replacement for the jumbo, whose operating costs are now too high. If Airbus were to proceed with its giant A3XX (the launch of which has been put back again, supposedly because of the Asia-led slide in the jet market) Boeing would be forced to invest heavily.

Bloodied, but strong

What does this mean to any predator? Here is a world-class company, with a brand name that is the best in the business and which has made three-quarters of the big jets flying today. Apart from the ageing 747 and the ailing 717, it has a healthy product range and two main businesses that are complementary (defence and civil jets), plus various space and infor-mation-systems activities, which have big growth potential. All it has lacked recently is the ability to extract value from this winning combination. Until now, analysts have thought that Mr Condit's job was on the line unless he improved Boeing in the first half of this year (despite the unfavourable turn of the civil market). But now he himself, to put the wind up his top managers, has raised the spectre of a takeover.

The new finance director has already commissioned a study which shows that about a quarter of Boeing product lines fail to create value. Top of the list, which has not yet been published, are probably the troubled 717 100-seater jet and the latest version of the big-selling 737, whose

production was most disrupted two years ago. Out of $13 billion of investment, she has identified about $2 billion that makes insufficient returns, and a further $1.3 billion that actually makes losses. More detail may be given in July, or whenever Boeing cancels programmes or sells something.

The man at the amiable Mr Condit's side, labouring to get Boeing's head up again, is Harry Stonecipher, his chief operating officer. He is an alto-gether tougher nut, coming from GE's aero-engine division via McDonnell Douglas, and imbued with the "fix it, sell it or close it" mentality that GE's boss, Jack Welch, has instilled in the company. And that is what lies behind the latest scrutiny. Intriguingly, GE is seeking to do a deal that would bind the companies closer than they have ever been.

Boeing's problem with a long-range 777, the product it needs most, is the huge engines required to power it. GE is offering to build such an engine in return for an exclusive contract to supply it. To land the deal, GE could offer to finance sales of 747s to hard-up Asian airlines. GE would be sharing some of the risks at the tail-end of the jumbo's career, but also helping Boeing to make the transition to a life without the aircraft that has made the bulk of its profits over the past 30 years.

It may be this degree of co-oper-ation that has led to rumours of GE launching a new bid for Boeing. For Mr Welch, it would be a dramatic finale to a stellar business career. On February 24th Mr Condit testily refused to comment on such suggestions. For its part GE flatly – and unusually – denied having any designs on the company. The rumours may have arisen only because GE is one of the few firms that could take on such a huge acquisition as Boeing. But they are also a comment on Boeing's management. GE's success is based on its ability to make assets sweat harder for shareholders. A Welch-like axe wielded over Boeing's wealth-consuming projects is just what is needed to chop away Boeing's loss-makers.

© *The Economist* Newspaper Limited, London (27 February 1999).

Company Profile 13
AT&T Corporation

Company overview

AT&T Corporation is one of the world's leading providers of communication services, with annual revenues exceeding $74 billion (1996). The company currently offers long-distance services to almost every country and territory in the world. It has operations, joint ventures and alliances in more than thirty countries, and employs more than 130,000 people worldwide. AT&T provides state-of-the-art communications networks, long-distance and wireless services, online services, access to home entertainment and local telephone services as well. The company also offers consulting, outsourcing, systems integration, customer-care services for larger businesses and manages one of the largest credit card programmes in the world. The corporate headquarters of AT&T is located in New York City.

Brief history

AT&T Corporation, formerly the American Telephone and Telegraph Company, was established in 1885 in New York as a wholly owned subsidiary of the American Bell Telephone Company to manage and expand the long-distance businesses of the company and its licensees. In 1899 American Bell sold all of its assets (except AT&T stock) to its subsidiary, AT&T, and as a result AT&T emerged as the parent company in the Bell Systems, assuming the holding company functions previously exercised by American Bell Telephone Company.

In the early 1900s the Western Electric Company, a subsidiary of AT&T, manufactured equipment to meet the needs of the world's telephone companies. A subsidiary of Western Electric, International Western Electric Company, had expanded its operations to London, Paris, Vienna, Milan, St Petersburg, Tokyo, Montreal, Berlin, Antwerp and Buenos Aires by 1914. In 1925 International Telephone and Telegraph Company (ITT) was formed and the International Western Electric Company was sold to ITT.

Until 1984 AT&T was the parent company of the Bell Systems. During the period of 1984–96 AT&T was an integrated provider of communication services, products, network equipment and computer systems. In 1991 AT&T merged with NCR. This gave AT&T the ability to meet its customer needs for networked computing. In 1993, through the acquisition of McCaw Cellular, AT&T was able to provide services in the fast-growing cellular services market. The continuous change in the industry and customers' needs shaped AT&T's evolution as an integrated telecommunication and information services and equipment manufacturing company.

On 20 September 20 1995 AT&T announced a major corporate reorganization and was split into three companies: AT&T, Lucent Technologies and NCR Corporation. Lucent became an independent systems and technology company on 1 October 1996; NCR Corporation became an independent computer business company on 31 December 1996; and AT&T became a communications services provider company. Currently, AT&T consists of Consumer Markets Division (CMD), Business Markets Division (BMD), AT&T Solutions, AT&T Wireless Services, AT&T Local Services Division, AT&T Universal Card Services, Network and Computing Services, and the AT&T Labs. In end October, 2000, AT&T has decided to split into four separate companies: broadband applications, wireless, consumer services and business services.

Innovation and significant contribution

Over the years AT&T Labs has developed new technologies, products and services to support the company's customers. According to AT&T, more than two patents are filed every business day to help shape the future of communications. AT&T's continuous efforts in product innovation have made significant contributions to the telecommunications industry around the world. In 1915 AT&T engineers experimentally transmitted the first human voice across the Atlantic Ocean via radio. In 1927 the company inaugurated the first commercial transatlantic telephone service using two-way radio. Through direct radio links, AT&T expanded its services to other countries as well. AT&T developed cellular wireless communication technology, communications satellites, commercial ISDN long-distance network services and optical digital processors, which have changed the way people communicate today. AT&T labs engages in R&D in networking, speech- and image-processing, computer science, communications systems, and a wide spectrum of new communications services concepts, technology development and implementation.

AT&T serves both large and small businesses, and government customers around the world with a wide range of advanced long-distance, local, wireless, video, data and Internet services. The company has also helped multinational corporations identify and realize through the power of networking new sources of value that link business, strategy, people, processes, organizations, structures and technology together. AT&T's leading digital PCS (personal communications service) provides a powerful combination of voice, messaging and paging communications in a single hand-held wireless device. The company's Wireless Services is also a global leader in aviation communication. AT&T has received the Malcolm Baldridge National Quality Award on three occasions (twice in 1992 for the manufacturing and service categories, and again in 1994 in the service category).

Challenges and opportunities

One of the major challenges for AT&T is to create and provide enhanced tailor-made services to its customers around the world. To increase its opportunities and compete in the emerging digital age and electronic commerce, AT&T has to make continuous efforts to provide state-of-the-art Internet and wireless communications, and an infrastructure that will allow the company to provide the best services to its customers. According to AT&T, the company has made efforts to integrate life-cycle environmental, health and safety considerations into its business decisions and activities in order to be recognized by the global community as a world-class company that contributes to human health as well as the global environment through innovation.

ROSALIE L. TUNG AND MOHI AHMED
SIMON FRASER UNIVERSITY

Further reading

Danielian, N.R. (1974) *AT&T: The Story of Industrial Conquest*, New York: Arno Press. (Provides a detailed case study of AT&T showing how scientific research can have a major impact on industrial development, employment and the earning of monopoly profits.)

Hamblen, M. (1998) 'AT&T makes comeback', *Computerworld* 32(3), 19 January: 114. (Gives financial analysts' perspectives on the company's financial direction.)

Hoover, G., Campbell, A. and Spain, P.J. (eds) (1995) 'AT&T Corporation', *Hoover's Handbook of American Business*, Austin: The Reference Press, Inc. (Gives a general overview of the company.)

Kanter, R.M. (1995) *World Class: Thriving Locally in the Global Economy*, New York: Simon & Schuster. (Provides guidelines on how companies can become globally competitive in their respective industries.)

Kleinfield, S. (1981) *The Biggest Company on Earth: A Profile of AT&T*, New York: Holt, Rinehart & Winston. (Gives an overview of AT&T.)

Quinn, J.B. (1992) *Intelligent Enterprise: A Knowledge and Service Based Paradigm for Industry*, New York: Free Press. (Discusses the management of knowledge-based service companies, including AT&T Bell Laboratories.)

Further resources

AT&T Corporation website
http://www.att.com

AT&T: The problems keep on coming

Business Week; New York; 18 October 1999

Abstract:

When C. Michael Armstrong arrived as CEO of AT&T 2 years ago, he could do no wrong. He lifted the moribund giant out of years of stagnation and charged ahead with a strategy to move AT&T into fast-growing markets. But something has gone awry. The company's long-distance is crumbling faster than expected, and Armstrong's bet that cable is the way out is hitting snags. As if that were not enough, the competition just got a whole lot scarier, with MCI WorldCom's announced acquisition of Sprint. AT&T stock, which had been on a tear since Armstrong's arrival, is in a swoon. Shares have tumbled 27% from their high in January, to 46 5/8, slashing AT&T's market capitalization by about $55 billion, to $149 billion. But Armstrong says concerns over AT&T's strategy are misplaced and overblown.

Alisa Daskarolis signed up for local telephone service from AT&T in mid-August, and she's not happy. "Can you hear that?" the 39-year-old math teacher asks as a loud hum interrupts a phone interview. She is using AT&T service that runs over a cable-TV network, new technology that is essential to the future of the company. But if this is the future, it has left Daskarolis wanting. She says she can't use her cordless phone in all the places she used to. "I can't go into the garage. I can't sit outside on a sunny day," she says. And she can't get over how her first month's billing got messed up when AT&T charged her $93, and she owed $53. After she complained, the company fixed its mistake, but it left her irked. "That's the kind of stuff that makes life frustrating," she says.

It's also the kind of stuff that AT&T can't afford right now. When C. Michael Armstrong arrived as CEO two years ago, he could do no wrong. He lifted the moribund giant out of years of stagnation and charged ahead with a strategy to move AT&T into fast-growth markets. But something has gone awry. The company's long-distance business is crumbling faster than expected, and Armstrong's bet that cable is the way out is hitting snags. As if that weren't enough, the competition just got a whole lot scarier: On Oct. 5, MCI WorldCom Inc. announced a $129 billion deal to acquire Sprint Corp., creating a powerhouse that nearly matches AT&T in long distance – while being far mightier in Internet services. "This merger allows us to compete head-on with AT&T," crows John Sidgmore, WorldCom's vice-chairman.

Indeed, the potent WorldCom-Sprint combo only brings AT&T's high-wire strategy into stark relief. Now WorldCom CEO Bernard J. Ebbers is packing a holster full of weapons to attack the industry leader – wireless, Net, long distance, international, and even local services. And Ebbers, a pragmatic former motel manager, will be using tried-and-true technology instead of the unproven cable-TV networks that the bold Armstrong is betting on. Armstrong has ponied up $110 billion to acquire two cable companies and will have to spend an additional $7 billion spiffying up the networks – mega-money that has Wall Street in a stew that AT&T will never see a payoff.

Making matters worse, just when Armstrong could use seasoned hands at his side, he's wrestling with turmoil in his top ranks. The latest development: On Oct. 6, Leo Hindery JR., the respected cable-industry veteran who was overseeing AT&T's push into cable telephony and Internet services, stepped down. That's the sixth top exec to depart in the past 21 months. Even John D. Zeglis, a brainy lawyer who has taken on the critical operational role of president, considered another job recently.

Defensive

AT&T stock, which had been on a tear since Armstrong's arrival, is in a swoon. Shares have tumbled 27% from their high in January, to 46 5/8, slashing AT&T's market capitalization by about $55 billion, to $149 billion. Over the same period, the Standard & Poor's 500-stock index is up 6%, and WorldCom's stock has slipped a modest 9%.

Suddenly, the seemingly indomitable Armstrong is on the defensive. Some have begun to question whether he will pull off his radical plan for transforming AT&T. After arriving from defense contractor Hughes Electronics Corp., the tough-talking, Harley-riding CEO quickly laid out a road map for making his new company less reliant on the long-distance business. His goal: to broaden AT&T into a communications behemoth, offering everything from speedy Net connections and telecom consulting to wireless and local phone service – to anyone, anywhere, by any means. It is a transformation on the scale of General Electric Co.'s makeover – from an appliance maker into a powerhouse in businesses as diverse as finance, entertainment, and jet engines.

Armstrong's task is no less onerous. He has broken from the pack by entering the $100 billion local telephone market through phone service over cable-TV pipes. The only problem is that cable systems are notoriously unreliable. That means he must make the cable networks as rock-solid as phone systems that have been fine-tuned for more than a century. While cable telephony has worked in the labs, the challenge of broad usage has defeated some of the country's best engineers. The conundrum: Cable phones operate on a network that customers share with their neighbors – so interference from the guy down the block can wreak havoc on phone quality. "I battled this for 10 years and threw in the towel," says Ralph Ungermann, who began working on cable telephony in the mid-1980s at Ungermann-Bass. "I think there are real serious technical problems."

"Execution"

Hogwash, says Armstrong. He characterizes concerns over AT&T's strategy as misplaced and overblown. Sure, a price war is battering his long-distance business, but he points out that the company is cutting costs so aggressively that it will continue to generate the cash that's essential to fund new businesses. And he is as committed as ever to cable. He believes that phone calls over fat pipes will become a formidable competitor to the existing phone networks as AT&T works out the kinks over the next year. "You know how in real estate the mantra is: location, location, location," he says. "Ours is: execution, execution, execution. We have the game plan and we have the technology. Now we have to make them work."

But can he? It will take near-flawless management to avoid the enormous pitfalls on every side. The long-distance business looks like a disaster in the making. And a massive rollout of cable telephony will be so complicated that it could very well take longer – and cost far more – than expected.

Here's what makes the task so tough. With Armstrong spending $110 billion in stock on two cable companies, earnings in the next few years will be watered down – because they're sprinkled across more shares. To boost income enough to make the deals contribute to earnings by 2004, Armstrong will need 7.6 million cable telephony customers paying nearly $800 a year, or $66 a month, and 5.6 million Net access subscribers paying $340 a year, or $28 a month. Those are ambitious goals, considering the company's customers now number a mere 3,000 for cable telephony and fewer than 1 million for Net access. Given the technology, marketing, and management risks, many investors are skeptical that Armstrong can hit such high targets. "I think he's screwed," says Sanford Rich, a managing director at GEM Management Capital, a money manager that invests in telecom stocks but does not hold AT&T.

If Armstrong can prove the skeptics wrong, though, the payoff will be enormous. He's banking that revenues from the cable operations will grow an average of 24% annually for the next five years, to $21.6 billion in 2004. That will more than make up for the slowdown in the long-distance business. Along with the vibrant wireless and consulting operations, cable would push AT&T's revenues up more than 10% per year, to nearly $100 billion in 2004.

Already, Armstrong is making progress. Thanks to innovative marketing and pricing plans, AT&T Wireless Services is soaring. One big reason AT&T still expects to hit Wall Street forecasts for this year is that the company figures wireless revenues will rise 40%, to $7.6 billion. AT&T Solutions, its consulting and outsourcing business, is expected to jump nearly 50%, to $1.6 billion. And the broadband Internet access service Excite@Home, in which AT&T holds a majority voting stake, boosted its number of customers 35%, to 620,000, between the first and second quarters.

Armstrong will need every bit of that to make up for troubles in the long-distance business, where AT&T still gets 72% of its revenues. Rivals MCI WorldCom and Spring Corp. unveiled aggressive new price cuts this summer that forced AT&T to respond with its own 7 cents-a-minute offer. The result: Revenues in the consumer long-distance market will decline as much as 5% this year, concedes Armstrong. At the same time, he says, growth in business long distance will slow to 7% or less, compared with the 9% that analysts were expecting. All told, AT&T's long-distance revenues will be roughly flat, at about $46 billion, vs. the $48 billion analysts originally predicted.

Maverick

And with Baby Bells such as Bell Atlantic Corp. preparing to enter the market, it's bound to get worse. That's especially true in the consumer long-distance market, where AT&T's revenues are expected to drop 8%, to $19.8 billion, in 2000, according to analyst Tod A. Jacobs of Sanford C. Bernstein & Co. "Wall Street is right to be worried," says Mark Bruneau, president of the business-strategy group at Renaissance Worldwide.

It doesn't help that AT&T is struggling with cultural clashes. Already, the mixture of the tradition-bound phone company, two maverick cable players, and a relatively new chief executive is showing signs of strain. There were tensions between Armstrong and Hindery before Hindery's abrupt departure, insiders say. Hindery lost much of the independence he had at TCI, while Armstrong felt Hindery wasn't committed enough to meeting his financial goals. That could foreshadow even more conflicts between the button-down CEO and the rough-and-tumble cable execs.

And Armstrong may soon lose another key manager. Zeglis, who was a serious candidate for the CEO post at AT&T when Armstrong was named, has suffered recent setbacks. When Hindery argued that he should report directly to Armstrong instead of to Zeglis, Armstrong agreed. Now Zeglis has no responsibility for the cable operations. And Zeglis didn't play much of a role in the MediaOne acquisition. He toyed with taking the top post at Compaq Computer Corp. before pulling himself out of the running earlier this year, and headhunters say he's willing to consider other jobs. Zeglis says only, "I'm doing thrilling things. No, I'm not out looking."

Executive turnover has prompted a number of questions about Armstrong's leadership style. While the company used to have a collegial culture, Armstrong is demanding and gruff. "Nobody ever got dressed down before, but Mike has done that several times," says one former executive. He's particularly tough on execs who don't deliver on revenues and expense targets. "If you're not on your numbers, there's a lot of fear and trepidation when you go to see him," says Tom Byrnes, a former AT&T manager.

At times, that has bruised egos and damaged morale. Some execs feel he has been dismissive of longtime AT&T managers and what they have accomplished in the past. "That has convinced some people to think about leaving," says a top manager who recently departed. Indeed, a survey of AT&T employees conducted in January and February showed that job satisfaction decreased the closer execs were to the top – the opposite of what personnel experts tend to find.

There are those, however, who say Armstrong's tactics are exactly what AT&T needs. "The culture is definitely changing, and some people who are lifers may not like that. But I think it's for the good," says Joel Gross, a former AT&T exec who is now chief financial officer of telecom startup Broadview Networks. Armstrong sets quantitative goals throughout the organization. Salespeople in the business-services unit must now meet revenue targets that range from $5,000 to $20,000 per month. "Yes, he's relentless," says Zeglis. "I think in our situation I would accept nothing less than a leader who is as demanding as Mike Armstrong. We have a lot to do."

For starters, AT&T is facing a regulatory battle over its proposed $62 billion acquisition of cable player MediaOne. Along with the acquisition of TCI that closed in March, the MediaOne deal could put AT&T over the Federal Communications Commission's limits on cable ownership, depending on how the FCC votes to revise its rules for cable ownership on Oct. 8. AT&T argues that it shouldn't have to dispose of any properties, but regulatory analysts say there's a chance AT&T may have to sell the 25% of Time

Warner Entertainment that MediaOne owns or other assets. "It's not a matter of if they're going to sell, it's a matter of how much they're going to sell," says analyst Scott C. Cleland of Legg Mason's Precursor Group.

Clouded

Just as crucial is how regulators affect AT&T's push into the business of selling broadband Net access. Through Excite@Home, the company is offering Net connections that are 20 times faster than today's traditional cable modems. But AT&T could get tripped up: Several cities say that because cable is a monopoly service, the company should have to let competitors such as America Online Inc. sell Internet access on its network. Portland (Ore.) officials plan to force AT&T to share its cable network, and earlier this year the city won a U.S. District Court ruling against AT&T upholding the decision.

Uncertainty will cloud the issue for several more months. The Ninth Circuit Appellate Court, which will decide an appeal of the Portland decision early next year. AT&T is confident that it will prevail, and most Wall Street analysts agree. But regulatory experts are less certain.

That's only the start of the problems with Excite@Home. There are simmering tensions between Excite and AT&T. Excite CEO Thoms Jermoluk wants to dish up content such as news stories and chat services along with Net access. AT&T, on the other hand, doesn't want Excite in the content business so it can market Net access with any content a customer wants, be it from AOL or Yahoo! Inc. "It would be a less valuable position for

us to saddle up to a particular content provider," says John C. Petrillo, the company's strategy chief.

The most critical challenge for AT&T, though, is rolling out cable telephony. In the Fremont trials, the experiences of customers such as Daskarolis suggest there's work ahead. Even glitches with the Excite@Home service are beginning to reflect on AT&T's phone service. Fremont resident Bruce J. Brown says the reliability of Net access is so spotty that he turned down an offer to be part of the phone-over-cable trial and receive $150 a month. "God, no, I'd never touch that," he says. "As far as I can tell, their infrastructure can't support reliable Internet service. Why would it provide reliable phone service?"

AT&T says cable technology is going to work just fine. It's operating in five test markets and is being sold commercially in Fremont and Chicago. The company plans to limit commercial and test users to 3,000 until the end of the year so that it can carefully work out any problems. "We're learning a lot about this business," says Curt Hockemeier, who is overseeing the effort. "In a word, the trials are going great."

So where does all this leave AT&T? The company's future may well be determined in the next year. If WorldCom gets approval to buy Sprint, the company will face a stronger competitor. How much of MediaOne it gets to acquire will affect the breadth of its reach in the U.S. And if AT&T can't get cable telephony to work on a massive scale at a reasonable cost, it will be in serious trouble. In the meantime, Armstrong's plans for a grand transformation hangs in the balance.

C. Michael Armstrong is named chairman and CEO Jan. 8, 1998

AT&T agrees to acquire upstart local phone company Teleport for $11 billion Jan. 26, 1998

Armstrong unveils strategic initiatives and plans to cut 18,000 jobs June 24, 1998

AT&T agrees to acquire cable giant Tele-Communications Inc. for $48 billion May 6, 1999

AT&T outbids Comcast to buy cable player MediaOne Group for $62 billion July 13, 1999

Florida's Broward County votes to force AT&T to let other companies use its cable network to provide Internet access Aug. 30, 1999

After aggressive price cuts by MCI WorldCom and Sprint, AT&T introduces 7 cents a minute long-distance plan Oct. 5, 1999

MCI WorldCom agrees to acquire Sprint for $129 billion Oct. 6, 1999

Leo Hindery, Chief of AT&T cable operations, resigns

AT&T's Six Challenges

Armstrong must overcome hurdles to transform the company from a long-distance player into a communications Goliath.

Long Distance

AT&T is troubled, and it's going to get worse. Because of a price war with Sprint and MCI WorldCom, AT&T's consumer long distance is projected to shrink about 5% this year, to $22 billion. The decline could accelerate when Bell Atlantic and other Baby Bells enter the market. AT&T's long distance for businesses is growing 6% this year, to $24 billion, although that's likely to slow in the future. Such pressures prompted AT&T to announce plans for $2 billion in cuts.

Wireless

This business is red-hot, thanks in large part to AT&T's Digital One Rate, which includes roaming and long distance for a flat fee of 11 cents to 15 cents a minute. The wireless business is projected to surge about 40%, to $7.6 billion, this year. Still, Sprint is adding more subscribers, and it's marketing wireless Web browsing that AT&T can't match. And the wireless joint venture between Bell Atlantic and Vodafone unveiled in September creates a major third competitor with national reach.

Local Phone Service

This remains a work in progress. AT&T has high hopes of selling local phone service over its cable-TV network, but there have been quality problems in its Fremont (Calif.) test market. AT&T has also announced a deal with Time Warner to offer cable telephony starting in February, but the two have yet to agree to final terms. Still, AT&T says it is on track to be in nine test markets with cable telephony by early 2000. It is selling service commercially in Fremont and Chicago.

Cable Television

Armstrong pulled off a coup by cutting a deal to buy MediaOne Group after Comcast appeared to have the company locked up. But he faces hurdles in getting the $62 billion deal closed. The FCC is concerned that AT&T could have too much of the U.S. cable market, and it may force the company to sell some cable properties, including perhaps MediaOne's stake in Time-Warner's cable business. If the deal closes, it will make AT&T the largest cable company in the country.

continues

International

After a previous international partnership floundered, AT&T created a joint venture with British Telecommunications last year to deliver services to multinational corporations. The venture has strong prospects. Both sides are chipping in assets that will generate a combined $10 billion in revenues, and they hired former Pacific Bell exec David Dorman to run the venture. If all goes well, this could well lead to an eventual merger between the two telecom giants.

Broadband

The cable-TV network has tremendous potential to deliver zippy Internet connections to U.S. homes. Excite@Home, in which AT&T has a majority voting stake, increased its cable-modem subscribers by 35% in the second quarter, to 620,000 people. But a strategic dispute is clouding relations between the two companies. Excite@Home is moving into content, while AT&T would prefer to sell Net connections without content. That way, it could market Net access with Excite rivals.

Turmoil At The Top

AT&T has lost several executives since CEO Mike Armstrong arrived at the company two years ago – and more could go. Jeffrey Weitzen, the former head of AT&T's business unit, left in January, 1998, to become COO of PC maker Gateway, lured by a $1.4 million signing bonus and an options package worth $21 million, according to Gateway's most recent proxy.

Gail McGovern

After Armstrong became CEO and Zeglis took the president post, McGovern, president of the consumer-services division, had no room to rise within AT&T. She left in August, 1998, to become an executive at Fidelity Investments.

Robert Annunziata

Annunziata came to AT&T as part of its acquisition of upstart Teleport, and was promoted to head up the business segment of AT&T. But he left in February to become CEO of hot telecom startup Global Crossing.

Daniel Schulman

The former head of AT&T's WorldNet Internet access business and, briefly, its consumer-services unit joined Internet startup priceline.com in June. He received a $300,000 salary and options on 3 million shares that now are underwater.

Leo Hindery Jr.

The well-respected former president of Tele-Communications came to AT&T as part of the company's acquisition of TCI in March. He ran the critical cable-television and cable-telephony operations until he resigned on Oct. 6.

Company Profile 14
Motorola Inc.

Company overview

Motorola is one of the world's leading companies in the area of wireless communication, semiconductors, advanced electronics systems, components and services. The company's operations are highly decentralized. It has six sectors and one group: Semiconductor Products Sector; Cellular Subscriber Sector; Cellular Networks and Space Sector; Land Mobile Products Sector; Messaging, Information and Media Sector; Automotive, Energy and Components Sector; and Motorola Computer Group. In 1996 the annual revenues of Motorola exceeded $27 billion, of which 58 per cent came from overseas. Motorola now maintains manufacturing, sales and services throughout the world and employs more than 139,000 people worldwide. The corporate headquarters of the company is located in Schaumburg, Illinois.

Brief history

The history of Motorola dates back to 1928, when Paul V. Galvin established the Galvin Manufacturing Corporation in Chicago. The major product of the company was the battery eliminator, a device to allow radios to operate directly from household electricity instead of batteries. In the 1930s the company commercialized car radios under the brand name Motorola, a new word suggesting sound in motion, and the product was very successful. In 1947 the company changed its name to Motorola Inc.

In the 1940s Motorola continued to expand and became a leader in military, space and commercial communication. In the 1950s the company built its first semiconductor facility and continued to grow in consumer electronics as well. In the 1960s Motorola started to expand its businesses into international markets and shifted its business focus away from consumer electronics. In the late 1980s the company became the major supplier of cellular telephones. Since the early 1990s Motorola has become the prime contractor for the satellite-based global communication system, and a major manufacturer and distributor of semiconductors, integrated circuits (including microprocessors) and digital signal processors. Since its beginning the company has come up with new product innovations and expanded its business activities.

Innovation and significant contribution

Motorola has made significant contributions in the area of wireless communication, semiconductors, and advanced electronics systems and services. The company states that Motorola 'enable[s] people to do the things they want to do'. Motorola's Semiconductor Products Sector designs, produces and distributes a wide range of semiconductors and integrated circuits, including microprocessors, digital signal processors, memories and sensors. The company's Cellular Subscriber Sector designs, manufactures and distributes the full range of wireless telephone products for the global market. Its Cellular Network and Space Sector designs, manufactures and distributes wireless telephone systems, and satellite communication for commercial and government customers.

Motorola's Land Mobile Products Sector designs, manufactures and distributes analog and digital two-way radio products, and systems for worldwide applications and wide-area communication. Its Messaging, Information and Media Sector designs, manufactures and distributes a variety of messaging products, including pages and paging systems, wireless data communications products, infrastructure equipment and systems. Its Automotive Energy and Components Sector designs, manufactures and distributes a broad range of electronic components, modules and integrated electronic systems, and products for automotive, industrial, transportation and communication markets. The Motorola Computer Group designs, manufactures and distributes system platform products for computers.

Motorola is widely recognized as a leader in total quality management (TQM). In 1988 the company received the Malcolm Baldridge National Quality Award for its company-wide TQM activities. Motorola collaborates with other organizations around the world. For example, it collaborates with Apple Computer to make the Power PC.

Challenges and opportunities

Improvements in the product innovation process, refocusing of investments in the areas of core competencies, customer satisfaction, and the design, manufacture and distribution of high-quality products at reduced costs are some of the major challenges confronting Motorola. To meet these challenges and to increase opportunities in the global marketplace, Motorola strives to engage in continuous innovation and improvement of marketing activities.

Rosalie L. Tung and Mohi Ahmed
Simon Fraser University

Further reading

Coy, P. and Stodhill, R. (1996) 'Is Motorola a bit too patient', *Business Week*, 5 February: 150–1. (Presents some key challenges facing Motorola.)

Engardio, P. (1993) 'Motorola in China: a great leap forward', *Business Week*, 17 May: 58–9. (Discusses Motorola's business expansion in China.)

Hoover, G., Campbell, A. and Spain P.J. (eds) 'Motorola, Inc.', *Hoover's Handbook of American Business*, Austin: The Reference Press, Inc. (Gives a general overview of the company.)

Jones, P. and Kahaner, L. (1995) *Say It & Live It*, New York: Currency Doubleday. (Presents the mission statements of fifty corporations.)

Krysten, J. (1997) 'Satellites: critical to the new global Telecommunications network', *Business America* 118(7), July: 13–15. (Discusses new global telecommunications networks via satellites.)

Further resources

Motorola Inc. website
http://www.motorola.com

A New Company called Motorola

Business Week, 17 April 2000, New York

Abstract:

Two years ago, the once mighty Motorola Inc. was in serious trouble. But over the past 2 years, CEO Christopher B. Galvin has taken dramatic measures to resurrect the company that his grandfather founded in 1928. He has cut costs by $750 million and slashed more than 20,000 of the 150,000 jobs at the company. He shut down semiconductor and paging plants and overhauled the rest of the company top to bottom. And to boost growth prospects, he agreed to the largest acquisition ever at Motorola, the $17 billion purchase of cable equipment maker General Instruments Corp.

In late March, when Janiece Webb and other Motorola Inc. executives visited the London headquarters of wireless giant Vodafone AirTouch PLC, they ran into unconcealed anger. The company's top brass were fuming over Motorola's past arrogance and its repeated blunders in delivering cutting-edge phones. "I don't want to waste my time with you guys," said Paul Donovan, Vodafone's marketing director, according to people at the meeting. But Webb, head of Motorola's Internet initiatives, promised the company would be more responsive and that it would speed innovative products to market. To prove her point, she showed off a splashy array of futuristic mobile phones capable of surfing the Web. Donovan, who only planned on staying for 90 minutes, ended up listening for eight hours, and

Vodafone agreed to start buying the phones this fall. "I cannot believe this is the same company," said Donovan at the time.

Good thing it's not. Two years ago, the once mighty Motorola Inc. was in serious trouble. The company that had invented the cellular industry was getting hammered by more innovative rivals such as Finland's Nokia Group. It was infuriating its customers by trying to dictate what kinds of mobile phones they could buy. And, in the ultimate embarrassment, the company that had won the Malcolm Baldrige National Quality Award was taking heat for shoddy products. In March, 1998, wireless carrier PrimeCo Personal Communications dumped Motorola in favor of Lucent Technologies Inc. because Motorola's gear lead to shutdowns of up to two hours.

But over the past two years, Christopher B. Galvin, the company's chief executive, has taken drastic measures to resurrect the company that his grandfather founded in 1928. He has cut costs by $750 million and slashed more than 20,000 of the 150,000 jobs at the Schaumburg, Ill.-based company. He shut down semiconductor and paging plants and overhauled the rest of the company top to bottom. And to boost growth prospects, he agreed to the largest acquisition ever at Motorola, the $17 billion purchase of cable equipment maker General Instruments Corp. "Everything has been modified or changed at the company," Galvin says.

Nothing more than Motorola's attitude toward the Internet. Once viewed as an oddball curiosity inside the company, the Net is now the core of everything Motorola does. With Galvin's blessing, Webb has been traveling the globe to convince wireless players that Motorola will offer the best lineup of Web phones in the world. Already, Motorola says it has shipped 1 million phones capable of browsing the Net – which analysts say is more than any other cell phone maker. And Motorola's wireless network gear is impressing customers with trials that zap data over radio waves at a speedy 64 kilobits per second, faster than today's typical computer modems. "Motorola is clearly rising to the mark," says Michael Reilly, head of market strategy at BT Cellnet, the British Telecom wireless unit that will roll out Net service with Motorola gear in May.

Warring tribes

To transform Motorola into a Net company, Galvin has had to rock the company's corporate culture. Once an environment of intensely warring tribes, the new Motorola is becoming a more cooperative place. To respond to changes at Net speed, managers are paid based on their ability to foster collaboration, and employees are evaluated on their customer service. "Being fast, smart, quick, agile – this is what will make the company different so we can avoid the issues that occurred in our past," says Galvin.

Galvin's shock therapy is working. Net income, excluding restructuring charges, hit $1.3 billion in 1999, vs. $347 million in 1998. And analysts expect the comeback will continue this year: Wall Street is expecting that Motorola's first quarter results, due out Apr. 11, will show a 25% jump in sales to $9 billion and a tripling of net income to $625 million. For 2000, profits are projected to climb 50%, to about $2 billion, and revenues to rise 24%, to

$38.5 billion, says PaineWebber Inc. The newfound optimism has done wonders for Motorola's stock. From its low of $38 in October, 1998, shares soared to $184 earlier year before dropping to about $134 during the recent market correction.

Still, Motorola will face plenty of challenges in the year ahead. The company needs to boost growth in its mobile-phone operation, where revenues increased a modest 13% in the fourth quarter, vs. 63% at Nokia. It also has to gain ground in the wireless equipment business against fierce rivals who have bested Motorola in the past few years. "They will have extensive competition for leadership of the market," says William Wiberg, president of wireless equipment at Lucent Technologies. And Galvin will have to figure out how to avoid serious financial liability for Iridium, the troubled satellite phone system. Motorola conceived of and helped finance Iridium, and now some bond-holders and shareholders think Motorola should pay billions to compensate them for their losses. Galvin readily admits the turnaround is not complete. "Success is a journey, not a destination," he says.

Investors who doubted Galvin's ability to turn the company around two years ago are beginning to trust his leadership. When the unproven executive took over in 1997, many suspected he got the job because of nepotism rather than talent. But Galvin, now 50, has weathered what appears to be his toughest storm. He seems to have struck the right balance between acting like an insider respectful of Motorola traditions and pressing for radical change. "He inherited a wreck, and he's done a good job of restructuring the company," says Jane A. Snorek, an investment officer at Firstar Corp., a Milwaukee-based money manager that has purchased Motorola stock.

So how did this icon of American ingenuity, so recently battered, recover? Interviews with 15 top Motorola executives, plus customers, rivals, and analysts, reveal the story behind the comeback. It's a cautionary tale about how the success of a company can breed such arrogance that only a steep decline can help it find the humility to reinvent itself.

Top-secret meetings

The seeds of Motorola's comeback were sown in the bleak days of early 1998. In March, Galvin huddled in top-secret meetings with Chief Operating Officer Robert L. Growney to figure out how to remake Motorola into a major Internet player. Galvin insisted that they would have to change the company's culture. The internal competition it had prided itself on was now hurting product development and customer relationships. The two execs figured the company needed a sweeping restructuring. For two weeks, they locked themselves in the 12th floor conference room at Motorola's headquarters, writing ideas on an electronic white board.

In April, Galvin presented his plan to 50 of the company's top officers at the Ritz Carlton in Chicago. He told the group that Motorola would combine all of the 30 units that make cell phone, wireless equipment, satellite, and cable modem products into one large communications division. Many executives would no longer have profit-and-loss responsibility, answering instead to the head of the whole division. The goal, Galvin told the group, was to create a

Motorola for the Digital Age. It could not longer be dominated by engineers focused on building gee-whiz products. Instead, employees had to pour all their energy into working together to give people easy-to-use ways to stay wired to the Net – from home, the office, the car. The devices for tapping the Web could be cell phones, pagers, cable modems, or something nobody has yet envisioned. "The market size for [these] solutions is infinite," Galvin says. "Someone has to make all this stuff work."

The restructuring didn't come easily. Growney thought that Motorola should have a separate group within the communications division to coordinate Internet strategies. But others thought the business units should develop their own initiatives. In the hallway at the Ritz, Growney and top Net strategist Randy Battat got into a tense argument over the issue. Later, Galvin gave the task of deciding how to structure the 70,000-person communications group to Merle L. Gilmore, a rising star who had run the company's overseas operations. Ultimately, Gilmore sided with Growney. In July, Gilmore decided to create two business units charged with fostering cooperation. One would be responsible for getting all the communications businesses working together to meet customers' needs. The other, headed by Webb, would coordinate Net strategies among all of Motorola's operations. Cooperation would be rewarded with stock options.

Courting Cisco

As the new communications structure was put in place that summer, Galvin and Gilmore tackled Motorola's troubled wireless equipment business.

After the top two executives of the group left for a startup, Gilmore recruited Bo Hedfors, the CEO of top equipment maker Ericsson's U.S. operations. After 30 years spent competing against Motorola, Hedfors knew precisely the holes in the company's technology. Most critically, he understood that wireless-phone companies needed a way to migrate from the big switches used for voice traffic to the routers that could handle Internet traffic as well as voice calls. To fill the void, he courted Cisco Systems Inc., the top maker of routers that direct Internet traffic. After months crafting the relationship, Hedfors penned a four-year, $1 billion pact in February, 1999.

While the venture is promising, Motorola still has much to prove in the wireless network business. The company has landed six trials for its high-speed data equipment, but it's still behind some competitors. "They're not doing the business that Ericsson and Nokia are," says analyst Matthew Hoffman of SoundView Technology Group.

"Go faster"

Galvin was feeling the heat. In early 1999, Dataquest Inc. released figures that showed the company had lost its lead in the mobile-phone market for the first time ever to Nokia. Even Motorola's own execs felt Galvin wasn't responding quickly enough to the company's troubles. At a meeting near Chicago days after the Dataquest numbers came out, one exec stood up while the mild-mannered CEO was on stage. "We want to go faster," he said, according to one onlooker. "We've got great leadership, but by God, we want it out of your head and in your heart."

By then, the Internet was coming to the wireless world. In early 1999, cellular operators were getting ready to buy millions of data-rich wireless phones. Analysts forecast that smart phones and Web-enabled phones would account for 9%, or 35 million, of all wireless phones sold in 2000, up from 0.1% in 1999. Motorola couldn't afford to let rivals beat it to market with the next generation of handsets. "It was like sheer panic through the place," recalls Webb.

Panic may have been just what Motorola needed. Back in 1998, the company's executives had had a showdown with engineers over Web browsers being built into its phones. The engineers didn't see much urgency in developing Web-enabled phones. But Webb and other executives insisted that Motorola should offer trial equipment by early 1999. Over the first few months of 1999, Motorola was letting customers try out the equipment. By May it had browsers embedded in nearly every phone. By comparison, rival Nokia promised a browser phone last summer, but has yet to deliver. "Motorola has outshined them," says Andrew J. Sukawaty, the chief of Sprint Corp.'s wireless business. "Motorola shipped browser phones on time."

In the spring of 1999, Galvin began worrying that Motorola was missing an opportunity in the cable equipment market. The company held the top position in the cable-modem market with a 37% share, but he wanted a larger presence in the growing industry. So in late May, Galvin dispatched Gilmore to see Ed Breen, the CEO of General Instrument, the No. 1 maker of television set-top boxes. After more than three months of negotiating, Galvin signed off on a deal for the largest acquisition in Motorola history: The company would buy GI for $17 billion. Just 10 weeks after the merger closed in January, Gilmore says it's paying off because Motorola has "deeper" strategic discussions with major network providers such as AT&T.

While Gilmore was cutting the GI deal, Webb was hot on the heels of the Internet's content providers. She wanted Motorola to have more Web sites bookmarked on its phones than any rival – and she refused to settle for travel and weather sites. "Let's quit sneaking up on this," she told her team. "Go after the big boys." She led the charge. In November, 1999, Webb visited Yahoo! Inc. CEO Timothy Koogle, who had been telling analysts that phonemakers would be paying Yahoo to bookmark his site. Webb told him that wasn't going to happen. Her argument? One billion people would eventually tap the Web from mobile phones – they could either be directed to Yahoo or some other site. The pair talked for two hours, and Koogle relented. He agreed that neither company would pay the other. Webb then cut similar deals with America Online Inc. and Amazon.com Inc.

Today, with the big names of the Net backing its strategy, Motorola is becoming a company to once again fear in the wireless business. "This is a company that has moved beyond the beginnings of a turnaround to real leadership," says SoundView's Hoffman. Yet Galvin remains cautious. Sitting in the Motorola museum not far from displays of his company's long line of innovations, he calls the company's progress "early traction." And he can't help moments of wistfulness. "We want to learn from the past," he says. "But we want our dreams to wipe away our memories." If the founder's grandson remains focused on the Internet, the company may manage to wipe the slate clean.

Unfinished business

Even after its recent progress, Motorola has to address key challenges. All revenue figures are for 1999.

Wireless phones revenues: $11.93 billion

Motorola held 17% of the cellular-phone market last year, well behind Nokia's 27% share. To gain ground, Motorola needs to crank out new, innovative phones.

Wireless equipment revenues: $6.54 billion

Rivals such as Sweden's Ericsson swiped market share in the late 1990s and seem better positioned to sell wireless equipment for high-speed data transmissions. Motorola hopes a venture with Cisco will help it catch up.

Semiconductors revenues: $7.37 billion

The company has become the No. 1 maker of embedded chips in products ranging from automotive electronics to wireless phones.

Satellite, government services, and other revenues: $4.06 billion

Iridium, the satellite communications system Motorola dreamed up, has been a disaster. Motorola must now show that it can still develop its satellite business by selling equipment to other ventures.

Data: *Dataquest Inc.*, Soundview Technology Group Inc. (available online)

Motorola's comeback

The company is regaining its footing, but it was a long struggle

Jan. 1, 1997 Christopher B. Galvin, the grandson of the company's founder, becomes CEO.

August, 1997 Apple Computer interim CEO Steve Jobs pulls the plug on licensing the Macintosh operating system to others. Motorola has to fold its clone operation.

December, 1997 Motorola's neglect of digital phones helps send its share of the worldwide wireless phone market from 51% in 1996 to 34% in 1997, according to Herschel Shosteck Associates.

March, 1998 Cellular-phone company PrimeCo boots Motorola in favor of Lucent for a $500 million contract for wireless network equipment.

April, 1998 First-quarter earnings plummet to half those of a year earlier, and Motorola warns that profits will remain below forecasts for several quarters. The stock plunges 11%, to 58.

May 4, 1998 Motorola refocuses its money-losing semiconductor division on embedded chips with a new brand, Digital DNA.

June 4, 1998 Galvin says he will lay off more than 15,000 employees and take a $1.95 billion charge. This is part of a plan to cut costs by 4%, or $750 million.

July 9, 1998 Motorola announces the restructuring of its disparate businesses into one unit called the Communications Enterprise headed by Merle Gilmore.

July 21, 1998 Months behind its rivals, Motorola introduces a new lineup of phones, including digital handsets and a slim high-end phone, the V-series.

August 6, 1998 After low morale in the network equipment business contributes to the defection of two top executives, Motorola hires Bo Hedfors, an industry veteran from rival Ericsson.

October, 1998 Iridium, the satellite system Motorola dreamed up, finally goes commercial after suffering a delay.

January, 1999 Motorola loses its lead in the wireless phone market as its share for 1998 drops to 19.5%, behind Nokia's 22.5%, according to researcher Dataquest.

February, 1999 Striving to improve its infrastructure business and prepare for the wireless Internet, Motorola enters alliances with Cisco and Alcatel to build next generation networks.

April, 1999 Net income increases 20% to $171 million for the first quarter, suggesting that Motorola's strategies are beginning to pay off.

Sept. 15, 1999 Motorola makes its biggest acquisition ever, buying cable equipment maker General Instrument for $17 billion. The deal will help it sell more Net gear.

Oct. 7, 1999 Motorola demonstrates its first mobile phone capable of browsing the Web. Major carriers including BT Cellnet sign contracts to buy the phones, such as the Timeport P7389.

January, 2000 Motorola reports its best financial performance in more than eight quarters. Fourth-quarter operating profit hits $514 million, more than triple the previous year's mark, while sales climb 8% to $8.5 billion.

Feb. 28, 2000 Motorola partners with Amazon.com to put a bookmark on its Web phones and make them e-commerce devices.

Reprinted from April 17, 2000 issue of *Business Week* by special permission, © 2000 The McGraw-Hill Companies, Inc.

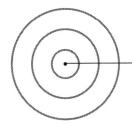

Part 2
Japanese Multinationals

In Part 1, an observation was made that even the best-run companies could experience major vicissitudes in their fortunes within a relatively short span of time – from one of high performance to one plagued by multiple problems in the course of a couple of years. In the case of Japan, the entire country appears to have undergone a reversal of economic fortunes within the course of one or two decades. In the 1980s, much of the western world was enamoured by the success of the Japanese economy and its companies, resulting in such superlatives as 'the Japanese economic miracle' and a 'Japan that can do no wrong'. By the early 1990s, however, the tide had begun to turn – the collapse of the bubble economy and Japan's continued inability to reverse an economic slowdown/recession, particularly against the backdrop of strong economic performance in the US, have led to growing negative characterizations of that country, such as 'a Japan that can do no right' and 'Japan's amazing ability to disappoint' (the cover story of the September 26–October 2, 1999 issue of *The Economist*). The truth about the Japanese economy and the performance of its companies lies somewhere between the accolades of the 1980s and the condemnations of the 1990s. The four entries selected for inclusion in this section seek to present a more balanced view of the current situation of the Japanese economy and the performance of some of its leading companies.

The first article from *The Economist*, 'Japan restructures, grudgingly', outlines the massive restructuring that is underway in different sectors of the Japanese economy. The second article, also from *The Economist*, correctly points out that despite the record number of corporate bankruptcies and the worst economic indicators in Japan after World War II, there are still many Japanese companies that continue to excel in their respective industries/sectors around the world.

The financial sector has often been faulted as a major source of Japan's current economic woes – in recent years, several major banks have collapsed and several others are on the verge of bankruptcy. Consequently, it is no surprise that major restructuring has and will continue to take place in this sector. The third reading in this section profiles the massive consolidation, including mergers and acquisitions, that has begun in the financial sector. The Bank of Tokyo-Mitsubishi, formed from the merger of Bank of Tokyo and Mitsubishi Bank, is an example of the corporate restructuring that has taken place in this industry.

The last entry in this section highlights the problems that Dentsu, a leading advertising agency in the world, encounters when it strives to go global. Many of these difficulties can be attributed to cultural differences. In advertising, as in the area of consumers' products, the need to be sensitive to variations in culture is perhaps more acute than in many other industrial sectors.

Japan restructures, grudgingly

The Economist, 6 February 1999

It is not enough that Japanese companies are being forced to change. They must actually want to change too

PRESSURE from outside, or *gaiatsu,* is a handy fig-leaf in Japanese politics. To help get a dirty job done, a politician's appeal to *gaiatsu* conjures up forces that are totally beyond his control, such as irresistible pressure from allies or trading partners. Yet the motive for lasting change, as everyone knows, really comes from within. Right now, the principles of *gaiatsu* are topsy-turvy among Japanese companies. Inside the boardroom, the desire to change appears as weak as ever. Yet the forces battering companies from the outside have become surprisingly strong.

On February 3rd Sumitomo Rubber, Japan's second-biggest tyre maker, announced plans for a string of joint-ventures with America's Goodyear. Under the agreement, Sumitomo Rubber will lose control of its businesses in Europe and America, in return for Goodyear's operations in Japan. The same day, Dupont, an American chemicals and plastics firm, announced a series of joint-ventures with Teijin, to create the world's largest polyester-film business, with annual sales of $1.4 billion. A few days earlier,

Nissan, Japan's troubled second-biggest car maker, in effect put itself up for sale. That such a bastion of Japanese manufacturing should be entertaining bids from foreign buyers would have been unthinkable six months ago.

Restructuring has been proceeding inside the country, too. In the search for economies of scale, Toshiba and Mitsubishi Electric are merging their big electrical-generator operations. Japan Energy and Showa Shell, an affiliate of Royal Dutch/Shell, are in talks to merge their petrol-distribution businesses, hoping to cut costs by halving the payroll. Sumitomo Chemical and Mitsui Chemicals are consolidating some loss-making resin plants, which make parts for the car industry. And Mitsubishi Chemical wants to merge its pharmaceuticals business with Tokyo Tanabe, a middling drugs company. In all, there were 908 deals involving Japanese companies last year, nearly 30% more than in 1997, and more than double the number of deals in 1993.

Yet few Japanese firms are pursuing mergers with the enthusiasm of their competitors in America and Europe. In most cases, the choice to merge has been the only one available. The deals are taking place against the backdrop of an economy in a dire state. Sales in the shops continue to slump; demand for new houses and cars has collapsed. This contraction is only adding to today's overcapacity in most big industries.

In the past, Japanese firms have been able to conceal just how badly they are doing. But in April, the country is switching to a more stringent system of consolidated accounting. Of the 54,000 subsidiaries belonging to the 1,000 or so big listed companies that produce consolidated accounts, only just over half, says Kathy Matsui of Goldman Sachs, are currently incorporated in the group accounts. Once the criterion for consolidation switches from majority ownership to "effective control", the finances of many more subsidiaries will be revealed. This will affect building and property firms, in particular, because they routinely create affiliates in which to bury losses. Car makers such as Nissan and Mazda will also suffer, because many of their loss-making dealerships will be included in the accounts for the first time.

Creditors are beginning to exert more influence, too. Since late 1997, the premium that the weakest companies pay over the strongest to borrow in Japan's corporate-bond market has doubled, to 1.2%. Banks can no longer afford to lend indiscriminately, and are themselves under pressure to tighten lending practices, from shareholders, foreign competitors and regulators. In the construction industry, tighter finances have already forced a few mid-sized companies into bankruptcy. Dozens more are pleading for debt-forgiveness from their banks – though, as Mark Brown of ING Barings, an investment bank, remarks, their fate turns in part on whether the builder has small enough debts to be allowed to fail.

As well as requiring more consolidation, new rules will also help to expose the underlying profitability of Japanese companies' main activities. From next year, companies must value their securities holdings at their market prices, rather than book values. These holdings are vast. The largest firms, for instance, own about ¥100 trillion-worth of each others' shares. When securities are valued at market prices, firms will no longer be able to support their sagging revenues from windfall profits made by selling or revaluing them. Department-store groups are particularly guilty of this legerdemain, but all sorts of Japanese firms have benefited from such "latent" profits. Since 1993, 12% of non-financial companies' pre-tax profits have, on average, come from cashing in their securities.

Once firms must mark their cross-shareholdings to market, there will be more incentive to unwind them. Those showing a loss on the shares will no longer be able to hide it by hanging on to them. On the other hand, those showing a profit will have to realise it in one fell swoop, after which it will make sense to reallocate the capital. It is possible even to be optimistic about what might follow. Once firms rid themselves of their stakes, some big blockages to mergers and takeovers could disappear. The Tokyo Stock Exchange might even become a market for corporate control, as are the exchanges in New York and London.

Even politicians are getting in on the restructuring game. Last week, the ruling Liberal Democratic Party (LDP) proposed a scheme that would allow companies to sell their cross-shareholdings to the government, rather than into the stockmarket. This would both ease the downward pressure of forced sales on share prices and also encourage more companies to sell – though, as always when a large sum of money passes through the LDP's hands, it risks ending up with party friends in the building and property industries.

The non-revolution within

Taken together, all this amounts to formidable pressure on Japanese businesses to restructure. Events so far, however, fall far short of a shareholder revolution. The reason is that for Japanese managers to change the habits of a lifetime, there must be incentives from within the company as well as from without.

At the moment those incentives are lacking. The efforts of Komatsu, a construction-machinery maker, are typical. While the firm is tidying up the group's treasury and merging two subsidiaries, its managers have neglected the problems at Komatsu Electronic Metals. This loss-making subsidiary makes silicon wafers for microchips, a highly competitive market dominated by specialist producers. Or take Kobe Steel, which squandered money diversifying out of the steel business in the 1980s, but still declines to get out of its semiconductor joint-venture with Micron, an American manufacturer.

All too often, firms are restructuring without regard for future profits. One example is Nippon Telegraph and Telephone (NTT), Japan's dominant domestic and international carrier. Last month NTT announced a reorganisation that was supposed to prepare for fiercer competition at home and abroad. Under a new holding company, there will be no fewer than 150 affiliated firms that together employ 220,000 people. That still leaves NTT with a cripplingly high wage bill and exorbitant costs for equipment sourced from its affiliated suppliers. Together, these two items account for 60% of NTT's expenses, up from 40% in 1985, when the company was partially privatised.

Restructuring in Japan will take off only when it is motivated from within firms – when, in other words, managers feel obliged to run their businesses more in the interests of shareholders. the introduction of performance-related pay, including the widespread use of share options, would help. So would the creation of a professional and mobile managerial class. The main goal of today's hopelessly conservative sexagenerians, who have picked their way through the ranks, is to scurry as quietly as possible towards retirement.

Some companies are waking up to these changes. From April Matsushita Electric Industrial, a consumer-electronics giant, plans to offer managers the choice of performance-related pay or the usual seniority scale. Fujitsu, a computer maker, is following Matsushita's lead. Yet boardroom reform and the use of share options are still novelties in Japan. Unless they become far more common, Japanese restructuring will proceed reluctantly, as the result of *gaiatsu* alone.

Japan's growth companies

The Economist, 26 June 1999

The disasters of corporate Japan are well known; less so its recent successes

AFTER shrinking continuously for the past 18 months, the Japanese economy has at last begun to stir. If growth can be sustained at anywhere near the 1.9% jump recorded in the first quarter – and that is doubtful, not least because the government's latest huge package of public-works spending will have petered out – Japan's economy could be truly back on its feet by early next year. For some companies, hope may come too late to prevent terminal decline or takeover. Many others will emerge permanently weakened. Yet it is premature to write off corporate Japan. Although much of big business is still struggling, leaner little brothers are even now emerging from the rubble – and they will be ready and able to take on the world.

The firms that have thrived during the recession include not only household names, such as Sony and Toyota, which already dominate the world's shopping malls and showrooms, but also new contenders that even the Japanese public has seldom heard of. Although many of these corporations operate chiefly in their domestic markets, practically all intend to move overseas. Their consistent strength is their attachment to that most unJapanese of management ideals: corporate focus.

The received picture of Japan still contains much that is true. It takes a great deal of will-power to reject the herd instinct to diversify into every fashionable new field, especially when a firm's main business is suffering. Japan's old growth-at-any-cost school of management assumed that it was always better to diversify than to face stagnation or (heaven forbid) redundancies – even if that meant entering fields where the company had no production facilities, no technology, no suppliers, no customers and no competence whatsoever. Because of their past addiction to investment, many Japanese firms are also still burdened with too much capacity, too much labour and too much debt.

Yet such old "corporate warriors", bent on catching up with America and aided by bureaucrats who like to pick winners, belong to the past. There is a "hidden" Japan; and its future is much brighter.

Japanese industry has reinvented itself once before, after the oil shock of 1973, when energy costs more than doubled. One way to spot tomorrow's successes is to look at how the ship-building, steel and heavy-engineering firms transformed themselves then. Hidetoshi Shioda, an analyst at Nomura Securities, notes that those firms that could afford to invest in energy-saving machinery managed to forge a lasting lead.

This time, firms need to spend on restructuring. Redundancies cost a Japanese firm some ¥24m ($200,000) per worker, about five times the going rate in Europe. But because borrowing is now more expensive than it was, Japanese firms that are relatively free of debt and can finance their restructuring out of cashflow ought to have a head start over their rivals.

Spotting the winners

In chemicals, an obvious winner is Asahi Chemical Industry, which sold its low-margin resin and synthetic-fibre businesses to other chemical firms, and its food interests to Japan Tobacco. With its low debt and high cashflow, the company is probably in better shape today then it was before the bubble burst in 1990. The chemicals businesses owned by the Mitsubishi, Mitsui and Sumitomo conglomerates, although nowhere near as successful, have likewise shut plants, streamlined product lines and disposed of non-core businesses. They, too, will one day again be strong.

In industrial electronics, Fujitsu is the most promising restructurer. It has long since streamlined its overseas operations, got out of low-margin microchips, expanded its software and computer-services businesses and (most recently) merged its European computer operations with Siemens. Hitachi still has remnants of its former excellence, but it has been slow to deal with the shortcomings of its semiconductor and power-generation businesses.

As well as these restructurers, Japan also boasts firms that have thrived all along. Most still have their founders around – if only in the background – to ensure that the visionary flame burns on. As businesses, they tend to be frugal, self-sufficient and mostly provincial. Few have allowed their headcounts to get out of line.

One way to spot them is by their return on assets. Whereas the average return for Japanese companies is little more than 2%, the best firms achieve American-like returns of 8% or more. On this count they have been even more frugal, resourceful and energetic than the firms that prospered through the oil shocks in the 1970s. In those days, the average return on assets of such companies was around 6%.

The best are such familiar names as Sony, Canon, Bridgestone, Toyota and Honda. Indeed, these stars qualify as "20-20" companies – the term that was coined to describe the couple of dozen American corporations with market capitalisations in excess of $20 billion and a record of expanding profits by 20% a year.

Those are demanding criteria, given the severity of Japan's recession. So Garry Evans, a strategist with HSBC Securities in Tokyo, has relaxed them, looking instead for "10-10" firms with capitalisations of more than ¥1.2 trillion that have boosted their net profits by at least 10% a year, averaged over the past five years. He has found 12, mostly in high-growth fields such as electronics, telecoms and pharmaceuticals.

By definition, all of Japan's 10-10 companies (including the handful of 20-20 superstars) have good growth records. To see how consistent they have been, Mr Evans reran his calculations using net profit and market-capitalisation figures for previous years. Although the list then became shorter, most of the same names cropped up. A few dropped off, such as Kyocera, a Kyoto-based maker of ceramic packages for microchips.

Sankyo, Japan's second-largest drug firm, had the longest record among all the 10-10 performers. As investments, all of the 10-10 companies have outperformed the Tokyo stockmarket in recent years by anywhere from 20% to nearly 50%.

A dozen or so industrial starts are hardly enough to rebuild Japan. However, beneath them reside dozens of firms which, for various reasons, have outperformed the rest. The 820 non-financial firms listed on the Tokyo Stock Exchange's first section, for instance, saw their revenues fall during the financial year that ended on March 31st by an average of 8.9% and their net profits decline by 63.6%. But the average is misleading. No fewer than 87 of these firms actually reported record profits.

What have they been doing right? Some are pioneers. Yamato Transport, which found a way round government regulations that prevented trucking companies from operating nationwide, has close to half of the parcel-delivery business in Japan and is now spreading abroad. Secom was the first to appreciate that automatic security systems were needed even in law-abiding Japan. Profitable for 35 consecutive years, Secom has a commanding 60% share of the domestic market and is also expanding abroad.

Others have built international reputations through their technical excellence. Although it is not in the same league as Merck or Glaxo Wellcome, Takeda, Japan's largest drug firm, has a string of original drugs in the pipeline – including a fast-acting alternative to Viagra. The Osaka-based drug firm currently ranks only 14th worldwide, but it could soon be among the top ten. Another firm, Noritsu Koki, supplies half the mini-photo processing labs used in camera shops and kiosks

around the world. Mabuchi Motor has half the world market for tiny electric motors used in electronic gadgets and computer drives. Hoya has huge world demand for its patented process for melting and annealing optical glass, which shrinks production times from 26 days to three days.

A third group to watch are those that respond to customers' changing tastes with a stream of improvements. Kao has been profitable for 18 straight years by sticking to its detergents, household products and cosmetics. The firm employs proportionately three times as many people on R&D as does Procter & Gamble, and it has won awards in America and Europe with Bioré pore packs, sticky strips that are used to clean skin. Most semiconductor makers have been savaged by falling prices, but Rohm, the world's largest maker of specialist microchips, has maintained margins by adding extra functions to its devices. Yaoko, a supermarket chain, has had rising profits for the past ten years by freeing store managers to select goods to match local tastes. With its small cars and motorbikes, tiny Suzuki Motors comes out of the same mould as Honda, but is an even lower-cost producer. Suzuki is currently working with Opel on a new car for Europe. General Motors, which owns Opel, has a 10% stake in Suzuki.

Wired worry

Yet there remains something worrying about Japan's achievers. Although they are superb in their chosen fields, too many come from the traditional economy. Japan has been slower than most industrial countries to embrace the wired economy, and that is not just because of its recession. A reluctance to dismantle regulations has kept domestic telephone and data-transmission costs high. Restrictions on the use of share options and equity swaps, only now being gradually relaxed, have cramped entrepreneurs. What e-commerce there is in Japan is being supplied mostly by foreign firms, such as Yahoo!, Japan's biggest portal.

Iwao Nakatani, an economist at Hitotsubashi University, notes that the "e-economy" accounted for only 6.5% of America's GDP last year. And yet, because it expanded by a formidable 65%, the e-economy contributed four percentage points to America's overall growth in 1998. Meanwhile, the traditional economy stagnated. The problem in Japan is that the e-economy still represents a mere 1% of GDP.

The government sees the need to change that. Earlier this month, its industrial competitiveness council came out with its blueprint for doing so. Unfortunately, though, the plan simply designates information, telecoms, chemicals and materials as "strategic growth areas" – which sounds all too much like the past strategy of picking winners, the kiss of death for most entrepreneurs. Little was said about the real obstacles such as too much red tape or high taxes on capital gains.

The good news is that Japan's basic company law is being overhauled, after pressure from traditional firms. Ironically, the reforms that the captains of industry want, such as freedom to spin off divisions, break up whole companies, promote employee buyouts and encourage broader share-option schemes, will benefit Japan's entrepreneurs more than its metal-bashers. Given the chance, and given a genuine commitment on the part of the government to deregulation, the country's coming crop of e-businesses will surely play a big part in the eventual renaissance of corporate Japan.

© *The Economist* Newspaper Limited, London (26 June 1999).

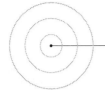

Company Profile 15
The Bank of Tokyo–
Mitsubishi Ltd (BTM)

Company overview

The Bank of Tokyo-Mitsubishi Ltd (BTM) is one of the world's largest financial organizations. The organization was formed on 1 April 1996 by a merger of the Mitsubishi Bank Limited (MBL) and the Bank of Tokyo Limited (BOT). BTM now has 326 branches, twenty-eight sub-branches and two agencies in Japan, and about 400 facilities in major financial and commercial centres around the world. The group operates in more than twenty-eight countries and employs about 19,300 people worldwide. The revenues of BTM exceeded $46 billion in 1996. The corporate headquarters of BTM is located in Tokyo, Japan.

Brief history

The origin of BTM can be traced back to the 1880s. The founder of the Mitsubishi industrial group, Yataro Iwasaki, established the Mitsubishi Exchange Office, a money exchange house, in 1880. The Exchange Office was succeeded by the Banking Division of the Mitsubishi Group. In 1919 the MBL was established and took over the Banking Division of the group. In subsequent years MBL continued to expand its businesses around Japan and overseas through a series of mergers and acquisitions. MBL was the main bank for the Mitsubishi group companies.

BOT was established in 1946. The bank was the successor of a special foreign-exchange bank, the Yokohama Specie Bank Limited (YSB), established in 1880. YSB had international banking networks including the United States, Europe, Africa and Asia. After World War II BOT was the only Japanese bank that was authorized by the Japanese Ministry of Finance (MOF) to establish offices abroad and to engage in foreign exchange and international finance. Thus until recently past the global network of BOT was more diversified than that of any other Japanese bank. After the merger of MBL and BOT, BTM became the world's largest financial organization, with assets in excess of $696 billion.

Japanese financial institutions are experiencing a severe business environment as a result of a downturn in the country's economy as well as structural reform plans, referred to as the 'Big Bang', in Japan. As a leading financial institution, BTM is also undergoing major structural reforms, the principal ones being a reduction in the number of directors and their pay, suspension of basic wage-rate increases and staff reduction, reduction in the number of domestic and foreign branches, sale of idle properties and reduction in general expenses, i.e. non-personnel expenditure.

Innovation and significant contributions

BTM's diversified global network and broad range of innovative financial products and services have made it a unique global financial group. The group is capable of providing total services to its customers around the world. Its innovative services in structured finance, corporate advisory and investment advisory services are also well recognized. The group's business activities include commercial banking, corporate banking, project finance, foreign exchange to housing mortgages, estate planning and real-estate management services.

The group's efforts to increase customer satisfaction and establish a reputation for reliability with global communities are significant. BTM has identified three pillars which guide its operations: 'Corporate Value' (customer satisfaction, preserving one's own integrity and contributing to the global community), 'Guiding Principles' (ensuring customer satisfaction, developing the skills and knowledge necessary to respond to challenges, maintaining professional ethics, and acting with responsibility and pride) and 'Corporate Objectives' (building a solid domestic management base to provide quality and diversified financial services in Japan and overseas, and acquiring a reputation for reliability among customers, employees, shareholders and communities).

Challenges and opportunities

As BTM was formed by a merger of two Japanese giant financial institutions with very different corporate cultures, a major challenge for the organization is to integrate the two systems to improve efficiency. While the merger has combined the former MBL's huge domestic branch networks with the extended international networks of BOT, the challenge now confronting BTM pertains to its internal management. Besides, BTM also has to contend with the challenges arising from Japanese economic turmoil and the restructuring programmes of the Japanese government.

To meet these challenges and to take advantage of new opportunities, BTM has implemented risk-management systems, advanced management information systems and efficient management practices. The group has taken measures to respond to rapid technological changes in information and telecommunications, globalization and social transformations worldwide. To meet the challenges in the fast-changing global marketplace and to increase its opportunities in the emerging electronic commerce (e-commerce), BTM has to improve its speed of delivery and enhance its strategic partnerships with other organizations.

Rosalie L. Tung and Mohi Ahmed
Simon Fraser University

Further reading

Economist (1997) 'And it finally came to tears', *Economist* 345(8045), 29 November: 77–9. (Discusses changes in Japan's financial system.)

Smith, C. (1996) 'The bashful giant', *Institutional Investor* 30(11), November: 133–6. (Discusses the challenges facing BTM.)

Further resources

Bank of Tokyo–Mitsubishi website
http://www.btm.co.jp
http://www.btmny.com

Rebuilding the Banks

Business Week; New York; 6 September 1999; Brian Bremner

Abstract:

A mad mating dance is sweeping Tokyo's once-placid Ohtemachi banking quarter. Ever since the collapses of several big banks and Toho Mutual Life Insurance last year, every financial executive has been in crisis-management mode. Now, hardly a week passes without news of a major deal, alliance or merger in Japan's financial industry. The latest deal is by far the biggest to date. In August, three money-center banks, Industrial Bank of Japan, Dai-Ichi Kangyo Bank and Fuji Bank, unveiled plans to form the world's biggest financial holding company. Japan's banks, lumbered with billions in bad debts, inspire more pity than awe. Ladles full of government cash saved the banking system from collapse. But the banks are not home-free. The government may have to rein in some of its life support to banks because overall government borrowing now equals 100% of GDP.

A mad mating dance is sweeping Tokyo's once-placid Ohtemachi banking quarter. Ever since the scary collapses of Yamaichi Securities, Long-Term Credit Bank of Japan Ltd., and Toho Mutual Life Insurance in the past year, every financial exec in town has been in crisis-management mode. Now, hardly a week passes without news of a major deal, alliance, or merger in Japan's once-cosseted financial industry.

The latest deal is by far the biggest to date. On Aug. 19, three money-center banks, Industrial Bank of Japan, Dai-Ichi Kangyo Bank, and Fuji Bank, unveiled plans to form the world's biggest financial holding company, with $1.2 trillion in assets. The monetary Godzilla will dominate Japanese retail, wholesale, and investment banking, and will make about 30% of all corporate lending. It will pit itself against the world's best. "We aim to rank among the top five [global] lenders in terms of capital, profitability, and services," says Masao Nishimura, president of Industrial Bank of Japan Ltd., who will co-chair the operation with Fuji Bank President Yoshiro Yamamoto.

Such ambitions would have alarmed rivals from Wall Street to Frankfurt a decade ago. No longer. Now Japan's banks, lumbered with $600 billion of bad debts, inspire more pity than awe abroad. About a year ago, Japan's top banks were seen as such poor credit risks that they had to pay a huge one percentage point more than Western banks to borrow dollars on global markets. Ladles full of government cash – $500 billion of capital and deposit insurance for ailing banks plus $200 billion in aid to bolster their customers – saved the banking system from collapse.

Rickety institutions

Japanese banks are not home free, however. The government may have to rein in some of its life support to banks because overall government borrowing now equals 100% of gross domestic product. Bad debts continue to grow apace. Impending accounting rule changes will flush out billions more of bad corporate debts now hidden in the books of subsidiaries. They also will lift the veil on $660 billion of unfunded pension obligations that will cast a pall over the creditworthiness of some of the banks' customers.

Meanwhile, some of Japan's 100-plus regional banks are rickety. And there are big worries about the financial health of the nation's massive life-insurance industry, which is squeezed between large-scale policy cancellations and a growing inability to cover claims from premium and investment income.

All the same, Tokyo Stock Market investors embraced the Aug. 19 bank deal. Bank stocks soared 20% in the week following the merger's announcement and have now doubled in value since October. That euphoria may be rewarded if the merger proves to be the first step in a huge consolidation of Japan's financial industry. Hakuo Yanagisawa, head of Japan's Financial Reconstruction Committee, certainly wants to see just that. If he gets his way, Japan's 18 money-center banks will be knocked into four or five $1 trillion behemoths that can compete globally.

Odd bunch

At first blush, the new partners seem an odd bunch to achieve that goal. Each has flaws. Dai-Ichi Kangyo Bank Ltd. is tainted by recent scandals over payoffs to racketeers. Fuji Bank Ltd. lost $3.5 billion in the year through Mar. 31, 1998, after making heavy write-offs. Even IBJ, the soundest, has lost government guarantees on the five-year bonds it uses to finance itself.

To be sure, the new combine towers over the likes of New York-based Citigroup or Germany's Deutsche Bank in assets. But it will be years before the trio will match the smarts, reach, or profits of rivals. Japan's money-center banks are the least profitable in the industrialized world, racking up measly 2% to 3% returns on equity, vs. a typical

15% to 20% in the U.S. Lousy lending is partly to blame – but so is the woeful tardiness of Japanese lenders in grasping how to use mergers to spread huge information technology costs over a bigger base, cross-market products from mutual funds to insurance on a global scale, and ruthlessly cut costs.

True, the trio's leaders promise to ax expenses by $1 billion. They plan to meld all their computer operations, for instance. Added to that, about 6,000 jobs will disappear from their combined 35,000 payroll, along with 150 out of 700 branches. But the cuts will be spread over five years – hardly the pace of a new breed of Japanese financiers who Yanagisawa wants to see "make decisions quickly with a real sense of crisis."

The deal isn't even a full-blooded merger. Once the holding company is formed next year, the banks will take two years to gradually inject their operations into it. Such activities as securities operations might be merged. But most work will be carefully carved up between the banks. Foreign employees will get the chop first as the new outfit eliminates duplicate branches abroad.

But the biggest potential for cost savings is in Japan, where DKB's and Fuji's branch networks overlap extensively. The new bank's leaders are leery of stepping into this hornet's nest. And with good reason: Japanese bank mergers often result in turf battles and failure to deliver promised savings. But unless managers act boldly to hack out domestic fat, the Financial Reconstruction Committee's reform plans will fall flat. Pessimistic analysts warn that the deal could turn into a reincarnation of the Ministry of Finance's notorious "convoy system", by which dud banks were coupled with healthier ones rather than closed.

Since being tapped by Prime Minister Keizo Obuchi last December, Yanagisawa and his 50-strong team of bank examiners and lawyers have attempted to make a break with the past. They have nationalized two giants, Long-Term Credit Bank and Nippon Credit Bank Ltd. If they succeed, Japan's sprawling banking industry will be slimmed down to a handful of sleek global contenders and a larger group of smaller banks that focus on domestic business or specialties such as asset management. Up to a third of Japan's 100-plus local banks will be merged or shut.

Yanagisawa is being helped by Japan's 1996 Big Bang financial reforms, which only now are succeeding in tearing down barriers between banks, brokers, and insurers. Foreign players like Fidelity Investments, GE Capital Services, and Goldman Sachs are adding to the pressure by making inroads into mutual funds, insurance, and asset management. New York investment group Ripplewood Holdings has even set up a $13 billion fund for its bid to buy LTCB from the government.

Cozy ties

Still, progress will be painful and slow. Urgent work in identifying viable regional lenders has barely begun. In April, 2001, the government will stop fully guaranteeing all bank deposits. Instead, it will set an $86,000 limit per account. The change could prompt runs on the weak lenders that lack adequate capital reserves. But government will still play a large role in banking: Its agencies guarantee 12% of all loans in Japan, while the Bank of Japan is now the main intermediary in the local commercial paper and interbank markets.

Despite the hurdles facing reformers, though, the bad old days of state-directed credit may be numbered thanks to budget constraints. The emergence of shareholder capitalism and internationally accepted lending and accounting practices could turn Japan's postwar economic model on its head by loosening collusive ties between banks and big companies. "Japan really is changing now," insists Yoshifumi Nishikawa, president of Sumitomo Bank Ltd. "The old rules won't come back."

Old rules? Consider this: At the start of the decade, the Ministry of Finance had undisputed control over every bank, broker, and life insurer. Top lenders even maintained bureaus that wined and dined MOF bureaucrats to trawl for inside dope on rivals or to lobby to keep foreign players out. As recently as a year ago, such cozy ties allowed the nationalized LTCB and Nippon Credit to set up dummy affiliates.

Bank lending used to be all about relationships, not risk assessment. Even after Japan's bubble economy collapsed, the easy lending continued until late 1996. Lax accounting practices made it devilishly tough to figure out whether a borrower was really solvent or not.

Once accounting reforms start to click in this year, giving bankers better numbers to work with, institutions may finally get their risk assessment skills up to snuff. Then they could become less reliant on low-margin lending to big corporate customers. At Sanwa Bank Ltd., new President Kaneo Muromachi sees no future in such business. Instead, he is forming a comprehensive tie-up with three insurance companies, as well as Toyo Trust & Banking Co. and broker Universal Securities Co., to offer products such as 401(k) plans to corporate customers. And on Aug. 24,

Sanwa announced plans to sell mutual funds managed by Morgan Stanley Dean Witter.

Muromachi is also trying to get middle managers to think creatively rather than passively following orders from the top. "We can no longer cruise along. I need ideas from a variety of people," says Muromachi. So Muromachi now reads a dozen E-mail messages a day from his staff. And during a roadshow in New York last month, he even asked global investors for advice on refining his strategy.

If managers such as Muromachi can revive Japan's banking system, the potential payoff will be substantial. Japan needs to triple the return on its massive savings pool, to 7.5%, figures Deutsche Bank Asia economist Ken Courtis, to pay the costs of caring for its graying population.

"Nonsense"

And instead of throwing good money after bad into old and inefficient companies, banks could bankroll Japan's emerging entrepreneurs. That's why Internet kingpin and Softbank Corp. founder Masayoshi Son is working with Nasdaq to set up a new over-the-counter market in Japan next year. "It takes about 20 years for a young company to have an initial public offering in this country," says Son. "It's nonsense." He knows: Two decades ago, he had to beg bankers to finance his then-fledgling software-distribution company.

Japan's backward financial system has cost the economy dearly. The hope now is that out of the ruins of the old Japan, something new and more dynamic can emerge. The creation of the first trillion-dollar bank might just

signal that Japan's long financial nightmare is finally drawing to a close.

Tom Wagner/SABA

...But Big Challenges Still Loom Ahead

Money-center banks

Bad loans are still increasing sharply. Newly merged players still need years to catch up with Western financial giants in profitability and financial knowhow.

Regional lenders

Four have been shut down this year, and workouts are just beginning at others. Deposits are shrinking as savers fret about the end of 100% deposit insurance in April, 2001.

Life insurers

Big failures of Nissan Mutual and Toho Mutual have cast a shadow over other giant insurance companies. Policy cancellations are up, and many insurers don't earn enough on investments to cover promised returns on policies.

Data: *Business week*

Japan's First Trillion-Dollar Bank

Together IBJ, Dai-Ichi Kangyo, and Fuji Bank have loads of clout ...

Assets	$1.2 trillion
Staff	35,000
Branches	740

... And a raft of problems

Bad debts	$45 billion
1998 Losses	$8.5 billion

Data: *Company Reports*

Reprinted from September 6, 1999 issue of *Business Week* by special permission, © 2000 The McGraw-Hill Companies, Inc.

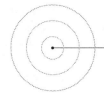

Company Profile 16
Dentsu Inc.

Company overview

Dentsu Inc. is one of the world's largest advertising companies. The firm employs 5,629 people and had revenues in excess of $1.3 billion in 1996. With its headquarters in Tokyo, Japan, Dentsu has offices in thirty-five countries. The slogan of the company is 'communications excellence'. It began operations as a news telegraph service and advertising firm. Later Dentsu expanded its activities to encompass nearly every aspect of creative communication. The major services offered by Dentsu are creative market development, market research, strategic planning, sales promotion, event promotion, corporate communication and media/digital advertising.

Brief history

In 1901 Dentsu Inc. was founded by Hoshiro Mitsunaga. It began as a news telegraph service and advertising firm in Tokyo and later evolved into a leader in the communication industry. In 1986 Dentsu redefined its role as a full-service communications company and implemented a new management philosophy to accomplish this mission. This new management philosophy has guided its corporate objectives, the qualifications it seeks in its employees (communication, planning, creative and production capabilities) and ten principles governing work. According to the company, the ten principles are:

1 Initiate projects on one's own instead of waiting for work to be assigned.
2 Take an active, not passive, role in all one's endeavours.
3 Search for large and complex challenges.
4 Welcome difficult assignments.
5 Complete a task once it is started, i.e. never give up.
6 Lead and set an example for one's fellow workers.
7 Set goals for oneself to ensure a constant sense of purpose.
8 Move with confidence.
9 At all times challenge oneself to think creatively and find new solutions.
10 Since confrontation is inevitable in the course of progress, when confrontation arises do not shy away from it.

This management philosophy was put forward by Hideo Yoshida, Dentsu's fourth president, to inspire its employees to attain the corporate slogan. These guidelines have helped Dentsu grow to become one of the largest advertising companies in the world.

Innovation and significant contributions

Dentsu has broadened the domain of the traditional advertising firm from one of providing mass-media services to encompass total communication. This has opened new opportunities for the company and other firms in the industry. The firm has also contributed towards the enrichment of people's lives by enhancing communication. It has also tried to stimulate creative talent, which is so important in the advertising industry, by providing an environment where employees are free to develop their own ideas.

Dentsu has begun efforts to create solutions for the emerging digital network era, and has won numerous national and international awards for its innovative advertisements.

Challenges and opportunities

Of the top fifteen advertising companies in the world in 1996, only eight are publicly owned. In 2001 Dentsu will make the transition from private to public ownership. This change is designed to help the firm meet the challenges of expanding its global presence in order to take advantage of increasing opportunities around the world. Initially, the company will focus on Asia-Pacific. To facilitate this development, it has established education exchange projects with China and Korea.

Emerging digital technologies have created challenges as well as new opportunities for marketing and advertising companies such as Dentsu. The increase in multimedia use, Internet advertising, cable-television systems and satellite broadcasting are some issues that these firms have to contend with in the years ahead.

ROSALIE L. TUNG AND MOHI AHMED
SIMON FRASER UNIVERSITY

Further reading

Japan 1998 Marketing and Advertising Yearbook, Dentsu Inc. (Gives a detailed overview of the company.)

Rehak, R. (1996) *Greener Marketing & Advertising: The Key to Market Success*, Dentsu Inc. Japan. (Discusses the advertising industry's growing concern with environmental issues.)

Further resources

Dentsu website
http://www.dentsu.co.jp
http://www.dentsu.co.jp/ENG/index.html

Growing pains

Marketing Week; London; 30
September 1999; David Kilburn

Abstract:

Dentsu's agenda to become a major global advertising agency has been in place for more than a decade. However, extending its power outside Japan has proven difficult. Account conflicts in the US hindered the growth of Dentsu/Y&R joint ventures. Now that the Japanese market is shrinking, margins are under pressure, and competition in Japan from international agency brands is increasing. Patience about international expansion is no longer permissible. Dentsu's major stumbling blocks have been cultural. There were mistakes in personnel training. Management's belief that the strength of the brand name in Japan would win and retain business overseas was flawed.

Dentsu's ten-year-old goal to become a major global player is looking tired, yet has become more urgent than ever as competition from international agencies in Japan increases.

Dentsu's calendar has been much the same in recent years. New Year begins with a stirring speech from agency president Yutaka Narita emphasising the need to go both global and digital. This refrain recurs in the summer on Founder's Day. As autumn leaves begin to fall, there are rumours of a partnership with Leo Burnett outside Japan.

Dentsu's agenda to become a major global player has been in place for more than a decade. Its dominance at home, where it holds 23 per cent of the world's second largest advertising market, ranks it as the world's largest agency brand, but extending that power outside Japan has proved difficult.

International goals were formalised in an international development plan at a Dentsu board meeting as far back as April 1990. Most of that plan's objectives were to be accomplished within five years. These included increasing overseas billings, which accounted for about ten per cent of Dentsu's total in 1989, to 20 per cent.

To achieve this, Dentsu's planners reckoned they needed not one but three international networks to handle overseas the many competing brands Dentsu serves at home. Winning as many of these brands as possible abroad was crucial if goals were to be met.

Fortune smiled on Asia. Dentsu's partnership with Y&R, first broached in 1975 and which led to a small joint venture in Tokyo in 1981, blossomed. Despite four name changes, DY&R has become the third largest multinational agency network in Asia, trailing McCann-Erickson and JWT. DY&R's Asian billings topped $1.1bn (L687.5m) in 1998 from an equal mix of Japanese, Western multinational and local clients. Separately, Dentsu's network of wholly-owned agencies rank in the top ten in most of their Asian markets.

Elsewhere, the going has been difficult. Account conflicts in the US hindered the growth of Dentsu/Y&R joint ventures, HDM, a European partnership with Y&R and Eurocom, briefly gave Dentsu a major European network in 1988. But this dissolved at the end of 1990 when the French opted out and went ahead to build EURO-RSCG Worldwide by themselves. CDP meanwhile neither regained its former lustre in the UK nor became a major springboard to Europe.

Patience about international expansion was allowable while domestic business was good and margins wide. But now the Japanese market is shrinking, margins are under pressure, and competition in Japan from international agency brands is increasing.

That patience is no longer permissible, according to Fumio Oshima, the Dentsu managing director who won control of international this July. "In two years we'll become a public company. The goals [my predecessors] set are best described as long-term intentions. Now we must decide both what is truly feasible and how we will achieve it."

While new targets have yet to be set, at least the starting point has been defined. For calendar year 1998, says Oshima, Dentsu's gross billings outside Japan were yen 229 billion (£1.35bn), dropping to yen 139 billion (817m), an equity adjusted basis. By comparison, Dentsu's consolidated gross billings for fiscal 1997/98 (the closest period for which comparable data is available) were yen 1,569bn (£9.2bn). Against this yardstick, equity-adjusted international billings register only 8.9 per cent.

Considering that Dentsu has spent at least $1bn (£625m) over the past decade, striving to build not one but three strong networks, this is not a major achievement.

In fact, Dentsu's major clients have been so much more successful overseas that the pressures to perform better outside Japan are heightening. Oshima says: "Our major Japanese clients have developed into global enterprises whose budgets outside Japan are bigger than those at home. Take Toyota for example, we reckon their overall communications budget outside Japan is over $3.5bn (£2.19bn). Our share of

this is less than ten per cent." In contrast, Toyota Japan's largest advertiser and Dentsu's largest client – spends most of its $1bn (£625m) domestic advertising budget through the agency.

The implications are profound. Oshima explains: "It is only a matter of time before one of our major clients decides to run a campaign in Japan, created originally for the US or elsewhere. We have to become global ourselves, the alternative simply is not an option."

Why has so little been achieved internationally? Mark Gault, McCann-Erickson regional director for Japan and North Asia, says: "Dentsu's dominance in Japan is unchallenged. In Japan, you do not have a choice other than to respect them. In media buying terms, they are formidable."

"They have contacts and connections most other agencies can only dream about, and which they use ruthlessly. But it is this dominance in their home market which has not driven Dentsu to break out of its Japan-centric, insular culture."

Dentsu's major stumbling blocks have been cultural. There were mistakes in personnel training. Management's belief that the strength of the brand name in Japan would win and retain business overseas was flawed. An outmoded management model encouraging direct day-to-day control from Tokyo rather than local empowerment was also a failure.

The US was especially intolerant. The pain threshold rose each year as staff defected, clients deserted, and agencies imploded. One dark day, in 1990, a group of workers dismissed from DCA took grievances to the EEOC and sued. Out poured tales of cultural insensitivity, alienation and misunderstanding. These problems have been fixed, however, since Narita became Dentsu president in 1993.

But there are still many cultural differences between Dentsu and its international peers, which may limit what can be achieved outside Japan. Oshima says: "Other groups have been more aggressive in M&A, but in Japan we don't do things that way. Buying and selling companies is not part of our culture in the way it is in the West, especially in the communications industry. That is why, many years ago, we decided to form a joint venture with Y&R and why we are now seeking a partnership with Leo Burnett."

Additionally, Dentsu's board of directors is an exclusively male club, mostly comprising graduates of the agency's media department. No non-Japanese has ever been a candidate for board membership. "There are no foreign candidates fluent in Japanese," explains Oshima.

"In many ways, Dentsu is still a deeply conservative organisation," says Hotaka Katahira, professor of marketing science at Tokyo University. "Even so, it is a highly creative company, but while its culture allows many divergent views to flourish, it has been less successful at focusing all that energy on achieving specific goals."

International expansion is a case in point. There is no intrinsic reason why a strategy based on partnerships rather than ownerships should fail to deliver. Perhaps all it needs is a more open culture to evolve in Dentsu's bureaucratic Tokyo headquarters.

Evolution is also the name of the game for Y&R, Dentsu's international partner for so many years. This July, Y&R took equity control of DY&R's Asian agencies while Dentsu took the majority of their three joint ventures in Tokyo – DY&R Japan, Dentsu Wunderman Cato Johnson, Dentsu Sudler and Hennessy.

Overall, the joint venture continues as a 50:50 partnership but with Y&R for the first time having equity control of a significant Asian network.

Oshima says: "Y&R, as a global agency, needs a network in Asia. In addition to DY&R, we have a network of our own agencies in Asia, and now we are negotiating with Leo Burnett as well.

"We are going to have three networks in Asia, but for Y&R, DY&R is their sole network in Asia and they only held 50 per cent of this which, in some [clients'] eyes, looked weak. Therefore, we agreed to rearrange our equity relationships. To Western minds it might seem that our relationship is weakening, that we are drifting apart, but this is not so."

Though a year has passed since Dentsu and Leo Burnett began to explore an alliance, the two have started working together. This August, they formed a media agency in Seoul to handle P&G's AOR for South Korea.

The new agency, called Unison PDS (Phoenix, Dentsu, Starcom), is a 50:50 arrangement between Leo Burnett and Phoenix, one of Dentsu's Korean agencies.

Could more such ventures be imminent? "We have not finalised things, but I am sure we will be signing an agreement within a few months," says Oshima.

But perhaps the defining characteristic of Dentsu's approach to international expansion is that after more than ten years of planning and investment, it is in a board room in Chicago, not Tokyo, that the critical decisions will be taken which will determine much of Dentsu's international future.

Reproduced with permission of *Marketing Week*.

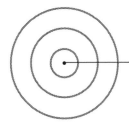

Part 3
Knowledge Management

A distinguishing feature of the new economy is almost instantaneous access to information anywhere in the world and rapid knowledge creation. Thus, an organization that can generate and manage effectively such new knowledge will gain ascendancy in the highly competitive global marketplace.

In Part 3 the focus is on knowledge creation and management. Three companies are selected for inclusion here. The first entry pertains to Wal-Mart. It illustrates how information technology (IT) is central to Wal-Mart's success and dominance in the field of general merchandising. While low prices are important, it is Wal-Mart's ability to move merchandise as efficiently as possible within its huge network that makes both consumers and employees happy, thus keeping the company at the top in its sector. This capability is made possible through the company's substantial investment in IT.

The second entry looks at Xerox, a pioneer in knowledge management. Xerox, which name is synonymous with photocopying, repositioned itself in 1990 to be a 'document company' to provide document processing capabilities to companies to enhance their productivity. The selected case, 'Xerox shares its knowledge', discusses how the knowledge-sharing culture at Xerox has allowed the company to retain its technological superiority. More recently, however, the company has fallen upon hard times as it has lost ground in both the copiers' and printers' market. In end October, 2000, Xerox reported its first quarterly loss in 16 years. The company plans to undertake massive restructuring through cost cutting, slashing jobs, and selling off billions of dollars in assets. Whether Xerox, a company built upon technological innovations and its ability to manage such knowledge, can overcome its present problems – stemming in large part from its efforts to reorganize around business rather than regions – and reverse its decline remains to be seen.

The last entry in this section examines how 3M, already one of the most progressive companies in the world, seeks to become the most innovative company in the world. 3M believes that innovation is a 'cultural and organizational issue' as well as a technological one. There appears to be much support for this argument as was seen in the P&G case presented in Part 1 where the consumer products' giant tries to change its organizational culture to facilitate its transition from one of marketing to that of innovation.

Company Profile 17
Wal-Mart Stores Inc.

Company overview

Wal-Mart Stores Inc. is one of the world's largest general merchandisers. The Wal-Mart stores consist of roughly forty departments ranging from apparel for women, men, girls, boys and infants to paper products, sporting goods, pharmaceuticals, personal care and healthcare products, food, toys, car supplies, small appliances, electronics, hardware, furniture and garden supplies. The annual revenues of the company exceeded $106 billion in 1996 and more than 675,000 people work for the firm. The corporate headquarters of the Wal-Mart Stores Inc. is located in Bentonville, Arkansas.

Brief history

The founder of Wal-Mart, Sam Walton, opened the first large-scale variety store, Wal-Mart Discount City, in 1962. In 1969 Sam Walton incorporated his firm as Wal-Mart Inc. and established a general headquarters and a distribution facility in Bentonville, Arkansas. By 1970 the company had established thirty-two outlets (eighteen Wal-Mart discount and fourteen variety stores) in four states, with net revenues reaching $31 million. In 1970 the firm changed its name to Wal-Mart Stores Inc. By 1980 there were 279 Wal-Mart Stores in eleven states, with net revenues exceeding $1 billion. During the 1980s Wal-Mart continued to expand. In 1983 Sam Walton opened Sam's Club, a membership warehouse club, to further expand the businesses.

In 1985 the firm inaugurated a Buy American programme and Sam Walton became one of the richest people in the United States, with a fortune of $2.8 billion. At that time the firm had 1,114 stores, with $6.4 billion in annual revenues. By 1990 Wal-Mart had a total of 1,531 stores in twenty-nine states, with net revenues totalling $25.8 billion. In 1992 Wal-Mart entered into a joint venture with CIFRA, Mexico's largest retailer, to develop and expand its businesses in Mexico as a part of its international expansion effort. In 1995 the firm entered into Hong Kong and Chinese markets by establishing joint-venture operations with local organizations. By 1995 the firm had more than 1,990 stores, with revenues reaching $82.5 billion. By 1997 Wal Mart had 2,744 stores in the United States, 136 stores in Canada, 145 stores in Mexico, eleven stores in Puerto Rico, five stores in Brazil, six stores in Argentina, two stores in Indonesia and two stores in China.

The firm's Supercenters concept, which combines groceries and general merchandise in a one-stop shopping facility, has become very popular around the world. The firm's small-town origins, strategic location of stores in the area of small communities, where local merchants were its principal rivals, and strategic absorption of businesses for miles around the stores contributed to the success of Wal-Mart.

Innovation and significant contributions

Wal-Mart has succeeded in establishing a reputation for its low-cost merchandising and high-quality customer services, including quick-response merchandise supply and innovative supply-chain management systems. The firm's RetailLink private network for sharing inventory and sales data with merchandise suppliers represents one of the most innovative implementations of information technologies (IT) in the general merchandisers industry. Wal-Mart's 'data warehousing' and 'data mining' have contributed to the firm's competitive edge in the retail industry. The firm's state-of-the-art IT system allows each store to customize the merchandise collection to match the needs of the community it serves. Wal-Mart also seeks to contribute to the communities in which it is located through fundraising activities for local children's hospitals, by educating the public about recycling and other environmental topics, and by awarding industrial development grants each year to towns and cities which foster the development of the local economy.

Challenges and opportunities

Cutting costs, reducing out-of-stock items and ensuring the efficient distribution of goods to its stores in international locations are the major challenges confronting Wal-Mart. The firm has tried to meet these challenges through strategic expansion in international locations, establishment of partnerships with its suppliers around the world and implementation of one-stop shopping concepts in the international marketplace. Strategic expansion and continuous innovation of the firm's distribution system and effective management of the supply chain in the emerging era of electronic commerce (e-commerce) will bring further success to the firm.

ROSALIE L. TUNG AND MOHI AHMED
SIMON FRASER UNIVERSITY

Further reading

Hoover, G., Campbell, A. and Spain, P.J. (eds) (1995) 'Wal-Mart Stores, Inc.', *Hoover's Handbook of American Business*, Austin: The Reference Press, Inc. (Gives a general overview of the company.)

Vance, S.S. and Scott, R.V. (1994) *Wal-Mart: A History of Sam Walton's Retail Phenomenon*, New York: Twayne Publishers. (Presents the perspective of Sam Walton.)

Wilder, C. (1997) 'Chief of the year: Wal-Mart CIO Randy Mott innovates for his company's and customers' good', *Information Week* 662, 22 December: 42–8. (Discuss implementation of IT at Wal-Mart's distribution centres.)

Zellner, W., Shepard, L., Katz, I. and Lindorff, D. (1997) 'Wal-Mart spoken here', *Business Week*, 23 June: 138–44. (Discusses the international expansion strategies of Wal-Mart.)

Further resources

Wal-Mart website
http://www.wal-mart.com

Chief of the year: Walmart CIO Randy Mott innovates for his company's – and customers' – good

Informationweek; Manhasset; 22 December 1997; Clinton Wilder

Abstract:

Wal-Mart Stores Inc.'s senior Vice President and CIO Randy Mott, InformationWeek magazine's 1997 Chief of the Year, is profiled. In a year when competitive pressures and a relentless pace of change have made the IT-business partnership absolutely imperative to the bottom line, *InformationWeek's* readers and editors have chosen Mott and his innovative IT division at Wal-Mart as the preeminent model of success. For good reason: Mott judges every IT investment, development decision, and technology choice by only one measure: how it will help the business. Mott, 41, has lived this philosophy since joining Wal-Mart, the world's biggest retailer, as a 21-year-old programmer in 1978. One of his early tasks involved coding applications for Wal-Mart's first remote automated distribution center, more than 200 miles away in Searcy, Arkansas.

On Dec. 1, the first Monday after the long Thanksgiving weekend, things were hopping in Bentonville, Ark., home of WalMart Stores Inc. The retailer's NCR Teradata database was fielding more than 20,000 queries as both Wal-Mart buyers and outside suppliers eagerly tried to get an early read on the start of the holiday shopping season. They got it – and then some. Wal-Mart's IS group, led by senior VP and CIO Randy Mott, gave the buyers and suppliers access to the previous 65 weeks' worth of sales figures for each of the retailer's nearly 2,800 U.S. stores, super-centers, and wholesale clubs. Some buyers even mined data from the checkout baskets of individual shoppers in a quest to make better decisions about merchandising and store displays. For nearly two decades, delivering that type of strategic information has been the modus operandi of Mott, *InformationWeek's* 1997 Chief of the Year. In a year when competitive pressures and a relentless pace of change have made the IT-business partnership absolutely imperative to the bottom line, *Information Week's* readers and editors have chosen Mott and his innovative IT division at Wal-Mart as the preeminent model of success. For good reason: Mott judges every IT investment, development decision, and technology choice by only one measure: how it will help the business.

Business first

Mott, 41, has lived this philosophy since joining Wal-Mart, the world's biggest retailer, as a 21-year-old programmer in 1978. One of his early tasks involved coding applications for Wal-Mart's first remote automated distribution center, more than 200 miles away in Searcy, Ark. The assignment helped Mott form his business-benefit above-all philosophy. "It was a big step for the company to have a lot of the merchandise in a place where they couldn't go out and touch it," Mott recalls.

Today, Wal-Mart's IT departments instill that kind of thinking in all of their 1,370 employees. "The greatest reward is to accomplish something in

IT and see it in action, making associates [Wal-Mart's term for its employees] and customers happy," says Mott. "It's tough to get any better than that."

Mott's philosophy has paid off handsomely – and pulled Wal-Mart out of some sluggish times. Two years ago, although the company's revenue had grown handsomely, to $93.6 billion, profit growth had stalled. To help, Mott embarked on an aggressive program to increase IT development staff by nearly 40% and quickly deliver applications aimed at reducing store inventories and speeding the supply chain. He succeeded. For the first nine months of Wal-Mart's current fiscal year, profits grew by 14% on a 12% sales jump; third-quarter profit jumped by 16% on an 11% revenue advance. Crucially, third-quarter inventories at Wal-Mart's U.S. stores were lower than year-earlier levels, an achievement directly attributable to better and faster information in the supply chain.

One result: Wal-Mart stores used to receive just one shipment of seasonal items for the Christmas season; now, each gets three to five shipments. "Wal-Mart controls losses from inventory better than any other retailer," says Bill Eisenman, senior VP of computer systems at NCR in Dayton, Ohio. "It's a major reason why they can keep costs down and advertise 'Always Low Prices. Always Wal-Mart.'"

By all accounts, Mott is a humble, self-effacing man who finds his greatest professional rewards in helping others succeed. "I see a lot of good CIOs," says Eisenman, "but what separates the real good ones is they don't just get the requirements from the business and deliver them. They view themselves as major catalysts for improving the business. That's Randy Mott to a T."

Wal-Mart's business executives couldn't agree more. In September, they promoted him to the company's 14-member executive committee. The appointment recognizes the fact that even though Mott has spent his entire 20-year career at Wal-Mart in IT, he has never once looked at technology only for technology's sake.

"First and foremost, he is absolutely a retailer," says Sue Brann, the IT division's people director (Wal-Mart parlance for head of human resources). "He tells every associate that they're going to understand a process before they automate it." Adds Kevin Turner, Wal-Mart's VP of application development: "He's not a fiery-for-effect kind of manager, but a solid, everyday contributor who earns your respect. He's one of the true gentlemen in our profession. You just want to be around him. It's hard not to kill yourself working for him."

Mott has kept Wal-Mart on the leading edge of innovation. Since his promotion to senior VP and CIO in May 1994, Mott has either pioneered or continued Wal-Mart's leadership in quick-response merchandise replenishment, use of massively parallel processing, and supply-chain management.

Wal-Mart has certainly been an IT pioneer. The retailer ran extranets – albeit not on the Internet – well before the term had even been invented. Its RetailLink private network for sharing inventory and sales data with merchandise suppliers was one of the first large-scale examples of vendor-managed inventory. It now shares data with more than 4,000 suppliers and is moving to the Net, with the rollover scheduled for completion by March. Wal-Mart's CarrierLink network for firms that haul goods to its distribution centers will also move to the Net next year. And its client-server decision-support application will move to the corporate intranet in 1998.

Wal-Mart's biggest ground-breaking IT advancements under Mott have come in data warehousing and data mining. It's not just having a database of 24 terabytes; it's the way the retailer has mined the data to better understand which items sell, which don't, which tend to sell with other specific items, and what types of people shop at particular Wal-Mart stores. That means better decisions in merchandising, inventory, and pricing. "No two Wal-Mart stores are alike," says Mott.

Warehousing evangelist

Impressive as that is, Mott has gone several steps further. He's taken on the role of data-warehousing advocate and evangelist, not just at Wal-Mart, not just in the retail industry, but for all kinds of potential users worldwide. Mott has hosted visits in Bentonville from more than 60 companies interested in data warehousing, and earlier this year, he spent a day and a half in Tokyo with retail customers of NCR Japan.

Yet Mott is no pushover for his vendors. In fact, he demands that vendors provide the same business benefits to Wal-Mart that he asks from his own IT organization. "[Mott] expects a quality product at the right price, and usually faster than we can deliver it," Eisenman of NCR says with a chuckle.

Also, Mott has a near-total commitment to using applications developed in-house. With only a few exceptions-such as a human resources system from PeopleSoft Wal-Mart eschews packaged apps, and Mott is adamant about it. "I know I think a little differently from some of my peers," he says, "but there's something fundamentally wrong when you have to ask your people to modify the business to fit a software package."

Mott has also taken a leadership position in easy communication across the supply chain. He serves on the executive committee of Voluntary Inter-Industry Commerce Standards in Washington, an association that promotes communications standards among retails and suppliers. Mott is also a member of the Research Board in New York, a prestigious group of CIOs from the country's largest corporations.

Wal-Mart, perhaps more than any other $100+ billion company, has remained true to the down-home roots of its founder, the late Sam Walton. Mott fits in perfectly. He's lived almost his entire life within 30 miles of Bentonville, attending high school in neighboring Rogers, Ark., going to college just 20 miles down U.S. 71 at the University of Arkansas in Fayetteville, and now living back in Rogers. "I wanted to join a growing and progressive IT organization and figured I'd have to move to Dallas or Houston," says Mott. "As it worked out, I was happy to be able to stay here and raise a family in northwest Arkansas."

Mott and his wife, Shannon, a registered nurse, have two sons and a daughter. A yearly ski trip to Colorado is a family tradition. Another of Mott's favorite pastimes is cheering his kids on at football, soccer, and basketball games – once again, reveling in others' successes.

Mott's local roots and long Wal-Mart career help the company attract IT talent to Bentonville, says HR director Brann. "He gets involved in the hiring process, even with college students," she says. "He's able to articulate what it means to work here from personal experience."

Mott insists his organization's best days are still ahead. "A lot of people look at retail technology and automation and think it has arrived. But it's not a finished product, and you have to continue to work at it," he says. "We still have a long way to go."

© CMP Media Inc. 22 December 1997.

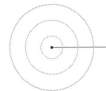

Company Profile 18
Xerox Corporation

Company overview

Xerox, which name is synonymous with photocopying, is a global company with revenues in excess of $17 billion in 1996. Xerox was founded in 1906 in Rochester, New York, as the Haloid Company and renamed Xerox Corporation in 1961. Xerox produces and sells copiers, printers, scanners, fax machines, document management software, and associated products and services in about 130 countries around the world. About one-third of Xerox revenues come from digital products. The company employs about 86,700 people worldwide, including 46,000 in the United States (1996). Its corporate headquarters is located in Stamford, Connecticut.

Brief history

The Haloid Company, which manufactures and sells photographic paper, was founded in Rochester, New York, in 1906. In 1938 Chester Carlson invented the first xerographic image in his lab in New York. Haloid acquired the licence to Carlson's basic xerographic patents and introduced the first xerographic copier, the Model A, in 1949. In 1953 Haloid established its Canadian sales subsidiary, the first subsidiary outside of the United States. In 1956 Rank Xerox Limited was established as a joint venture between the Haloid Company and the Rank Organization PLC. In 1958 the Haloid Company changed its name to Haloid Xerox Inc., and the company was renamed again, as Xerox Corporation, in 1961.

In 1962 Fuji Xerox Co. Ltd was established as a joint venture between Rank Xerox Ltd and Fuji Photo Film Co. Ltd of Japan. In 1965 Rank Xerox opened a manufacturing plant in the Netherlands. In 1969 Xerox Corporation acquired a majority interest (51.2 per cent) in Rank Xerox. In the same year Xerox moved its corporate headquarters from Rochester, New York, to Stamford, Connecticut. In 1975 Xerox ceased manufacturing and selling mainframe computers. During the 1970s Xerox's market share dropped tremendously as a result of severe competition in the global marketplace. Its major competitors include Canon, Sharp, Toshiba, Siemens, Kodak and Hewlett-Packard. The company has successfully responded to this challenge by adopting a strategy known as 'leadership through quality'. Through reduced cost, higher quality, participatory management and benchmarking, Xerox was able to recapture much of its lost market share.

In 1991 Xerox and Fuji Xerox established Xerox International Partners to market its printers in the global market. After significant corporate restructuring, Xerox announced its corporate identity as 'The Document Company, Xerox', in

1994. The company continued to expand its products and services around the globe.

Innovation and significant contributions

Since the beginning, Xerox has made important innovations and contributions in the area of document processing. Xerography, the laser printer, Ethernet networking, bit mapping and the graphical user interface are examples of major technological innovations by Xerox – all these innovations have revolutionized the way people work. To many people, the word 'xerox' is synonymous with 'photocopying'. In 1970 Xerox established the Xerox Palo Alto Research Center in Palo Alto, California, which provided a focal point for its R&D efforts. In 1989 Xerox Business Products and Systems received the Malcolm Baldridge National Quality Award. The company has continued to receive awards for quality from around the world.

Xerox uses only recyclable and recycled thermoplastics and metals, and has adopted designs in its products to facilitate assembly and disassembly for cleaning, testing and reuse of parts. In 1992 Xerox received the Gold Medal for International Corporate Environmental Achievement from the World Environment Centre and the Environmental Achievement Award from National Wildlife Federation.

Its joint venture with Fuji Photo, in addition to being one of the earliest joint ventures between an American and a Japanese entity, has been cited as an example of a highly successful cross-national collaborative agreement. In fact, the joint venture itself has made major innovations, which were, in turn, introduced into the parent companies.

Challenges and opportunities

To continue to innovate and expand, Xerox has entered into collaborative arrangements with other entities around the world. In 1987 Xerox established technology alliances with Sun Microsystems Inc. In 1992 Xerox entered into an agreement with Apple Computer to market Apple-brand supplies for Apple printers; and in 1993 Xerox formed a partnership with Microsoft to integrate personal computers and document processing products. In 1995 Xerox began partnerships with the American Foundation for the Blind to donate Reading Edge machines to blind people, and in the same year Xerox established a subsidiary, Xerox (China) Limited, to manage existing Xerox manufacturing and marketing operations in China. To increase opportunities in China, Xerox also established its first Document Technology Center in Beijing in 1996.

Linking technology and market is one of the major challenges facing Xerox. To remain one of the most innovative and competitive firms around the world and further develop opportunities in the competitive global marketplace, Xerox must make continuous advances in digital technologies and cost reduction, and must broaden its products and services distribution networks throughout the world. In end October, 2000, Xerox reported its first quarterly loss in 16 years. The company plans to undertake major restructuring, including cutting costs and jobs and selling off billions of dollars in assets. Whether these efforts are adequate to turn the company around remains to be seen.

ROSALIE L. TUNG AND MOHI AHMED
SIMON FRASER UNIVERSITY

Further reading

Hoover, G., Campbell, A. and Spain, P.J. (eds) (1995) 'Xerox Corporation', *Hoover's Handbook of American Business*, Austin: The Reference Press, Inc. (Gives a general overview of the company.)

Jones, P. and Kahaner, L. (1995) *Say It & Live It: 50 Corporate Mission Statements That Hit the Mark*, New York: Currency Doubleday. (Presents the mission statements of fifty companies, including Xerox's.)

Kiely, T. (1994) 'Innovation congregations', *Technology Review* 97(3): 54 (MIT, Cambridge). (Discusses Xerox's approach to encourage innovation and experiments among its employees.)

Rosenbloom, R.S. and Spencer, W.J. (eds) (1996) *Engines of Innovation: U.S. Industrial Research at the End of an Era*, Boston, MA: Harvard Business School Press. (Focuses on R&D and change management at Xerox.)

Smart, T. (1993) 'Can Xerox duplicate its glory days', *Business Week*, 4 October: 56–8. (Discusses the challenges facing Xerox in the areas of technology, products and markets.)

Smart, T. (1997) 'Out to make Xerox print more money', *Business Week*, 11 August: 81–2. (Outlines the mission of Xerox's president, ex-IBM CFO Richard Thoman, to create a new Xerox.)

Smith, D.K. and Alexander, R.C. (1988) *Fumbling the Future: How Xerox Invented, Then Ignored, the First Personal Computer*, New York: William Morrow & Company. (Gives an insight to Xerox's change management process.)

Xerox Quality Solutions (1993) *A World of Quality: The Timeless Passport*, Milwaukee, WI: ASQC Quality Press. (Examines TQM principles, practices and their importance at Xerox.)

Further resources

Xerox website
http://www.xerox.com

Xerox shares its knowledge

Management Review; New York;
September 1999; Michael Hickins

Abstract:

A competitive edge based on technological superiority is now measured in weeks rather than years, providing a head start at best. But companies can regain that edge by leveraging their knowledge to get more mileage out of their innovations and bring them to market faster than the competition. Xerox Corp., an emerging leader in knowledge management practices, is an interesting example of how the process is done right. Xerox's reputation as a leading knowledge company has been built on a strong knowledge-sharing culture. This culture has become a catalyst for the company's development of knowledge-intensive products. In Xerox's case, the innovations happen to be KM tools – technologies for efficient knowledge sharing developed on the basis of the company's existing copier, printing, and scanning technologies. Xerox also aligns its KM practice with its business plan, which calls for the company to use its strength and customer base in traditional document management products to evolve into a total digital network solutions company.

An acknowledged leader in knowledge sharing, Xerox puts its culture front and center in the effort to leverage employee know-how.

Reality check du jour: a competitive edge based on technological superiority is now measured in weeks rather than years, providing a head start at best. But companies can regain that edge by leveraging their knowledge (or intellectual capital) to get more mileage out of their innovations and bring them to market faster than the competition. Xerox Corp., an emerging leader in knowledge management practices, is an interesting example of how the process is done right.

A pioneer in knowledge management (KM) research and development, the Stamford, Connecticut-based company has been consciously managing knowledge since 1990, when it repositioned itself as a "document company" as part of a new 15-year strategic outlook and adopted its Year 2005 plan. Today, Xerox [www.xerox. com] is one of the top five "Most Admired Knowledge Enterprises" chosen by senior executives at Fortune's Global 500 companies and leading KM practitioners in a survey sponsored by *Business Intelligence* and the *Journal of Knowledge Management*, both of the UK.

Xerox's reputation as a leading knowledge company has been built on a strong knowledge-sharing culture. This culture has become a catalyst for the company's development of knowledge-intensive products. In Xerox's case, the innovations happen to be KM tools technologies for efficient knowledge sharing developed on the basis of the company's existing copier, printing and scanning technologies. But even nontechnology companies can leverage their knowledge in this manner.

Xerox also aligns its KM practice with its business plan, which calls for the company to use its strength and customer base in traditional document management products to evolve into a total digital network solutions company. At the same time, it expects to improve staple metrics such as quality and time-to-market. Since the company now defines documents as any information structured for human comprehension, its business has expanded to include products and services that touch on document and knowledge management, including a KM consulting service.

Consistent with that strategic alignment is the active encouragement and support that senior management gives to each business unit's KM effort. The leadership believes that the company can gain a significant competitive advantage by leveraging the knowledge contained in the heads of 90,000 employees, its archives of patents and processes, and countless documents stored around the world in various digital formats.

While many companies' KM initiatives have failed, Xerox has been able to make KM work because it has focused on the right thing from the start. Rather than emphasizing the IT infrastructure of knowledge sharing and forcing employees to either adapt or fail, Xerox has gone to great lengths to tailor its KM initiatives to people by understanding how they do their jobs and the social dynamics behind knowledge sharing.

Eye on the prize

Xerox's overarching KM strategy is to create added value by capturing and leveraging knowledge. This strategy is rooted in the lessons learned from Xerox's near collapse in the 1970s, when many of the company's most profitable patents, notably in copiers, expired. It also had failed to exploit numerous advanced technologies it had developed, such as the mouse and pull-down menus that were later commercialized by Apple. These lost opportunities led to the thinking behind the Year 2005 plan.

Considering that documents are more than just paper, Xerox today calls itself a "digital document company." President and CEO Richard Thoman has said that documents are the DNA of knowledge – the blueprint of an organization's intellectual capital. As communications manager Sandy Mauceli puts it, "Documents are not physical things, they are the crucible of knowledge."

Dan Holtshouse, one of the architects of the Year 2005 plan and now director of corporate strategy and knowledge initiatives, believes that Xerox's clients will gain a strategic advantage by managing knowledge better than the competition. Xerox applies this thinking internally as well. Thus, its goal is to develop products that manage the "crucibles of knowledge" be they hard copies or electronic documents and make them accessible to a large number of people.

But Xerox did not create a KM strategy out of thin air. Instead, KM is the nomenclature for an overall cultural focus on knowledge sharing. KM programs are the enablers that allow Xerox employees to share their knowledge. Chairman Paul Allaire says that aligning KM and its related technologies with the way people function in the workplace is key. "Fundamentally, the way we work is changing, and we have to look at ways to help shape the workplace of the future through technology," he says. "Because work has become much more cooperative in nature, technology must support this distributed sharing of knowledge."

Knowledge sharing

At Xerox, the sharing of knowledge translates into accelerated learning and innovation. Eventually, that is where its competitive advantage lies. Indeed, it was the internal reflection on

KM that led Xerox away from the analog copier business to digital copiers in the mid-90s and to digital document networking today.

In a sense, Xerox has put itself on a different level from its traditional rivals in the copier business. And it is frankly pinning its competitive hopes for the future on knowledge sharing. As Bob Guns, senior manager of knowledge management at Pricewaterhouse-Coopers, notes, "It is a competitive advantage if your company is learning faster than the competition."

Learning begins with sharing at Xerox, according to Holtshouse. In companies where power is acquired by hoarding knowledge, learning cannot take place effectively. William Latshaw, knowledge manager for consulting firm Arthur D. Little, says, "In the past, power was derived from having the knowledge. Unless you address this, the knowledge management system will founder."

But knowledge sharing is more than telling hoarders to play nice. It is about capturing the tacit knowledge locked in people's heads. In the experience of David Owens, vice president of knowledge management at Unisys Corp. and vice chair of The Conference Board's Learning and Knowledge Management Council, "Only 2 percent of information gets written down – the rest is in people's heads."

For Xerox, the challenge is to capture and transform such knowledge into a sharable form – a tall order when tens of thousands of people are involved in the sharing. One example: Xerox has 23,000 repair technicians around the world who repair copiers at clients' sites. Some of the solutions exist only in the heads of experienced technicians, who can solve complex problems faster and more efficiently than less experienced ones. By drawing on the tacit knowledge they've accumulated over the years, they can save time and costs, reduce customer aggravation and increase customer loyalty – a significant foundation for business growth.

Xerox realized that such knowledge could be documented and shared among technicians, allowing all to achieve the same positive results. In 1996, it developed Eureka, an intranet communication system linked with a corporate database that helps service reps share repair tips. To date, more than 5,000 tips have been entered by Xerox technicians, and they are available to all via their ubiquitous laptops. For employees who are scattered around the world and travel often, the ability to share such knowhow means they don't have to miss out on the kind of knowledge that's typically exchanged at the watercooler.

Holtshouse says this knowledge-sharing technology has had a significant impact on the culture of the entire workforce. "We're starting this knowledge-sharing initiative as a cultural dimension inside of Xerox," he says. "Knowledge sharing is going to become part of a fabric inside the company, for all employees."

Making KM work

Xerox is not alone in trying to make KM part of its corporate life. Many companies create a KM system, replete with IT glitter such as expert databases and intranet sites, and then foist it on a workforce that already has plenty to do. Employees often resist the added burden, and even the best intentioned may throw up their hands in frustration.

The problem is that technology itself can be off-putting. Employees may have a difficult time remembering the computer-generated passwords needed to use database systems, for example, says Stephen Cunningham, information resource consultant for Roche Diagnostics in Indianapolis, Indiana. Often, the users are embarrassed to call the systems administrators for help and simply give up.

Another problem is that people are loathe to spend time adding content to a knowledge repository. And everyone knows that a database is only as good as the information it contains. Mark Mazzie, chief knowledge officer at Barnett International, a consulting firm in Media, Pennsylvania, says, "Don't create extra work for the people who use knowledge management systems – that's the best way to kill a program."

That's one minefield Xerox has managed to sidestep, despite the technological focus of its business. Laura Tucker, manager of the company's technical information center, emphasizes that KM at Xerox is not technology-driven. "It's people-driven," she says. Internal KM experts say that 80 percent of designing KM systems involves adapting to the social dynamics of the workplace. Only 20 percent involves technology as an enabling mechanism.

With Eureka, for instance, the goal was to develop a system that would suit field technicians and a database they would populate with content. Hence the link to laptops, which are standard issue at Xerox. The company also discovered that the technicians were more than happy to add tips to the database because they received credit for their contributions, which enhanced their standing among colleagues. Indeed, when management suggested attaching financial incentives to the tips, technicians resisted the idea. They felt this would diminish the value of their contributions.

Xerox also avoided the pitfall of poorly designed electronic yellow pages. Those arranged by name and title, for example, do not necessarily help users identify sources of information. In the yellow pages at Xerox, employees identify themselves by areas of expertise, which are as varied as digital networking, cuneiform and workplace psychology. Each employee also qualifies the degree of his or her expertise – broad knowledge, some knowledge, hobby, etc. – so that those seeking help in a given area or subject matter can identify sources. People must register themselves to use the database, says Tucker, so that they are available to others as they use the resources.

Social dynamics

Xerox's KM practice is successful because of the priority it gives to people. The company examined how social dynamics shape the pattern of knowledge sharing to create technologies that reflect factors such as work habits, the perceived benefits of sharing and the contexts in which sharing is natural.

DocuShare is a good example of this. According to Holtshouse, the tool was first developed in 1996 to enable the 500-plus employees at Xerox's research labs in Rochester to share information. Now, it is available companywide and allows work teams to create a "virtual" office space on the corporate intranet – a 3-D room where visitors can navigate through and access filing cabinets containing electronic documents.

Individual users set codes to determine who can have access to their documents and who cannot. All members of a group can visit any filing cabinet in their "room" and give access codes to employees from other work groups. The tool encourages typically closed-lipped scientists to share information with colleagues while respecting their need for privacy. In the end, it helps break down the barriers of distance and the product silos that usually exist in larger companies.

Brian Falkenhainer, manager of Xerox's DocuShare project, offers one example of how the tool has helped speed up his work: In this case, he had waited until the last minute to prepare for a presentation at a conference, but he knew that a colleague had made a similar presentation. Rather than having to hunt him down in the hallway and ask for a diskette or hard copy, he used DocuShare to find the presentation on the intranet. This saved hours of work recreating a document that already existed. Falkenhainer says this tool reflects a very different work atmosphere at Xerox. "It's very different from how we used to operate internally two years ago."

By allowing the same information to be reused, DocuShare also reduces development costs and potentially stimulates new applications for the same knowledge, which ultimately increases the information's absolute value.

DocuShare also takes into account what motivates people to share knowledge. During the early design phase, Xerox hired anthropologists to help understand how scientists at the labs generally worked, both individually and in groups. It then decided that certain conditions were required for these scientists to use a common knowledge-exchange platform – no training needed to use it, no maintenance and no bureaucracy. It also discovered how scientists set criteria about which information to protect and which to make accessible. These social dynamics affected the technological specifications for the tool.

Thus, Holtshouse says that while KM solutions may appear to be technical, successful ones come from an understanding of the social dynamics of a particular workforce. "A lot of what you know about the social aspects can actually be expressed in the product," he says.

The germ of Portals, another KM tool used at Xerox, developed at the company's Palo Alto Research Center (PARC) facility in California. Portals is a digitally networked tool that uses the scanning technology inherent in copiers to build electronic links between copiers and corporate databases, says Mark Hill, vice president and general manager of the Document Portals business unit. Instead of just making copies, employees can use Portals to scan in hard copies of documents and transfer them to a hard disk. They can also retrieve documents from anywhere on the corporate database and print them out from Portals. This allows them to capture, search for and retrieve knowledge more efficiently.

Like DocuShare, Portals was developed from an understanding of people's work habits, says Hill. Rather than inventing a new digital scanning device, he decided to combine existing copier technology with people's preference for simple operations. In his own words, people are "used to hitting the little green button to make copies." By paying attention to the details of the workplace (that little green button), Xerox developed a tool that enhances the number of ways that documents – and knowledge – can be shared.

Holtshouse sums up Xerox's approach of fitting technology to people instead of the other way round: "We started with an intense search around workers what makes them tick, what's important, what problems they are solving – and then picked technology that suits the solutions."

A pat on the back

It goes without saying that any KM program requires strong leadership support. At Xerox, a consistent communications strategy from senior management demonstrates that support. Hotshouse says that public comments from the top executives are critical. The validation of CEO Thoman shows that KM is important and strategically relevant over time.

Besides giving verbal support, senior managers have adopted a hands-off policy toward KM projects to ensure that the process of innovation isn't hindered by bureaucracy or budgetary considerations. This does not mean that KM project teams are a free-wheeling endeavor. But rather than setting specific KM goals in stone, senior management sets more traditional organizational goals, such as quality and time-to-market. Associates can then develop KM projects that will support those goals.

The top executives aren't looking for quick wins, and the biggest strides have come from a grassroots, project-by-project approach rather than grandiose, management-driven initiatives. As Holtshouse notes, "In my experience, Xerox has a little more respect for the unknown, of not knowing what the grand picture is to begin with."

Eureka and DocuShare are examples of KM solutions that began as modest grassroots projects. Management funded those ventures without knowing exactly where they would lead. Portals grew out of conversations between Hill, based in Rochester, and chief scientist John Seely Brown and others at PARC in California. This sort of cross-boundary discussion can be called a community of practice, which Joe Horvath, a senior consultant at IBM Consulting Group, defines simply as "a group of people bound by interest in a common set of problems." These communities spring into being spontaneously, adds Holtshouse, and cannot be "ordered" up. "The critical knowledge in any society is living knowledge," he says.

Dale Bennett, a longtime Xerox employee who works out of his home without a specific title (a "freewheeling idea generator" is how he describes himself) says communities of practice are an informal kind of cross-functional teamwork that generates innovation. "It's cross-pollination where you say, 'Oh, he's doing that over there, I could use that over here.' And those 'aha' moments when you realize, 'Oh yeah! That's a great idea and this is how I'd use it.' That process is what really gives you access to creativity and creates a competitive advantage."

But even at Xerox, Tucker notes, "You have to have some deliverables eventually – not necessarily related directly to the community of practice, but with regards to your own job. Otherwise it's just a coffee klatch."

Copying Xerox (again)

The French philosopher Pascal said that the human race is like a man who never dies, always gaining knowledge. This immortality of knowledge is the aim of learning organizations – to get all the knowledge in people's heads written down somewhere. By most accounts, the know-how most vital to companies as they struggle to compete, innovate and improve shareholder value is undocumented in any form.

So while the importance of knowledge sharing is not in doubt, implementing a KM project is still a challenge to many. Xerox is a technology company and can create many of its own KM solutions. But that isn't the point. Despite the technological nature of its business, Xerox assumes that KM initiatives can be as low-tech as notes on a refrigerator door or as high-tech as its intranet-based virtual office solutions.

Other companies can and should emulate Xerox's implementation strategy, which is based on aligning knowledge sharing with business goals and allowing workplace habits – not IT – to drive the process. Furthermore, the process shouldn't be static. Says Holtshouse, "We need to enhance what we do inside around knowledge sharing so that we continually learn, so that we can be a leader on what we know about this."

For Holtshouse, who worked for NASA earlier in his career (and still holds some patents), this isn't rocket science. It's just smart. MR

What you buy is not always what you get

Knowledge management (KM) is an internal practice at Xerox – and would be, even if the company produced paper clips. But as it happens, Xerox produces technological tools that enable KM. This does not mean that purchasing Xerox products alone will give you its KM capability. Without a corporate philosophy that embraces learning and sharing, even the best KM technologies won't put you ahead of the competition.

But companies that adopt KM as a basic principle do tend to produce more knowledge intensive products. One example is Monsanto Co., which also embraces KM as a guiding post. It is branching into increasingly sophisticated products in both of its core areas – agricultural and pharmaceuticals – and new areas of development, which it has spun off as its life sciences division. According to Jane Rady, vice president of prospecting, knowledge management at Monsanto, KM is a core value that helps the company develop better products and bring them to market faster.

In one case, the company found a way to imbed intelligence into seeds, which have essentially been a commodity product. Its new seeds are genetically engineered to fend off parasites, which reduces costs for farmers because they don't have to spray the crops and also benefits the environment.

For Monsanto, the seeds breathe new life into its agricultural business. Farmers generally use seed crop – the portion of their crop used to grow future plants – to avoid buying more seeds. But genetically engineered seeds pose a new challenge as their novel qualities are lost in succeeding generations. That means farmers must go back to Monsanto for more parasite-resistant seeds every year.

Rady credits Monsanto's KM philosophy with helping the company to leverage the intellectual capabilities of various departments (such as R&D and marketing) in the formerly highly siloed organization. "Surprising insights can be created thanks to knowledge sharing across a wide spectrum of the organization," she says.

KM consulting as a new strategy

Knowledge management (KM) is a vital tool that can serve two purposes, as consulting companies have discovered. Managing their own knowledge is critical to their survival, while KM also is a consulting product they can market. So it should come as no surprise that not only Xerox, but also IBM, Unisys and other technology companies are developing consulting practices in this field.

Xerox is counting heavily on its relatively new consulting business, which it considers a natural extension of its core business. CEO Richard Thoman recently said that he expects Xerox Professional Services (XPS), which includes the consulting business, to generate at least 50 percent of the company's revenues within 10 years.

According to Bob Couture, XPS vice president and general manager, the division's mission is to leverage business with existing Xerox customers and build on the company's growing reputation in KM to help its clients better manage documents – and, by extension, knowledge and information.

To this end, Xerox recently reorganized its activities by industry group rather than geographic region. "This helps us better understand and help our clients address issues that are important within their industries," says Couture.

But while XPS may rely on existing Xerox copier clients for business, Couture says XPS does not necessarily recommend Xerox hardware or software solutions. "We do not have a measurement system and will not have a measurement system that compensates Xerox consultants for placing Xerox products – there is no inherent incentive to do that."

On the other hand, the KM practice at XPS, headed by Priscilla Douglas, owes its intellectual legacy and competitive edge to the work done by Xerox scientists and thinkers at the Palo Alto Research Center. The KM practice focuses on clients' work practices and processes to help determine which kinds of documents need to be captured and the best ways of doing so. Unlike consulting companies that offer a broad array of services, XPS focuses exclusively on document lifecycles and document management. According to Douglas, "This intellectual foundation, which developed a social and technical approach to capture knowledge, is really what differentiates us in the market."

With a workforce of 2,500 worldwide, XPS acquired XL Connect (since renamed Xerox Connect) in 1998 to augment its technological infrastructure and provide clients with on-site technical assistance. "XPS is not an incidental part of the corporation. We're square in the middle of the strategy," says Couture. – M.H.

© American Management Association September 1999.

Company Profile 19
Minnesota Mining and
Manufacturing Company (3M)

Company overview

Minnesota Mining and Manufacturing Company (3M) is one of the most innovative global companies, with revenues of about $14 billion in 1996. It employs 74,000 people worldwide, 39,000 of whom work in the US. The company started out in a small town in Minnesota in 1902. It now operates in more than sixty countries, with manufacturing operations in forty-two international locations and laboratories in twenty-two locations around the world. 3M's business units fall into one of two major sectors: industrial and consumer sector (automotive and chemical markets, electronic/electrical and communications, consumer and office, industrial markets) and the life science sector (dental, medical, pharmaceuticals, traffic and safety, diaper closures, commercial graphics, advertising markets). According to the company, its key strengths lie in 'market leadership', 'technological innovation', 'customer focus', 'global reach' and 'employee initiatives to advance the lives and businesses of its customers and provide an attractive return for shareholders'. 3M seeks to become the most innovative firm and the preferred supplier in these two business sectors.

Brief history

3M was established in Minnesota, near the Lake Superior town of Two Harbors. It began in mining, but as the mineral deposits proved to be of little value the company quickly turned its focus to sandpaper products and, in the process, moved its business to the Duluth area. In 1910 the company relocated to St Paul, and grew through technical and marketing innovations.

In 1925 a young lab assistant at 3M invented masking tape, the first of many Scotch-brand pressure-sensitive tapes. In the 1940s 3M also produced defence materials for the US military for use in World War II. In the 1950s 3M introduced the thermo-fax copying process, Scotchgard fabric protector, videotape and many other electro-mechanical products. Between the 1960s and 1980s 3M continued to expand through other innovations, such as Post-it Notes in the 1980s and liquid-display films in the 1990s. Since the early 1990s the company's annual revenue has reached the $14 billion mark, 30 per cent of which comes from product innovations introduced in the preceding four years.

Innovation and significant contributions

At 3M innovation is key. 3M provides an example of how continuous innovation can contribute to the continued growth of a company. 3M operates in more than thirty technology platforms spanning virtually all disciplines of science. 3M has received numerous awards for its innovations, including the National Medal of Technology in 1995, the highest honour bestowed by the President of the United States for technological achievement. In 1997 3M's dental products unit received the Malcolm Baldridge National Quality Award in recognition of its achievements in quality and business performance.

3M conducts R&D at three levels. The first level is the division laboratories, where scientists work closely with the company's customers to come up with developments that support existing product lines and technologies. At the second level scientists in the sector laboratories try to anticipate technologies that will serve the market in the next five to ten years. At the third level, the corporate research laboratory, scientists try to predict what will be needed in the market ten to fifteen years hence. Besides in-house technical innovation, 3M has formed alliances with its customers and suppliers, including PSI Telecom, Hoechst Marion Roussel and Catholic Materials Management Alliances.

Challenges and opportunities

3M serves a diverse group of markets ranging from consumer products to construction/maintenance, automotive, office products, telecommunications and transportation. The company has made efforts to meet the challenges of market leadership, technological innovation, customer satisfaction and global reach. These can be daunting challenges since the company operates in such a diverse range of products and markets. In the past 3M's approach has been to offer integrated solutions by providing technologies, products and services to its customers. It is likely that 3M will continue with this approach, which has enabled it to remain in the forefront of its industry for such a long time. Continuous innovation has been a cornerstone of 3M's success in the global marketplace. As the concern for ecological and economic efficiency continues to grow, companies such as 3M must come up with ecologically efficient products and services.

ROSALIE L. TUNG AND MOHI AHMED
SIMON FRASER UNIVERSITY

Further reading

Business America (1997) 'Four US companies are named winners of the Malcolm Baldridge Quality Award', *Business America* 118(11), November: 33–4.

Hoover, G., Campbell, A. and Spain, P.J. (eds) (1995) 'Minnesota Mining and Manufacturing', *Hoover's Handbook of American Business*, Austin: The Reference Press, Inc. (Gives a general overview of the company.)

Kanter, R.M., Kao, J. and Wiersema, F. (eds) (1997) *Innovation: Breakthrough Thinking at 3M, DuPont, GE, Pfizer, and Rubbermaid*, New York: Harper Business. (Presents perspectives on innovations at several leading companies, including 3M.)

Further resources

3M website
http://www.mmm.com

Knowledge management and innovation at 3M

Journal of Knowledge Management; Kempston; September 1998; Adam Brand

Abstract:

3M's objective is to become the most innovative company in the world. To be innovative in highly competitive industries and global markets requires the effective use of Knowledge Management. 3M employs a wide range of Knowledge Management systems, but the appropriate environment has to be in place before people will be motivated to input and access such systems. 3M concentrates on the tacit to tacit area in the belief that if this is functioning well, other aspects of Knowledge Management will fall more readily into place. The willingness to share knowledge between individuals is directly affected by the culture within a company. How 3M creates and sustains its innovation and learning culture is outlined.

Knowledge management: a cultural issue

More than technology

3M sees Knowledge Management more as a cultural and organizational issue than a technological one. The company has many systems in place and is continually adding to them. Formal training programmes, learning by doing, help desks, intranet, Internet, Lotus Notes (TM), video conferencing and IT based databases are available to a vast range of employees. The Technical Planning and Coordination Group updates and maintains best practice and key player databases. For its more than two dozen core technologies, the company knows who are the people working in each area on what subject, and it is also linked to many universities specializing in areas of particular interest to 3M. An important requirement is that a company knows what it knows and 3M continually maps on databases what and where the technological skills it needs are located.

But if a company invests in a Knowledge Management infrastructure similar to 3M's it will not find this the sole answer to achieving a Knowledge Management environment. Of the four key areas of Knowledge Management outlined by Nonaka, 3M puts its major emphasis on the 'tacit to tacit' area (the transferring of an individual's experience and knowledge to other individuals). People have to be motivated to access and share information and to convert that information into knowledge. If the business processes are in place and the context is appropriate then Knowledge Management systems can flourish and people will input their knowledge into systems for access by others; but in the wrong context a Knowledge Management infrastructure will atrophy.

Effective Knowledge Management has parallels with effective innovation. For innovation to take place, a company needs caring people who are willing to share for the greater good of the company and creative people who have the ability to turn ideas into practical products and services.

Generosity, freedom and safety

A company cannot order people to be caring and creative. All it can do is attempt to create an atmosphere of generosity, freedom and safety in which innovation can flourish. Effective Knowledge Management is essential to innovation and it too needs an atmosphere of generosity, freedom and safety if it is to act as the river on which innovation can sail.

Since 3M's disastrous beginning in 1902, when a group of investors by mistake bought a mountain containing worthless mineral to start a business to mine corundum to manufacture sand paper – and the company did not achieve a profit for 14 years – considerable efforts have been made to create an atmosphere that will support innovation.

Requirements for successful innovation

For a company to be successful in innovation, 3M has stated that it needs vision (what it wants to be), foresight (a knowledge of where the world is going), an understanding of its core competencies (which will assist in setting Knowledge Management priorities), stretch goals (which in the case of 3M requires every single business, no matter what its history, to have at least 30% of its sales from products not in the line four years ago), freedom for employees to achieve those goals, and an atmosphere which enables and encourages people to give help and draw help from others.

To guarantee such conditions for innovation are in place and sustained over time requires a long-term commitment from top management, the recruitment and retention of the right people and a strong support and recognition programme.

Top management's long-term commitment

Total company involvement

Some companies appoint a New Products Manager and expect the person rapidly to launch new products. If that person struggles for 18 months and achieves little, he or she is moved to other duties or leaves the company. Such a situation could be repeated with newly appointed Knowledge Officers. Innovation cannot be farmed out to one or two individuals; it must permeate the entire fabric of an organization and every department within a company, not just technical or marketing. And in the same way Knowledge Management cannot be left to one or two individuals.

At 3M Knowledge Management does not just bubble up from middle management; top management see it as one of their major duties to encourage knowledge linkages. Share price is a constant issue for the board. 3M has an example of the positive effect on the share price when Knowledge Management programmes are explained, as witnessed by 3M's Vice Chairman, Ron Mitsch, when he spoke to New York financial analysts. He outlined the linkages salespeople from different industrial divisions have made to benefit customers and how, at breakfast meetings, they teach each other about their various products and discuss customer problems that can be solved by technologies from other groups.

Tradition

William Waldergrave commenting on what makes for an innovative scientific nation has written: "It needs order and institutional memory. It needs, in short, tradition."

3M encourages a sense of tradition. Lifetime employment and promotion from within are important traditional 3M policies – the average service at 3M is decades and employee turnover is low. Such experience in depth cannot by definition be duplicated quickly by competitors, even if those competitors have sophisticated Knowledge Management systems in place. An important role for Knowledge Management is, of course, to leverage the experience in the heads of employees so that downsizing, or staff turnover cannot damage the competitive edge and innovative ability of a company. Such a role for Knowledge Management is, however, at present, difficult and may, in its totality, be impossible to achieve. For 3M to follow other companies into short termism in the hope that Knowledge Management will fill the experience gap is considered detrimental to its long term competitive position.

Continuity

Promotion from within and lifetime employment policies mean that 3M people get to understand and know each other well. Senior people have worked in or visited many different countries. They have a personal connection with a wide variety of people and that makes knowledge transfer, using electronic communication, across different cultural boundaries effective.

Continuity of employment and global personal networks result in people helping others over and over again without immediate expectation of return. These people know, however, during the next ten or 20 years, that when they need help they will get it. The Canadian biologist, Dr. Hans Selye, summed up this concept by coining the words 'altruistic egotism' – helping others for one's own benefit. A sense of continuity allows that atmosphere to flourish.

Loyalty over time

Some companies, worried about long-term pension responsibilities and the need for head count flexibility, employ people on short-term contracts under the mistaken belief that fresh new employees along with Knowledge Management systems will generate innovative ideas. These short-term people may, however, not be interested in loyalty to the company and the sharing of knowledge for long-term innovative success. Their interest may focus primarily on their profession, and making sure their CV looks attractive to their next employer. They may not be looking for freedom to innovate; they may not be looking for an opportunity to help others who in the long term may be in a position to return that help.

In the short term they know they will be leaving to work elsewhere. What they want is specifically structured experience that is quantifiable and measurable. But innovation often happens at the margin and it does not always start as an Eureka shriek. It can be a gentle flame that needs fanning. But who has the time to do that nurturing if job horizons are short? So innovation happens and Knowledge Management works best when employees trust their company will be loyal to them over time.

Tolerance of mistakes

Long-term commitment at 3M also allows for mistakes to be tolerated. Top management taking the long view can tolerate a few mistakes. Lew Lehr, a recent chairman, commented, "As befits a company that was founded on a mistake, we have continued to accept mistakes as a normal part of running a business."

3M's ceramic business began as a result of mistakes in the development of a new abrasive grit. The Post-it Notes adhesive was developed be Spence Silver from a mistake. The unique quality of the Post-it Notes adhesive was that it was weak, but unlike other weak adhesives, it did not get harder or softer over time, but stayed consistently weak, and a new stationery product using the special properties of the adhesive was invented by Art Fry.

On the other hand, short termism may increase intolerance. Mistakes will be considered an expensive waste. Investigating mistakes, learning from them, will be time consuming, and if horizons are short, mistakes will be ignored or squashed. As William McKnight, another 3M chairman, said, "Mistakes will be made, but if a person is essentially right, the mistakes made are not as serious in the long run as the mistakes management will make if it is dictatorial." He said that in 1944, well before the empowerment movement started.

Story telling

Top managers who joined the company when they were young and who have absorbed the company's traditions and stories, re-tell those stories to reinforce the values and atmosphere that encourage innovation. A case in point is the story about Dick Drew ignoring his boss in the 1920s when asked to stop developing ScotchTM masking tape and yet he carried on successfully. This story was used by Lew Lehr in the 1950s when he was ordered to stop developing adhesive backed surgical

drape, but he also continued successfully. Richard Miller, the inventor of immune response modifiers, in the 1990s again had the story in mind when he carried on working with his ideas even after his project had been officially terminated and he had been put on the unassigned list.

Top management at 3M, all of whom know these stories, continue to allow a healthy disregard for management. They are loath to say no to anybody passionately working in an area of their choice and as a result innovations of tremendous importance to the company have been developed.

Flat organization

Top management's tolerance for mistakes is in line with its policy of establishing a flat organizational structure and allowing important decisions to be made at all levels. 3M's aim is not just to try and achieve 'a sustainable competitive advantage'. Its aim is continuously to develop, to adapt and to search for new sources of temporary advantage. That is why 3M has done laboratory work in space and has invested considerable time in becoming the first western company with a wholly owned subsidiary in the People's Republic of China. When everything is considered tentative, everybody has to remain flexible and to keep learning. 3M wants to be swiftly adaptive and it knows that the best adaptive systems are the ones which are self-organizing.

The above points were summarized many years ago by the 3M statement: "Make a little, sell a little, make a little more and keep learning with the market." The company has been compared with a nickel and dime store many times over. Rather than a hierarchy, it is a collection of networks.

Innovation approaches

But doing these things are not enough to generate innovation. Management needs to be in touch through Knowledge Management processes with all the various opportunities for innovation. For example, trend intersections, an example being Warner's 'edutainment', need to be studied. Technology inflection points such as electronic chips becoming memory chips need to be assessed. Multi-technological approaches and how the company can alter fundamental customer value, such as CNN's 24 hour news, need to be examined. 'Synectics'(R) type brainstorming, and 'Idon'(TM) type scenario planning need to be carried out to generate ideas that can become new industries.

With the above options in mind 3M has taken two main approaches to innovation: firstly defining needs that could use 3M technology – 'knowledge by design'; and secondly, developing new technologies that then require product applications to be found – 'knowledge by emergence'.

'Knowledge by design'

In the area of needs seeking technologies, top management is involved by initially defining, through planning systems, those customers it wants to work with and then encouraging technical people to become part of those end-user customers' adaptive systems. This way technical people are in a position to define the customers' unarticulated needs which may lead to new innovations.

An example here is 3M's graphic business, which began when panels of flexible plastic material were screen printed to create advertising and informational displays on the side of truck trailers. From this experience, the business learned to use the material for graphics around petrol stations and on the sides of buildings, and then for 'floor graphics' as advertisements in supermarkets. Another example, Thinsulate(TM) material, launched as a warm lining for ski and climbing jackets, has spread into camping gear, uniforms and acoustic dampening for cars – a continual learning process combining what 3M has to offer with what the market might need.

'Knowledge by emergence'

As for the second approach where technologies, often emerging from serendipitous situations, are looking for a product definition, there are a number of examples. 3M obtained its first fluoro chemical patents in 1945. One hundred lab scientists worked on the programme until 1953 without any application being discovered, until during that year, a lab scientist, Patsy Sherman, dropped some chemicals on a tennis shoe and found that it was dirt resistant. The result was Scotchgard(TM) chemicals to protect textiles and Scotchban(TM) chemicals to protect paper. Another example is random web technology which was supported for six years before an application – floor matting – was developed.

Cross divisional co-operation

Top management's long-term support for innovation is important to prevent groups becoming 'turfy', that is, people protecting their own patch and keeping out possible new ideas. Internal monopolies are more difficult to maintain when Knowledge Management systems are in place, but nonetheless managers who fight for territory can be damaging. At 3M top management's long-term commitment to innovation encourages cross divisional co-operation.

An example here is 3M's microreplication technology developed by Roger Appledorn. Microreplication produces three dimensional patterns in plastic film. It was first used in the 1960s as a thin film with tiny grooves for replacing the glass back plate in overhead projectors, and enabled 3M to become a leader in the field. Because of the stretch targets placed on all 3M businesses for new product sales, other groups were motivated to assess the new technology and see where it fitted into their work. As a result, the technology was picked up by the traffic sign business, to make a brighter surface; it was used to enhance the liquid crystal displays on personal computers which resulted in a greater brightness at a lower battery usage; and it was used by the abrasives group to design a far more effective sandpaper which produced a finishing system requiring fewer belt changes. It is also being used for new fasteners and as anti-counterfeiting for bank notes.

Coping with chaos

The path of innovation rarely runs smoothly, especially where technology is the driver. Companies like to have clear objectives, to develop a plan, then take action, check the variances and take new actions if it is necessary to bring a project back in line. But innovation in its early stages is a 'loose' activity and can follow a chaotic path. Standard Knowledge Management approaches and processes will be vital for effective 'tight' implementation, but may not always be capable of igniting the spark in the first place. People create that spark, so top management

must make allowances and not move too fast to judge, assess and audit projects. Pulling up a tender plant to see if it is still alive kills it.

Recruiting and keeping the right people

If innovation and effective Knowledge Management is furthered by having people with a depth of experience, it is important the right people, who fit the culture, are recruited in the first place.

3M has found the ideal people are those who want to start things rather than inherit businesses. They are interested in freedom to do their own thing rather than money or power. They are action orientated and prepared to take some risk with their future. 3M recruiters search for people who are creative (those people who can live in contradiction and perceive opposites as true at the same time), have a strong worth ethic, are self-motivated and resourceful, and are problem-solvers with broad interests.

Broad interests seem to be a distinguishing feature because it is often people with broad interests who are eager to learn, willing to explore ideas with others, have a multi-disciplinary approach, and are happy networking both face to face and by electronic means.

To retain such people requires a culture in which they can flourish. Cultures found within companies range from the 'innovative' (divergent and learning) with its opposite of 'controlling' (convergent and efficiency conscious) to 'supportive' (empowered and caring) with its opposite of 'directive' (profit before people). 3M's culture is one of learning and experimenting, but in a highly competitive environment there have to be strong cost control systems. As Lawrence and Dyer have pointed out: "For the readaptive process to be sustained, organizational members need to learn in order to be innovative and need to strive in order to be efficient."

A balance between learning and efficiency is the target. Processes for improving efficiency can take a long time to set up, but cannot be allowed to become too rigid. Intuition is needed to trigger the moment when it may be necessary to jump out of the process for the sake of innovation.

Programmes for supporting a knowledge management environment and innovation

Organizational structures

To maintain the balance and ensure that there is not an over emphasis on efficiency and controls at the cost of learning, 3M has put a number of organizational structures and recognition programmes in place. The organizational structures relate to fairs, technical audits, special interest chapters and the 15% rule.

Fairs, technical audits and chapters

Fairs consist of displays of technologies which are available for product development. 3M people are invited from around the company to examine ideas on a confidential basis to assess whether the technologies can be applied in the various markets in which 3M operates. Technical audits of the various labs take

place on a regular basis and are carried out by a team from other labs around the world. An example might be the technical director of the library systems group auditing the abrasives laboratory activities.

Bringing together people, face to face, or by video conference, who have diverse backgrounds in a supportive review environment can result in the generation of new ideas. In addition, the company allows work time for special interest chapter groups to discuss issues across divisions.

15% rule

An important support for innovation is signalled by 3M's 15% rule which states that 3M people can spend 15% of their time working on innovative ideas of their own choosing. This figure of 15% is not a hard and fast percentage. Not everybody uses it – and some take far more than 15% time especially when a promising idea takes form as a likely product. But the message is clear; it is saying it is OK to try something not on the main line. The consequence of this 15% rule has been a number of important new businesses for the company.

Grants

Money as well as time is required for innovation. The 15% rule helps with the issue of time. Genesis and Alpha grants help with money. Technical people can apply for 3M Genesis grants to buy equipment to assist them in the development of the '15% ideas'. Or they can use the grant to pay for temporary labour to do some of their existing work while they spend their own time developing their '15% project'. The Alpha grant is for developing ideas, such as new processes, which fall outside the technical area.

Recognition programmes

Organizational structures and support programmes which encourage learning and knowledge transfer are underlined by the recognition programmes. 3M knows that the inventors of new industries and products are the critical people in the company. Through the dual ladder process they can be promoted to vice-president level without having to have any management responsibility. 3M also makes certain that inventors are known and recognized across the company through articles and presentations. As a result 3M people tend to know more about 'the heroes of innovation' than they do about senior management. To develop a new product for 3M is the commercial equivalent of immortality, so for others to see inventors recognized is a spur to their own activity.

There are a number of award programmes to recognize innovation. The Golden Step Award is given for reaching a certain sales volume with a new product; the Circle of Technical Excellence Award is for considerable technical contribution; while the highest accolade for an inventor is his or her admission to the 3M Carlton Society.

Awards are not confined to technical people. Sales, marketing, logistics, finance and production people are included in the Pathfinder Programme which gives awards to teams for developing and launching new products within a country. There is also an award to motivate marketing people to check what is going on elsewhere and overcome the issue of crossing boundaries. This is the Pathfinder Merchant Award presented to those teams that have taken an idea developed in another country and then launched it in their own country. To make certain learning from sales and marketing programmes and other areas is not lost, a Sales and Marketing Professionalism Award and a Quality Award programme are also organized and the results published.

It might be considered odd that in a British or non American culture employees are happy to cover their office walls and desks with plaques and award statuettes. But a well decorated office or work area gives the employee a greater chance of having his or her ideas listened to, especially if, at first, those ideas sound crazy. The plaques on the wall are a sign that the person has achieved great things in the past and could do so again. Somebody with a strong record but a possibly shaky idea may well attract support faster than a person without a strong record who has what seems on the surface an outstanding idea.

Motivation: the key to Knowledge Management

Knowledge Management processes are being used by companies to reduce the need and therefore the cost of face to face meetings. At 3M, where the three Ms are said to stand for 'meetings and more meetings' that is also the aim as demonstrated by 3M's efforts to ensure the effectiveness of dispersed teams. But it is 3M's experience that these systems work far more effectively if the appropriate culture is in place. Long-term personal relationships with people selected because their attitude and personality fit the free flowing innovative culture of a company seems to be the necessary condition to have in place if Knowledge Management systems are to work.

If the motivation is there and this is enhanced by the right atmosphere, people will use Knowledge Management systems, even in companies where the systems are not that sophisticated, to achieve their objectives. On the other hand, a sophisticated Knowledge Management system in the wrong environment will achieve little in the way of innovation.

3M's record proves it is open to new ideas and it will continue to incorporate the best of the Knowledge Management approaches into its strong culture to ensure it achieves its mission to be 'the most innovative' company in the world.

Reprinted with permission of *Journal of Knowledge Management,* 2:1, 1998.
© MCB University Press.

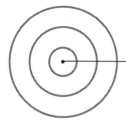

Part 4
Mergers and Acquisitions

The wave of cross-border mergers and acquisitions (M&As) that began in the 1980s has continued unabated into the new millennium. By 1999, cross-border M&As account for 2 per cent of the world's GDP. These activities have resulted in consolidation in many industries and sectors, including petroleum, financial, automotive and pharmaceuticals. Such M&As have created a number of mega-corporations of unprecedented size around the world.

A major objective of M&As is to generate synergies brought about by greater economies of scale in production, marketing, and research and development. Studies have shown, however, that these desired outcomes might prove elusive in many cases, at least in the shorter-term. Based on an analysis of 115 mergers created between 1993 to 1996, A.T. Kearney found that the most difficult aspect associated with such deals is in managing the relationship between the partners rather than finding a partner or negotiating the terms of the transaction. Such difficulties have contributed to the finding that 58 per cent of these mergers fail to 'add value', a statistic consistent with another study by Mercer Management Consulting that 57 per cent of such M&As failed (*Wall Street Journal,* October 6, 1998, p.4). The entries in this section examine the consequences and implications of such M&A activities at three giant multinationals.

The first case investigates the situation at DaimlerChrysler a year after the much-publicized merger of the two automotive giants. One year into the merger, Chrysler increasingly felt that they had been acquired rather than being a partner in a merger of two equals, as the deal was touted to be at the time of its inception. Chrysler's co-chairman has stepped down, two years ahead of his planned period in office. A new book, *Taken for a ride: How Daimler Benz drove off with Chrysler*, by Vlasic, Bradley and Stertz (William Morrow and Company, 2000), though written primarily from Chrysler's perspective, captures the sentiments on the American's part.

The second entry on General Motors discusses the problems confronting the American automotive giant. While the case does not pertain specifically to M&As, General Motors is partner to many strategic alliances around the world. The company's latest attempt at reorganization was undoubtedly affected by and will affect the consolidation that is taking place in the automotive sector worldwide.

The final entry in this section investigates the experience at Novartis, the life sciences company created from the merger of Ciba and Sandoz, two giant Swiss multinationals, in 1996. Several years into the merger, Novartis continues to experience difficulties in combining the businesses and products of the two formerly independent companies. In fact, there has already been devolution of some sort, such as the creation of Ciba Specialty Chemicals shortly after the merger.

Company Profile 20
Daimler Chrysler

Company overview

Daimler-Benz AG is one of the world's largest transportation and services groups. The group offers products and services that encompass various modes of transportation on land and sea, and in the air and outer space. Daimler-Benz has twenty-three business units, which fall into four major divisions: Passenger Cars, Commercial Vehicles, Aerospace and Services. Other industrial business units of Daimler-Benz are rail systems, micro-electronics and diesel engines. The group's principal profit-generating unit is Mercedes-Benz, manufacturer of luxury cars. The annual revenues of Daimler-Benz exceeded $71 billion in 1996. The group has operations in fifty countries and employs about 290,000 people worldwide. The corporate headquarters of the group is located in Stuttgart, Germany.

In May 1998 Daimler-Benz merged with Chrysler, the largest industrial merger in the world, with annual revenues around $130 billion.

Brief history

Daimler-Benz was established in 1926 through a merger of two German companies, one established by Gottlieb Daimler and the other by Karl Benz. The group's history dates back to the 1880s, when the two founders were doing business separately. In 1883 Benz & Co. was established and started car manufacturing. In 1890 Daimler Engine was incorporated; it started manufacturing motorcycles and began the sale of motor engines to French car manufacturers. The businesses of both companies were severely affected by the World War I. After the merger of Daimler and Benz in 1926, the new company began to recover. During the World War II the company started to manufacture military vehicles and aeroplane engines, but most of its factories were destroyed during the war.

During the post-war recovery period in the 1950s there was a heavy demand for cars and trucks in Germany and this created opportunities for Daimler-Benz. In the 1970s sales of its luxury cars continued to grow and brought benefits to the rest of the group. Growing competition in the automobile industry forced the group to diversify and make efforts toward sustainable innovation. During the 1980s the group expanded its businesses, and in 1993 the group established its first Mercedes factory in the United States to manufacture fuel-efficient and less expensive cars. The group has made continuous efforts to innovate and further diversify its business through the development of new products and services.

In May 1998 Daimler-Benz merged with Chrysler to form the world's fifth largest car company (after GM, Ford, Toyota and the VW Group). The group will be managed by two bosses, Jürgen Schrempp from Daimler-Benz and Robert Eaton from Chrysler, from two headquarters, Stuttgart (Germany) and Michigan (USA). Daimler Chrysler will be owned 53 per cent by the largest industrial firm in Germany and 47 per cent by the third largest automobile manufacturer in the United States.

Innovation and significant contributions

Daimler-Benz's contributions to the industry are significant. The group promotes innovation throughout its management, including the analysis of social trends, the monitoring of innovative global technologies and the adoption of sustainable technology strategies in all of its product segments. The Research and Technology unit of Daimler-Benz supports the development of technology strategies, secure integrated innovation and technology management through networks and knowledge-based cooperation with its business units to compete in the rapidly changing global marketplace. According to the group, the Research and Technology unit is the nerve centre for technological innovations in the group.

In 1997 Daimler-Benz introduced emission-free fuel-cell city buses powered by hydrogen. The group is currently developing a new electric car, the NECAR 3. To come up with new product innovations, besides relying on in-house efforts, Daimler-Benz also collaborates with partners around the globe. For example, the group has entered into a partnership with Ballard Power Systems Inc. (Canada) and Ford Motor Co. (US) to facilitate the development of fuel-cell technology for use in energy-efficient cars.

Daimler-Benz has also developed a prototype passenger car equipped with state-of-the-art communication systems which will allow Internet access on the road. According to the group, it should be able to mass produce this car by the twenty-first century. Mercedes-Benz has entered into a joint venture with Swatch AG to manufacture Smart, a sporty little car, another trend-setting effort in the industry. The Smart car is designed specifically for use in the city and is environmentally friendly. The Smart project represents the first of the group's efforts to collaborate with firms in completely different industries to compete and adapt to the changing global business environment. This is an example of the strategies of 'co-evolution' and 'collaborative advantage' espoused by the group. The group has also developed a road-side assistance programme and other services for its Mercedes-Benz customers by using satellite communication systems. The group is focused on quality products and services and sustainable innovation.

Challenges and opportunities

The major challenges confronting the group are rapid technological change and increased competition in the automobile industry, continuous advances in information and communication technologies (ICTs), and growing concerns with sustainability. The group has tried to increase opportunities by taking advantage of ICTs and innovative technologies developed by the group and other firms around the world. It also seeks to become more competitive through strategic alignment of individual divisions and related subsidiaries to take advantage of opportunities as they arise.

According to Maryann Kellyer, an American car analyst, the merger of Daimler and Chrylser will pose formidable challenges, principal of which is the difference in corporate cultures of the two companies. 'When it comes to the cultures of these two companies, how they think and act and what drives their decisions, they're oil and water' (Kellyer 1998: 62). Another issue pertains to the future of Daimler's businesses in other sectors, such as aerospace and services. The question is how these other sectors will fit into the mission of a car company.

ROSALIE L. TUNG AND MOHI AHMED
SIMON FRASER UNIVERSITY

Further reading

(References cited in the text marked *)

Chalsma, J. (1994) '1994 Mercedes-Benz E420: easy to get used to', *Machine Design* 66(2), 24 January: 124–5, Cleveland, OH. (Compares Mercedes Benz E-420 series to its Japanese competition) *Economist* (1996) 'Selling fuel cells', *Economist* 339(7967), 25 May: 86. (Discusses trends in the automobile industry, including electric vehicles.)

Heller, R. (1997) *In Search of European Excellence: The 10 Key Strategies of Europe's Top Companies*, London: Harper Collins Business. (Presents the key strategies of major European companies.)

* Kellyer, M. (1998) 'A new kind of car company', *Economist*, 9 May: 61–2.

Spain, P.J. and Talbot J.R. (eds) (1995) 'Daimler-Benz Aktiengesellschaft', *Hoover's Handbook of World Business 1995–1996*, Austin: The Reference Press, Inc. (Gives a general overview of the company.)

Templeman, J., Woodruff, D. and Reed, S. (1992) 'Downshift at Daimler', *Business Week*, 16 November: 88–90. (Identifies the challenges facing Daimler-Benz.)

Further resources

Daimler website
http://www.daimlerbenz.com
http://www.daimlerchrysler.com

Year later, DaimlerChrysler struggles with identity

Reuters, 8 November 1999, Ben Klayman

One year after DaimlerChrysler AG executives launched their new auto colossus with worldwide fanfare, head-hunters are literally circling the automaker's North American head-quarters.

On a recent fall afternoon, employees at the former Chrysler Corp.'s sprawling Auburn Hills, Mich., office looked to the sky to see a plane pulling a banner from a local employment agency that asked whether they were looking for a new job and listed a name and telephone number.

All is not well at the former Chrysler, the No. 3 U.S. automaker that merged on Nov. 17, 1998, with Germany's Daimler-Benz AG to create the world's No. 5 automaker. More than ever, employees at all levels are quitting or looking to leave, company insiders said.

The picture that emerges from numerous interviews with employees and sources close to the Stuttgart-based firm is one that includes poor communications within the combined company. Also, there's the inevitable culture clash between Americans used to flat organizations and easy access to senior executives and the German firm's highly political, structured hierarchy.

Merger of equals?

The deal was originally billed as a dual-country "merger of equals." The idea was the new firm would couple Chrysler's high profits and free-wheeling atmosphere with Daimler's strong luxury brand image and technical resources.

One year later, the merger looks more like what Chrysler employees feared: a Daimler takeover of what was considered one of the U.S. auto industry's most creative companies.

"The original (company) slogan of 'Expect the Extraordinary' has turned into 'Anticipate the Ordinary,'" one employee said.

The seeds for today's problems may have been planted on the first day. In the rush to assuage fears, Chrysler Chairman Robert Eaton and Daimler Chairman Juergen Schrempp, who share the top spot in the new automaker, emphasized equality.

Sources close to the automaker suggested such talk worked against the two firms' integration, while several sources said former Chrysler executives may have been naive. "The senior people at Chrysler went in very trusting," one source said of the merger talks. "I believe they were out-negotiated."

Eaton did not see it that way then, and still doesn't. "Chrysler needed to be teamed up with somebody that gave us additional scale, the technology, the broader brand segmentation, (and) the international presence that would allow us to grow," he told Reuters recently.

However, insiders, all of whom requested anonymity, said the equal partners idea did not take root from the beginning and was undercut further by the September board shakeup that ousted North American President Thomas Stallkamp, Chrysler's popular No. 2 executive who led the integration effort.

Chrysler executives have not been powerless, torpedoing the acquisition of a stake in Nissan Motor Co. Ltd. and plans for a Mercedes minivan. The decision last Wednesday to kill the Plymouth brand was championed by new North American President James Holden and would have occurred regardless of the merger.

'Get over it'

In a move to boost morale and regain Chrysler's nimble attributes, Holden announced last month the automaker's North American unit would operate with more autonomy.

Earlier this week, he acknowledged the company mishandled communication issues, leading to morale problems. But he insisted they've been ironed out, and the old Chrysler is a major contributor to the new firm's profits and management. "The conclusion we've come to as a board is 'Get over it. It doesn't matter anymore,'" he said.

That hasn't slowed down headhunters. One official at a large executive search firm said resume activity among U.S. employees has surged in the last six months. "I've been at this 10 years, and the disenchantment is more than I've ever seen," the executive said.

Competitors have been quick to benefit. General Motors Corp. and Ford Motor Co. have hired away both top and midlevel employees in communications, engineering and manufacturing. David Cole, director of auto industry study at University of Michigan, predicted more will follow.

Culture clash

Cultural differences, both corporate and national, have made the transition harder, Cole said. "With the disclosure practices led to a two-day, 15-percent slide in the stock price after disappointing second-quarter earnings."

The tensions are not felt solely by U.S. workers. Many Germans took umbrage at the designation of English as the official company language, sources said. German executives also have been frustrated by the Chrysler unit's dealings with U.S. safety regulators, believing the standard U.S. disclosure of recalls and defect reports reflect poorly on company quality.

Meantime, Schrempp has told board members that Chrysler's executive staff wasn't as strong as he initially believed, sources close to the automaker said.

Ironically, the dynamic, hard-charging Schrempp has been unfairly attacked for acting like any U.S. executive after an acquisition, said Bob Rosen, chief executive of consulting firm Healthy Companies International.

"The U.S. is having a complicated reaction to the fact that non-American companies are taking major roles in traditionally American businesses," he said. "It bumps up against our sense we are the best in the world and our intense patriotism."

Eaton insists that no culture will be trampled. "We're not going to try to Americanize the Germans or Germanize the Americans."

In the end, both German and American workers will have to adapt, a process that seems to have begun and, some say, could take as long as three years. One of the top-selling books ordered by U.S. DaimlerChrysler workers from online bookseller Amazon.com Inc. was "The German Way," Amazon said.

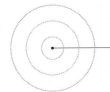

Company Profile 21
General Motors Corporation
(GM)

Company overview

The world's largest industrial corporation, General Motors (GM), is a full-line vehicle manufacturer. Established in 1908, GM has a presence in more than 190 countries. The company employs over 647,000 people worldwide and its revenues exceeded $168 billion in 1996. The General Motors Corporation is made up of General Motors North American Operations, Delphi Automotive Systems, General Motors International Operations, General Motors Acceptance Corporation, Hughes Electronics Corporation, General Motors Locomotive Group and Allison Transmission. Its corporate headquarters is located in Detroit, Michigan.

Brief history

GM was founded in 1908. In 1920 it completed the GM building, and in 1924 it began to assemble vehicles in Denmark, in its first assembly facilities outside the United States. Alfred P. Sloan who was the president of GM during the period 1923–37, implemented innovative management systems which are still considered to be management guidelines for many modern high-technology industries. Sloan, along with Pierre Du Pont of DuPont Chemicals was credited with 'applying the principles of decentralization and the use of staff services in senior management' to large-scale manufacturing companies in the private sector. Sloan was also 'responsible for influential developments in consumer marketing, for innovations in the use of specialist expertise in management, and for numerous developments in ways of obtaining, presenting and using data needed by decision makers' (Glover 1996: 4481). On 11 January 1940 the company manufactured its 25 millionth car. During World War II it continued to expand its products and adopted innovations.

In 1978 GM established the Cancer Research Foundation, and in 1981 it opened its European assembly plant in Saragossa, Spain, one of GM's largest overseas expansion projects. In 1985 GM established a Medical Committee for Automotive Safety and developed the crash dummy to measure forces exerted during side impacts as a part of its safety-related R&D programme. In 1997 GM introduced fourteen new models, the biggest launch in the company's history.

Innovation and significant contribution

Since its beginning, GM has made significant contributions to the automobile industry. Its many innovations include the electric headlamp for automobiles (1908), the electric self-starter (1911) and the all-steel body (1912). In 1924 GM opened the first automotive proving-ground test facility, and it introduced shatter-resistant safety glass in 1926. GM set the industry standard by introducing the column-mounted gearshift in 1938 and curved glass windshields in 1949. GM also introduced power steering and automatic windshield wipers as standard equipment for automobiles.

GM established the world's first safety test laboratory in 1955 and conducted atmospheric R&D. The company shares its findings with industry and government. GM's guidance and navigation system, for example, contributed to the Apollo II mission. GM introduced the first airbags in 1974. In 1988 GM won the Car of the Year award, and in 1990 it introduced a nearly pollution-free gas-electric-powered vehicle. Its electric vehicles were also a significant contribution to the automobile industry.

Challenges and opportunities

GM's major challenges include the need to make continuous improvements in productivity, to shorten product development time, to reduce cost and to increase market share around the world. According to GM, the firm is now making efforts to increase opportunities in the global marketplace through a coordinated approach. Since 1984 GM has established a joint venture with Toyota as New United Motor Manufacturing Inc. (NUMMI) in Fremont, California. Through the joint venture, GM seeks to learn from Toyota with regard to reducing time and costs in production. The joint venture allowed Toyota, on the other hand, an opportunity to apply its production systems in an American work environment. The NUMMI joint venture has proved to be very successful.

Continuous efforts in R&D for environment-friendly automobiles and social marketing will create further business opportunities for GM in the future.

ROSALIE L. TUNG AND MOHI AHMED
SIMON FRASER UNIVERSITY

Further reading

*(References cited in the text marked *)*

* Glover, I. (1996) 'Alfred P. Sloan', in M. Warner (ed.) *International Encyclopedia of Business and Management*, London: International Thomson Press. (Gives a biographical account of Alfred P. Sloan.)

Hoover, G., Campbell, A. and Spain, P.J. (eds) (1995) 'General Motors Corporation', *Hoover's Handbook of American Business*, Austin: The Reference Press, Inc. (Gives a general overview of the company.)

Kanter, R.M. (1989) *When Giants Learn to Dance*, New York: Simon & Schuster. (Offers guidelines on how large companies can engage successfully in collaborative agreements with other entities.)

Kerwin, K. (1993) 'Can Jack Smith fix GM?', *Business Week*, November: 126–35. (Discusses the challenges facing GM.)

Sullivan, T. (1996) 'GM shifts direction to gain global clout', *Marketing Week* 19(34), 15 November: 20–1. (Discusses corporate re-engineering at GM.)

Taylor, A. (1997) 'GM: time to get in gear', *Fortune* 135(8), 28 April: 94–102. (Discusses the challenges that lie ahead for GM.)

Womack, J.P., Jones, D.T. and Roos, D. (1990) *The Machine that Changed the World: Based on the Massachusetts Institute of Technology 5 Million Dollar 5 Year Study on the Future of the Automobile*, New York: Rawson Associates. (Provides some guidelines for auto manufacturing and production management systems.)

Further resources

GM website
http://www.gm.com

The decline and fall of General Motors

The Economist, 10 October 1998

America's biggest industrial company has announced its biggest reorganisation in a decade. Even so, General Motors has still to grapple with its products and its culture

ALL empires contain the seeds of their own destruction. The ideas on which they were founded cannot adapt to changing times. Their wealth creates bureaucracy and complacency. Meritocracy gives way to an introverted oligarchy that wastes its talents vying for position within the imperial court, rather than expanding the empire's borders. Even as the empire shrinks, an air of unreality persists – right up to the moment when the Goths break into the imperial city.

Nowadays, General Motors' sole claim to imperial status is size: its 608,000 employees and $166 billion in sales. Yet for most of this century, GM was also the world's most important company. The management system pioneered by Alfred Sloan at GM in the 1920s became the basis for the multidivisional modern corporation. Haunted by Henry Ford, Sloan built a company that could run itself, independent of the whims of one man. This explained GM's decentralised structure, with its autonomous operating divisions; its rigid system of command and control, where every detail had to be planned; and its vertical integration, in which GM undertook to make nearly all the parts that went into its cars.

In the 1940s, when Peter Drucker invented management theory, he chose GM as his subject. In "The Concept of the Corporation", he praised GM's decentralisation, but criticised it for treating its workers as a feudal cost centre, rather than a source of knowledge. This infuriated GM, but Japanese car firms learnt from it. "Lean production", Toyota's management creed, which relied on putting workers into teams and just-in-time delivery, is now as popular as Sloanism once was.

Meanwhile, decentralisation – at least in GM's sense of creating many different divisions that compete with each other – has fallen out of fashion. With each division having its own marketing and engineering, GM incurred unnecessary overheads. "As the world opened up to free trade," says Jack Smith, GM's chairman, "Sloan's system was not competitive."

Today, GM pops up in management books only as an example of what not to do – blamed for not introducing products quickly enough, for poor labour relations and so on. Nobody denies that GM's empire, no less than that of Rome or Byzantium, has some excellent parts: its research, its Eisenach manufacturing operation in Germany, to name a couple. When GM puts its weight behind a project, as it did this week when it announced a huge marketing campaign for the new Chevrolet Silverado pickup truck, its sheer power is impressive.

But the suspicion remains that the firm's leaders – all GM men practically since birth – still think that the firm is too big ever to lose its dominance. In an age where "only the paranoid survive," the chief fear stalking the firm's new headquarters at the Renaissance Centre in Detroit is of the threat of another palace coup such as the one that removed Robert Stempel, Mr Smith's predecessor, in 1992.

Nowhere are the doubts about GM's management greater than on Wall Street. GM's shares have underperformed the stockmarket by around 70%

in the past decade, continuing a dismal tradition. Even more staggeringly, all GM's stockmarket value is accounted for by its financing operation (GMAC), its parts company (Delphi) and its 74% stake in Hughes Electronics. Other car firms also make money on financing and parts, but rarely do investors implicitly value the vehicle-making side as worthless, or even a liability. What GM's shareholders are saying, in effect, is that they would pay you to take the world's biggest industrial operation off their hands.

This is damning. But it is also a mark of GM's potential. If GM could only make cars as well as its competitors, it would be worth twice what it is today. At a time when virtually every other car firm is desperate to achieve economies of scale in a fast-consolidating industry, it is ironic that the biggest company of all is considered such a laggard.

The axe falls

So far GM's reorganisations have tended to fall into two categories – catastrophic and ineffectual. The most catastrophic was the huge restructuring in 1984, which set off an ill-fated $80 billion spending-spree on technology, and also split its American division into two groups – BOC (officially "Buick-Oldsmobile-Cadillac", unofficially "Big Over-priced Cars") and CPC ("Chevrolet-Pontiac-Canada" or "Cheap Plastic Cars"). Most of the restructurings since then have been incremental.

The changes over the past three months amount to the biggest revolution since 1984. Although GM's senior staff insist that change has long been in the works, two things speeded it up. The first was the recent takeover of Chrysler by Daimler-Benz. The second was a bitter strike by workers at two factories in Flint, Michigan. Over the course of seven weeks, GM ran up after-tax losses of at least $2 billion – and received fairly minor concessions. With investors angry and talk of another boardroom coup, Mr Smith knew he had to do something. Since August he has pulled four rabbits out of the hat:

- GM is trying to sell 100% of Delphi, thus giving up the Sloanist idea of being a vertically integrated company. Mr Smith argues that a firm as big as GM should have an enormous advantage in buying parts and raw materials. So far it has not, because most of that buying power has been applied chiefly to Delphi (ultimately at GM's own expense).

- GM will centralise its vast sales, service and marketing system for the six main American car divisions that provide two-thirds of its sales volume. This will not only save around $300m a year; it also obliterates the Sloanist idea that Cadillac, Pontiac and so on should function as autonomous divisions. Henceforth they will be little more than the nameplates bolted to the back of GM cars.

- The firm will build a network of new assembly plants. In America, where GM has been shutting factories rather than opening them, this is something of a novelty. But the new facilities will be far smaller than current GM assembly plants, use much less labour and require capital investments of "an order of magnitude" less than the sums GM has spent on existing plants, according to Mr Smith. These factories will follow the example set by Eisenach and a new Brazilian plant, called "Blue Macaw", which will rely on suppliers to pre-assemble "modules", such as entire instrument panels. The main task of GM's workers will be to put these modules together.

• This week GM announced it would consolidate its North American and international automotive operations into a single, global unit, reporting to Rick Wagoner, the firm's new president and Mr Smith's heir apparent. As well as cutting layers of bureaucratic fat (if something exists, GM has a committee for it) this should also help GM change the way that it designs and builds cars. Even after recent cuts, GM still has 16 car platforms. Mr Wagoner now says these will be slimmed to eight. And even though the firm expects to launch several new models of light truck, it will maintain the current eight truck platforms.

Entertaining Mr Sloan

There are two responses to these changes. The first is simply to have doubts about them. Insiders are suspicious about the lack of detail on both the timing and the benefits. In Detroit, the changes have been seen largely as more intrigue at the imperial court. The marketing changes were seen as a victory for Ron Zarrella, the marketing chief; this week's moves as Mr Wagoner's final victory over Lou Hughes, GM's international boss.

The second response, is to lament just how far behind GM has fallen. For instance, Volkswagen, Europe's largest car maker, plans to use just four platforms in its manufacturing. Already,

cars as different as the quirky Beetle and the staid Golf share everything from floor-pans to windscreen-wiper motors. Volkswagen has also introduced modular assembly at its plant in Resende, Brazil. Indeed, the factory was partly paid for by its main suppliers, which also employ three-quarters of the factory's workers.

However the company that GM is most obviously trying to catch up on is Ford. GM's domestic and international consolidation borrows liberally from Ford 2000, an ambitious plan to integrate the car maker's global car operations, launched four-and-a-half years ago. Ford 2000 has saved the company around $3 billion a year. But there were some wobbles along the way and at least one tactical retreat (the restoration of a Ford company to oversee European marketing). The plan survived only because it was zealously promoted by Alex Trotman and Jac Nasser, Ford's two chiefs.

If GM is to succeed, it will have to show some of the same commitment. At GM, re-organisations still tend to be disseminated by memorandum (the 1984 plan paralysed the organisation for nearly two years). If GM were to ask people to write their names on a "wall of commitment", as Ford's managers did at a famous rally in Florida, they might end up with a scrawl of nasty graffiti.

Can Mr Smith rally the troops? His main difficulty is in North America where GM's relations with the United Auto Workers have been poisonous. At present, GM has too many under-used plants employing too many old (and thus expensive) workers. GM's assembly plants usually come bottom of the league in any industry comparison. "We have 35,000 more people than the firms benchmarked best in class," admits Mr Smith. But he points out that the average age of his employees is 48, giving GM the chance to slim by attrition over the next five years.

Somewhere behind all this lies GM's unnecessarily confrontational culture. Over the past four years, the company has faced more than a dozen walkouts, while Ford has not faced one. Following this summer's strike, GM agreed to set up a new communications system, so that union leaders and senior management can air and resolve their grievances. But there are already problems, especially over the management's plan to hold separate wage negotiations after Delphi is spun off (components workers tend to be paid less than car workers).

Mr Drucker's warning of half a century ago still holds true – except the list of people that the company has irked has widened to include its suppliers and dealers. Many of the former have still not forgiven GM for the cost-cutting exercise instigated by Ignacio Lopez de Arriortua, its purchasing manager in the early 1990s. By tearing up contracts and banishing expensive suppliers, the Spaniard helped shave GM's parts bill by several billion dollars a year. But he also destroyed trust that the company could well use now.

Legionnaires

Something similar may be happening with GM's dealers. Just as GM has too many factories, it also has too many showrooms. The downstream part of the car business now accounts for a fifth of the sticker price. Mr Wagoner seems keen to take a more conciliatory line. Although he says that GM could eliminate as much as 20% of its current retail outlets, he stresses that those who survive the shake-out are likely to be making a lot more money, a formula that can overcome all sorts of dissent.

By contrast, the one area where GM's managers have often not been brutal enough is in their own ranks. For years the car maker was known by its white-collar workers as "Generous Motors". The "layer of clay" made up by GM's middle management has actively resisted many changes. GM's habit of rotating managers every couple of years has also made it easy for individuals to evade responsibility. Mr Smith's answer is to create "Vehicle-Line Executives", engineers charged with overseeing specific products for long periods – perhaps as long as ten years.

These sorts of cultural issues can sound vague. But they are entwined with GM's biggest challenge: to produce cars that consumers like. Most of GM's top managers, including both Mr Wagoner and Mr Smith, have backgrounds in finance. They are not what people in Detroit call "car guys" – unlike Messrs Trotman and Nasser or Ferdinand Piech (who led the turnaround at VW) and Bob Lutz (who was the brain behind Chrysler's revival).

Arguably, GM's focus on organisation rather than charisma and risk-taking dates back to Sloan and his worries about Henry Ford. In the past ten years GM's restructuring has been soulless. But even the most hard-bitten efficiency experts acknowledge that you cannot simply save your way to success – particularly now that most cars work reasonably well. "This is a product business," says Jim Harbour, a Detroit expert. "If you don't have the product people want, you are dead."

IF GM is going to have the influence on the next century that it has had on this one, it will need more creativity, alongside its new structure.

Messrs Smith and Wagoner both say they want to take risks with new cars. They might bear in mind what Edward Gibbon wrote of another empire in decline, "all that is human must retrograde if it does not advance."

© *The Economist* Newspaper Limited, London (10 October 1998).

Company Profile 22
Novartis AG

Company overview

Novartis was established in 1996 as a result of the merger of two giant enterprises, Ciba and Sandoz. Novartis is the world's leading company in the field of life sciences and the largest company in the pharmaceutical industry. In 1996 the company's revenues exceeded $29 billion. According to Novartis, the company's name came from the Latin term *novae artes*, which means 'new arts' or 'new skills', and the company's motto is 'New Skills in the Science of Life'. The core business units of Novartis are healthcare (pharmaceuticals, generics, consumer health, CIBA vision), agribusiness (crop protection, animal health and seeds) and nutrition (infant and baby nutrition, medical nutrition and health nutrition). The healthcare unit operates 126 affiliates in sixty-three countries; the agribusiness unit operates 116 affiliates in fifty countries; and the nutrition unit operates thirty-three affiliates in twenty-nine countries. Novartis employs about 116,000 people worldwide and its headquarters is located in Basel, Switzerland.

Brief history

Novartis was established in 1996 following the merger of Ciba and Sandoz. The history of both companies dates back to more than two centuries ago. In 1758 Johann Rudolf Geigy-Gemuseus began trading in all kinds of materials (chemical, dyes and drugs) in Basel. Before the merger in 1996, Sandoz, Ciba and Geigy had set up the Interessengemeinschaft Basel (Basler IG), an agreement which was disbanded in 1950. In 1970, Ciba-Geigy was formed as a result of the merger of Ciba and Geigy. In 1992 it was renamed Ciba. In 1886 a chemical company called Kern & Sandoz was established in Basel. It entered into pharmaceutical research in 1917. Later it expanded its business around the world. Sandoz established its first overseas subsidiary in England in 1919 and entered Latin America between 1941 and 1957. In 1960 Sandoz established its first subsidiary in Japan, and in 1964 the company established its first research centre outside Switzerland, in East Hanover, New Jersey. Ciba established a special biotechnology unit in 1980 and Ciba vision in 1987. After continuous transformations and growth, Ciba and Sandoz merged to create Novartis. The motives behind the merger were to remain competitive in the rapidly changing marketplace and to reduce the cost of operating in Switzerland.

Innovation and significant contributions

The mission of Novartis is to utilize 'scientific research, imagination, and new technologies to provide ever greater benefits for humankind'. The company seeks to innovate to serve its customers' needs in healthcare, agriculture and nutrition. Even prior to the merger, both Ciba and Sandoz were leading companies in the industry. Ciba's major products were pharmaceutical products, formulated pesticides, dyestuffs and pigments, synthetic resins and plastics, photographic equipment, materials and chemicals, and spectacles and lenses. The major products of Sandoz were miscellaneous chemical products for industrial use, pharmaceutical products, infant and dietetic foods, and textile raw materials.

Both Ciba and Sandoz have introduced several major breakthroughs in the life sciences. Calcium-Sandoz, for example, the foundation of modern-day calcium therapy, was developed by Sandoz. A Geigy researcher received a Nobel prize in 1948 for his discovery of DDT for use as an insecticide. In 1963 Sandoz began large-scale production of antibiotics and other substances developed on the basis of biotechnology. In 1977 the company began the production of anti-allergy drugs. In 1980 Ciba established a special biotechnology unit, and it continued to make efforts in R&D. Since the merger in 1996, the company has continued to innovate in its various business units: healthcare, agribusiness and nutrition.

The company has established the Novartis Foundation for Sustainable Development, which focuses on strengthening the development capacities of the developing countries; supporting the self-help efforts of the most deprived people in developing countries; developing and implementing innovative strategies for improving the effectiveness of programmes and projects; and researching and teaching in development policy issues. As the world's leading life sciences company, Novartis is now trying to introduce new products within a shorter period of time.

Challenges and opportunities

Novartis currently has about ninety projects under development and expects to introduce about seventeen new products by the turn of the century. This will create new opportunities for the company. According to the company, the goal of Novartis is not only to 'expand the horizons of science, but also [to] expand the horizons of life through science'. To avoid duplication of R&D efforts, the company realizes that it is important for its research activities to be comprehensively documented. To meet these objectives, Novartis has established a globally active group responsible for document management using state-of-the-art information and communication technologies.

Rosalie L. Tung and Mohi Ahmed
Simon Fraser University

Further reading

Financial Post Daily (1996) 'Sandoz–Ciba merger hailed as world's biggest', *Financial Post Daily* 9(21), 8 March: 5. (Discusses the merger of Ciba-Geigy AG and Sandoz AG.)

Henkel, N. (1997) 'Novartis creates global access to documents', *Document World* 2(6), November–December: 51. (Documents Novartis's efforts to avoid duplication in R&D efforts.)

Further resources

Novartis website
http://www.novartis.com

Healing Novartis

Business Week; New York; 8
November 1999; Kerry Capell and
Heidi Dawley

It's a mild mid-October day in Basel, and Daniel Vasella, the 46-year-old CEO of Swiss pharmaceuticals giant Novartis, is just back from a whirlwind tour of Asia. One of the highlights, he confides over lunch, was discussing the pros and cons of genetically modified food with the King of Thailand.

It's a topic he knows well. In 1996, when Swiss drugmakers Ciba-Geigy Ltd. and Sandoz Ltd. got together in a $63 billion merger to form Novartis, the former physician proudly proclaimed it the world's first life-sciences company. Vasella said that thanks to its world-class agribusiness portfolio, Novartis was in a unique position to apply technologies learned from plant genetics to both pharmaceuticals and agricultural businesses. He staked the company's future on genetic engineering.

Vasella bet on the wrong horse. The backlash over genetically modified crops is undermining the life-sciences concept upon which Novartis is based. Although Vasella still believes gene technology is the wave of the future, he admits that at least for now, the synergies between plant science and pharmaceuticals have proved marginal. At the same time, soft commodity prices and increased competition have cut into agribusiness sales. "The plan now is to focus on health care," Vasella says.

The shift in focus is likely to set off a new round of restructuring at Novartis. Vasella says he may spin off the agribusiness units to shareholders. He could use the proceeds to buy another pharmaceutical company, which would strengthen the more lucrative drug franchise. In the first half of this year, agribusiness sales fell 10%, to $3.2 billion, while drug sales grew 6%, to $6.1 billion. At the very least, a spin-off would buy Novartis time until revenues from new pharmaceutical products kick in, in 2001. The company has 11 new compounds in late stages of human testing or awaiting approval, more than most of its competitors. Vasella aims to increase sales of newly developed drugs from 18% of the total to 25% within two years.

That's a tall order. Novartis' drug portfolio is mature, and it faces increasing competition from generics. Three-quarters of its pharmaceutical products are at least five-years-old, and 50% of sales come from products that are off patent. More worrisome is declining market share in the U.S., currently the world's fastest-growing drug market. "In the next two to three years, Novartis is going to take a bath in profitability," says G. James, a former Ciba executive and president of Pharma Strategy Consulting in Basel. He reasons that the cumulative effect of shrinking market share, lack of blockbuster drugs, and a suffering agribusiness will bring growth to a standstill.

Strong balance sheet

It's a dramatic change in sentiment from 1996, when analysts assumed the company could deliver on cost-cutting and sales growth. Cost-savings from the merger have improved the company's results. Pretax profits in 1998 were $5.5 billion on sales of $22 billion, up from $3.9 billion on sales of $21.1 billion at the time of the merger. But sales remain sluggish.

Investors are sitting on the sidelines until they get answers on the fate of the agribusiness units and the commercial viability of the new drugs coming to market. Novartis' current price-earnings ratio of 22 times next year's earnings is among the lowest of any major drug companies. "The market is in a waiting position, and I don't blame it," says Novartis Chief Financial Officer Raymund Breu.

Vasella, a scientist who began his career in the drug business 11 years ago, is feeling the pressure. In addition to mulling over the prospect of spinning off agribusiness, he is bringing in new management and shedding peripheral units in consumer health. He also plans to seek a secondary listing on the New York Stock Exchange, which would help raise Novartis' profile in U.S. markets and give it access to a greater pool of capital.

But both Breu and Vasella say the pessimism is exaggerated, and that they are making progress in restructuring the group. Promised job cuts and new cost savings of around $1.4 billion are likely to be completed by yearend. Most of the money saved will go to improving the company's already strong balance sheet, which includes $12.8 billion in cash and marketable securities. The remainder of the freed-up cash will go to strengthening sales and marketing efforts, particularly in the U.S., which currently accounts for 36% of Novartis' sales.

The main problem is the weak performance of agribusiness, which includes fungicides, herbicides, seeds, and animal-care products. Despite a massive reorganization, the business continues to lose market share in herbicides and fungicides to competitors such as Monsanto Co. and AstraZeneca.

To offset agribusiness losses, Vasella is working hard to rejuvenate the company's drug portfolio. Novartis aims to increase the percentage of drugs under patent to 70% from 50% by 2003, says Joerg Reinhardt, the head of development for Novartis Pharmaceuticals. It hopes to put three new compounds from each of the company's seven therapeutic areas into the product development pipeline each year. If it succeeds, Reinhardt believes Novartis can increase the number of compounds that make it to market each year from 1 in 10 to 1 in 7 by 2002.

Several of the drugs under development will hit the market by the end of next year. The first is expected to be Visudyne, which is currently under priority review with the U.S. Food & Drug Administration. Visudyne is a treatment for macular degeneration, the leading cause of blindness in adults over 50. With potential sales of $1 billion within the next three to five years, it could rapidly become the largest-selling ophthalmic treatment in the world, says Richard R. Stover, a senior analyst at Arnhold & S. Bleichroeder Inc.

This will be followed by Zelmac, a treatment for irritable bowel syndrome, Starlix for adult-onset diabetes, and E-25 for treating asthma. Novartis will have an additional seven new compounds, including treatments for Parkinson's and Alzheimer's diseases, epilepsy, and asthma, on sale in the U.S. by the end of next year. In 10 years' time, Vasella estimates that Novartis will have spent a total of $1 billion to develop xenotransplantation therapies, which use genetically modified animal organs for transplantation in humans.

Vasella has initiated a number of promising changes. But he still needs a blockbuster, along the lines of a Viagra or a Prozac, to prove the worth of his merger. And he'd better hurry. Investors are losing patience.

What's ailing a giant

Gene fury

Backlash over genetically modified crops is undermining the life-sciences concept upon which Novartis was created three years ago

Slow growth

Patent expirations, generic competition, and an aging portfolio of drugs will result in two years of single-digit growth for the core pharmaceuticals business

Troubled agribusiness

Weak commodity prices, increased competition, and concerns over biotechnology, especially in Europe, are driving down margins and hurting sales

Data: *Business Week*

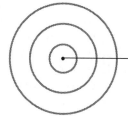

Part 5
Corporate Social Responsibility

A strategic challenge confronting world-class organizations is how to balance the often conflicting demands of their various stakeholders from around the world. Increasingly, in their decision-making process, companies have to factor into consideration the need to be socially responsible, i.e., to be perceived as good corporate citizens who are not out to make a quick profit but who also contribute to social and economic development in the countries where they operate. This perception by the general public and by various stakeholders could, in turn, affect the company's financial profitability in the longer term. In fact, more and more business schools now offer one or more courses in ethics and corporate social responsibility.

The four entries in Part 5 examine the scrutiny organizations, particularly large multinationals, are subjected to in their worldwide operations. The first entry looks at Shell, one of the most profitable companies in the world. Because of the nature of their business, Shell often has to operate in politically unstable regions in the world. As a result, their policies have often come under attack, including its relationship with military dictatorships and/or political regimes which do not have a good record of human rights' protection, and its pollution of the natural environment. The corporation has devoted considerable time and effort to allay the public's concern about its social accountability.

The second case focuses on Siemens, the German electrical engineering and electronics' giant. Class action suits demanding huge reparations have been filed against Siemens for use of forced labour camps during World War II. While these atrocities were committed over half a century ago, companies can be held liable for actions of their predecessors. The case of Siemens relates to the broader issue of product liability that corporations and their boards of directors have to assume for decisions made during their tenure.

The third entry presents the attempts made by the largest chemicals company in the world, Dupont, to conserve, not just protect, the environment. This might seem paradoxical as the chemicals industry has often been accused as one of the major polluters of the natural environment.

From time to time, many leading companies have to deal with unexpected crises, some of colossal proportions, which demand immediate and effective action. In general, the response of an organization to a crisis situation can fall into one of two broad categories: One involves immediate acknowledgment of responsibility for the problem and swift action to resolve the situation at hand. The other response is one of denial that the problem exists and/or attempts to shift blame to another entity, and in the process, delay rectifying the situation. Tylenol's response in the wake of cyanide lacing of some of its capsules is a benchmark of the first category of response. In the fourth case presented in this section, Dow Corning's mishandling of the silicone breast implant situation has been used as an example of the second type of response. In the end, Dow Corning had to file for bankruptcy. While Dow Corning is not Corning Inc., the company profiled in this section, both Dow and Corning have shared equity ownership of the now defunct Dow Corning corporation. This case makes for interesting analysis as companies can learn what constitutes appropriate and inappropriate responses to crises situations. Perhaps both Ford and Firestone could benefit from the experiences of Tylenol and Dow Corning in their handling of the latest debacle involving Ford Explorer sports utility vehicles and Firestone tyres where both companies sought to deny the problem at first and then lay blame on the other.

Company Profile 23
Royal Dutch Shell Group

Company overview

The Royal Dutch/Shell Transport and Trading Group, commonly known as Shell, is one of the world's largest and most profitable companies. The group employs more than 100,000 people in over 120 countries and its revenues exceeded $128 billion in 1996. Two parent companies, Royal Dutch Petroleum and Shell Transport and Trading, own the group in the proportion of 60 per cent and 40 per cent, respectively.

Brief history

In 1833 Marcus Samuel started a small shop in London's East End selling seashells. The company soon developed into an export–import business. Marcus Samuel, Jr, the founder's son, expanded into the oil-export business because he saw the huge opportunities there. At that time Standard Oil in America had a monopoly in the oil business, so Marcus Samuel, Jr, had to compete on the basis of lower price. During the 1890s a Dutch company (NV Koninklijke Nederlandsche Maatschapppijtot Exoplotatie van Petroleum-bronnen in Nederlandsch-indi) was engaged in the oilfield development business and built its own tanker fleet to compete with Marcus Samuel's company. However, both companies soon realized that they could do better by working together; consequently, they merged to form the Asiatic Petroleum Company in 1903. The partnership worked very well and four years later, in 1907, extended its operations worldwide with the creation of the Royal Dutch/Shell Group of companies. The two parent companies retained their separate businesses, however.

The group continued to grow into a giant multinational company, with its major businesses in the exploration and production of oil products, chemicals, gas and coal. The group is now extending into a fifth core business, renewables, which brings together the group's activities in solar energy, biomass and forestry. The most important and risky part of the group's business is in the exploration and extraction of raw materials, which are then converted into oil products, gas and coal. Some of the specialized outputs from the crude-oil refineries are subsequently converted into plastic and industrial materials. In the 1990s the firm has sought to expand its share in the fast-growing renewables market.

Innovation and significant contributions

The group perceives the continuous development of technology (primarily communication technology), globalization and trade liberalization as important forces that will shape the demand patterns and expectations of stakeholders around the world. To meet these challenges Shell uses 'scenario building' as an important management tool. Since the early 1970s Shell has used scenario building to help the company prepare for sudden changes, and to create a common culture and language throughout its disparate operations around the world. In the late 1990s Shell adopted the following two scenarios: 'Just do it' and 'Da Wo' Big me. In the first scenario it seeks to take advantage of the latest innovations in technology to implement new ways of doing business and solve problems; and in the second it seeks to develop relationships through the building of trust and mutual obligations. Besides sustaining its profitability, the group seeks to improve the working conditions of its employees by paying greater attention to employee safety and the comfort of its workers. In addition, the group seeks better to address the issue of global environmental protection.

Shell undertakes R&D to develop and implement new technology that can contribute to increased profits, improved safety and productivity, protect the environment through lower emissions or better use of resources, reduce capital expenditure and develop new materials (for example synthetic materials) that have new applications. The group has twelve main research and technology development centres, which are located in the Netherlands, the UK, the US, France, Belgium, Germany, Japan and Singapore.

The Royal Dutch/Shell Group is truly an international company and a remarkable example of a long-term corporate partnership between two companies from two countries. The group has also established other examples of inter-firm collaboration around the world (e.g. collaboration with GTE and collaboration with professional firms: legal, tax, human resources, planning, finances and investment services). Shell's timely and scenario-based strategic decisions have made it one of the world's most profitable companies.

Challenges and opportunities

The group focuses its corporate vision on 'wealth creation', 'customer satisfaction' and 'responsiveness to changing needs and expectations in the outside world'. The group is fairly decentralized and most of its companies operate locally in different countries. To coordinate its global operations, however, strategic decision and business support functions are performed by some 300 people in the UK, the Netherlands and Belgium. The ultimate decision-makers in the group are the directors of the two parent companies. Development of human resources is one of the group's top priorities. The company needs people who have the ability to get things done and who are interested in cross-cultural team-building. Shell has several extensive training programmes to develop these skills.

Like other companies, Shell faces new challenges arising from the changes in technology, globalization and trade liberalization. To meet these new challenges and to expand its business activities Shell needs the right people and the right technology at the right time. To sustain its competitiveness in the rapidly changing global marketplace the group must pay adequate attention to the issue of environmental protection.

ROSALIE L. TUNG AND MOHI AHMED
SIMON FRASER UNIVERSITY

Further reading

Gerreston, F.C. (1957) *History of the Royal Dutch*, vols 1–4, translated from the Dutch *Geschiedenis der Koninklinjke*, The Hague: Leiden. (Gives the detailed historical background of the Royal Dutch.)

Guyon, J. (1997) 'The world's most profitable company', *Fortune*, 4 August: 120–5. (Identifies major challenges and the diversification of the group.)

Schwartz, P. (1996) *The Art of the Long View*, New York: Doubleday. (Examines scenario planning in the Royal Dutch/Shell group.)

Spain, P.J. and Talbot, J.R. (eds) (1995) 'Royal Dutch/Shell Group', *Hoover's Handbook of World Business 1995–96*, Austin: The Reference Press, Inc. (Gives a general overview of the company.)

Further resources

Shell Group website
http://www.shell.com

Petroleum and human rights: The new frontiers of debate

Oil & Gas Journal; Tulsa; 1 November 1999; John Bray

Abstract:

Petroleum and politics have always made a combustible mixture, and human rights controversies have long been part of the brew. Recent high-profile controversies include: accusations concerning Royal Dutch/Shell's relationship with the military regime in Nigeria, arguments about BP Amoco PLC's links with the security forces in Colombia, and the campaign against investment in the offshore gas industry in Myanmar. These controversies reflect changing public attitudes in the West on the role of all large international companies, not just the petroleum sector. The sources of pressure for change are analyzed. How companies can meet the new challenges is discussed. The most sensitive issues in the current international debate and the likely way forward are identified.

Petroleum and politics have always made a combustible mixture, and human rights controversies have long been part of the brew.

Past examples include criticisms of the oil industry's relationship with the Shah of Iran and his notorious secret police or its relationship with apartheid South Africa at a time when much of the world was calling for a commercial boycott of that country.

But while the issues are not new, the debate is intensifying. Recent high-profile controversies include: accusations concerning Royal Dutch/Shell's relationship with the military regime in Nigeria, arguments about BP Amoco PLC's links with the security forces in Colombia, and the campaign against investment in the offshore gas industry in Myanmar.

These controversies reflect changing public attitudes in the West on the role of all large international companies, not just the petroleum sector. The problem is that change has yet to lead to a new consensus on the precise breakdown of responsibilities among companies, governments, and other actors, such as nongovernmental organizations (NGOs). The human rights debate is far from over.

This article has three objectives. First, it analyzes the sources of pressure for change. Second, it discusses how companies can meet the new challenges. Third, it identifies the most sensitive issues in the current international debate and the likely way forward.

Pressures for change

Reflecting on the lessons learned from the Ogoni affair in Nigeria, former Royal Dutch/Shell Group Managing Director Cor Herkstroter acknowledged that his company might have been "excessively focused on internal matters... 'a state within a state.'" Partly as a result, it failed to realize the implications of social and technological changes and how these affected public perceptions of the oil industry. To its credit, Shell has sought to learn from its mistakes, and other international companies can benefit from its experience.

Communications

Some of the most significant social and technological changes stem from the revolution in international communications.

No remote oil and gas field can now be considered obscure and, in an era of political fluidity, no historical secrets can now be regarded as confidential.

To give the first of two Southeast Asian examples, Myanmar may appear relatively infrequently on international television screens, but political and economic developments in the country – including the affairs of the offshore gas industry – are covered in an array of specialist internet and online information services.

Meanwhile, in Indonesia, the political succession from Suharto to a new government has opened the door to a series of investigations on past contracts and business practices. The energy sector has been subjected to particular scrutiny.

Advocacy groups

National and international NGOs have been quick to appreciate the benefits of the internet as a source of information. At the same time, the internet provides them with a "shop window" to promote their own viewpoints. More importantly, they also use the web as a means of coordinating campaigns involving widely scattered organizations with similar aims.

One of the most spectacular recent NGO campaigns involved an international institution, the Organization for Economic Cooperation and Development. In 1995, the OECD's 29 member countries began negotiations on a proposed Multilateral Agreement on Investment (MAI), which was intended to give foreign investors the same rights as domestic companies in signatory countries. Negotiations continued in comparative obscurity

until early 1997, when the MAI came to the attention of a group of North American NGOs. They argued that – among other failings – the draft treaty paid insufficient attention to environmental safeguards; undermined the sovereignty of host governments; and gave too much influence to multinational companies.

The NGO campaign was remarkable for the breadth of its international reach. In early 1998, the Council of Canadians used the internet to publish a joint statement on the agreement, which was endorsed by 560 organizations in 67 countries. The internet was used to disseminate information rapidly. As the council's chair commented: "If a negotiator says something to someone over a glass of wine, we'll have it on the internet within an hour, all over the world."

This campaign, which, from the OECD's point of view had suddenly "descended from nowhere," led directly to the formal suspension of MAI negotiations in the spring of 1998.

Legal action

In the US, NGO demands for corporate accountability on human rights and environmental issues have been backed up by legal action.

The two prime examples are the 6 year legal case brought by representatives of Ecuadorean Indians against Texaco Inc. and a similar case between representatives of Myanmar farmers and Unocal Corp.

In the Texaco case, lawyers acting on behalf of about 30,000 Ecuadoreans have accused the company of a combination of environmental negligence and racial discrimination during 1964–92. Meanwhile, Unocal has been accused of complicity in the Myanmar government's policy of forced relocation and other abuses in connection with the construction of a gas pipeline from the Gulf of Martaban to the Thailand border.

In both cases, one of the key issues is whether the companies can be brought to trial in the US on account of activities abroad. The legal arguments have been based on a new interpretation of an ancient law – the 1789 Alien Tort Claims Act – which allows foreigners to sue in a US federal court for violations of international law.

Regardless of the US legal technicalities, the two cases are symptomatic of a wider trend. Human abuses are increasingly regarded as offenses against international law, which are therefore open to trial outside the jurisdiction where the offenses are said to have taken place. Former Chilean leader Gen. Pinochet is all too well aware of this trend: He is currently in Britain contesting extradition proceedings to Spain on account of torture allegations in his home country.

Meanwhile, human rights lawyers have raised the possibility that companies as well as individuals could in future be brought to trial before the International Criminal Court, which is to be created under the terms of an international treaty signed in Rome in July 1998. The offenses for which companies might be liable could include complicity in human rights abuses apparently inflicted on their behalf.

Accountability, power, mandates

These developments raise new questions about accountability. What exactly are the mandates of international companies, and to whom are they accountable?

In the past, the answers appeared straightforward. Companies' mandates were strictly restricted to commercial activities and, provided they operated within the laws of the land, they were primarily accountable to shareholders. Oil executives were often tempted to dismiss human rights controversies as being beyond their remit: "Business is business, and politics is politics."

Now clear dividing lines have become increasingly blurred. At a minimum, it is now widely accepted that companies should be accountable to a broader range of "stakeholders" – such as local communities – who are directly affected by their operations. However, their influence and responsibility arguably goes well beyond this.

The companies' traditional claims to apolitical status are undermined when, for example, US-based energy companies are seen to exercise considerable lobbying power on issues relating to global warming. In doing so, they are clearly behaving as political actors.

Similarly, advocacy groups point to petroleum companies' potential leverage in economies such as Nigeria, Angola, or Colombia that depend heavily on oil for their foreign exchange earnings. They argue that the companies should use this leverage to press governments on issues relating to human rights or the distribution of wealth produced by their own industries. By contrast, companies argue that their influence on sovereign governments is limited both by the scope of their mandates and by competition. The power of governments may appear to be receding, but they retain the authority to dismiss "difficult" companies in favor of their competitors.

Meanwhile, other actors have made the human rights equation still more complex. Regardless of the precise balance of power between companies and governments, the influence of consumers – informed by NGOs and the internet – is growing. Few companies can now afford the taint of being associated – wrongly or rightly – with human rights abuses. In the information age, reputation is everything.

Emerging best practices

The first thing companies can – indeed, must – do is to take the human rights debate seriously. As will be seen, many key issues of the debate remain unresolved, but the fundamental principle is clear. International companies are expected to implement – and promote international standards in the field of human rights as much as in the environmental arena. Inevitably, human rights concerns overlap with other areas of best practice such as corporate ethics, employment standards, community liaison, and environmental policy. If these areas are properly addressed, human rights controversies are less likely to arise.

Policy statements

A company's commitment to human rights implies an explicit declaration in business principles or ethics codes.

Royal Dutch/Shell's Statement of General Business Principles includes a commitment to "express support for fundamental human rights in line with the legitimate role of business."

Similarly, BP Amoco's code expresses support for the "principles set forth in the UN Universal Declaration of Human Rights, recognizing the role and enforcement responsibilities of governments."

Assessment, monitoring, consultation

Principles are of limited value unless they are seen to be practiced, and this requires knowledge.

The need for risk assessment is most obvious when companies are planning a new project. The host government will be an essential source of information, but official views are not necessarily balanced.

In sensitive regions, companies will also need to seek information and advice from a range of other sources, including official and unofficial media and NGOs. No one source can be expected to have all the answers, and all must be viewed critically.

Staff policies

Human rights policies, like other aspects of a company's ethical code, must become an integral part of a company's operations if they are to be taken seriously.

This means training staff members in advance when they are likely to be operating in complex situations.

It also means incorporating business values in the regular appraisals and reporting structures of senior staff.

Further, it means making sure that there is an effective communications structure so that staff members can communicate problems – if necessary direct to senior management – if they have ethical concerns.

Community relations

Many of the classic political and human rights problems in the energy sector have arisen because of tensions between the central government and the outlying regions where, by the vagaries of geological chance, oil and gas reserves are often located.

The inhabitants of these regions often are poorly represented in the national administration. All too often, they bear the environmental costs of petroleum development and receive few of the benefits. Nigeria's Niger Delta region is an obvious example. Other regions where similar claims have been made include Baluchistan, Pakistan, and, Indonesia.

Companies operating in such areas will need to find ways of communicating with local communities, and this may well mean operating outside formal political structures. If the government machinery does not provide a means of consulting local stakeholders before a project takes place, then the company will need to find ways of going direct. Any such approach will need to be handled carefully, so that government officials do not feel undermined, but the need for it is clear.

Social programs, auditing

It has now become near-standard practice for companies operating in developing countries to devote a portion of their budgets to "good-neighbor" programs, such as health clinics or schools. Such programs constitute a valuable form of local diplomacy provided that certain guidelines are followed.

At a minimum, it is essential to consult the local communities to make sure that the programs address real needs. In practice, it may be more effective for companies to involve development agencies as partners that administer such programs, rather than seeking to run them directly.

External and internal financial audits have long been mandatory; environmental audits are increasingly considered mainstream, and many international companies are extending the principle to include audits of their social impact.

Problem areas

While the principles of best practices are beginning to emerge, there are several sensitive areas of debate that have yet to be resolved. Typically, these have emerged in crisis situations, and this underlines the obvious, but important, message that "prevention" is better than "cure." Once companies become involved in major controversies, they may find it hard to extricate themselves.

Community tensions

In recent years, mainstream companies have learned to take community relations questions much more seriously than in the past. Nevertheless, problems frequently arise because of a combination of local government failures and unrealistic expectations.

In Nigeria's Niger Delta region, local communities complain, with some justification, that the central government has neglected local development in areas such as health and education. They look to the oil companies to make up for the government's deficiencies. To some extent, the companies are able to achieve this through their social programs. However, these programs typically are designed to complement the government's development initiatives rather than to replace them.

The communities look for more and – if the government fails to provide it – turn to the companies instead. All too frequently, they back up their demands with violence. In the last 2 years, there has been an escalation of short term kidnappings of oil workers in Nigeria. A common theme has been demands for benefits that might reasonably have been seen as government responsibilities.

There is no single answer to such problems. Companies will need to do their utmost to ensure the security of their employees. At the same time, they will need to reinforce lines of communication with local communities, making it clear what they can and cannot realistically achieve in their social programs. This process is likely to prove both complex and time-consuming.

Security issues

Security arrangements are a second potent source of controversy.

Oil and gas employees have a right to work in a secure environment, and many companies establish their own guard teams to secure their immediate work sites and residence areas. However, they will depend on government forces for their broader security requirements, particularly in areas where there is political unrest or insurgency. If those forces are involved in real or suspected human rights abuses, the company is likely to be blamed. Companies have faced accusations of this nature in, among other countries, Nigeria and Colombia.

These accusations raise the question how far companies can or should influence government security forces. For example, the New York-based Human Rights Watch has called on BP Amoco to ensure that no soldiers involved in past human rights abuses are deputed to guard its operations. Most government forces are likely to regard any such vetting as unacceptable interference.

'Pariah' states

The final area of controversy is perhaps the most intractable. The profits from oil and gas operations frequently form a major source of income for host governments. To the extent that this revenue helps support repressive regimes, companies run the risk of being accused of complicity in government human rights abuses – even when these do not involve their operations directly. In such circumstances, should they be in the country at all? And who should decide? Such questions have arisen with regard to apartheid-era South Africa, the late Gen. Sani Abacha's Nigeria, and contemporary Myanmar.

Such questions may be tougher for petroleum companies by comparison with operations from other sectors. The investment required to finance, say, a clothing factory is much less than that required for an offshore oil rig. Once petroleum companies have moved into a country, they clearly will be reluctant to withdraw at short notice.

The classic defense for continuing to operate in so-called "pariah" states is that international commercial operations serve as a form of "constructive engagement", opening the host country to ideas and external contacts, as well as economic benefits. Total SA (France), Unocal (US), and Premier Oil PLC (UK) have presented this argument in relation to Myanmar but continue to face severe criticism from opposition leader Aung San Suu Kyi and her many foreign sympathizers.

Taking the debate forward

The debate on commercial involvement with pariah states (and on government-imposed sanctions) remains unresolved, and it would be unrealistic to expect an early consensus. Yet many of the most exciting oil and gas reserves are in complex and potentially unstable political environments. Risk-averse companies that avoid these regions completely may miss out on valuable commercial opportunities.

Meeting the political and human rights challenges will require companies to be "engaged" in the fullest sense: engaged with all sides, taking different points of view seriously, and finding innovative solutions.

There is no blanket formula for success, but the ingredients are likely to include skillful cooperation with a range of different interests at the local, national, and international levels. No company can afford to appear politically partisan; equally important, the most successful companies will be those that demonstrate a high level of diplomatic skill as well as technical expertise.

Used by permission of *Oil & Gas Journal* and Control Risks Group.

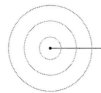

Company Profile 24
Siemens AG

Company overview

Siemens is one of the world's largest electrical engineering and electronics companies, with 1996 revenues totalling $63 billion. Siemens's businesses are in eight sectors: communication, transportation, information technology, lighting, health, energy, industry and trade, and electronic components. In 1966 Siemens & Halske AG, Siemens-Schuckertwerke AG and Siemens-Reiniger-Werke AG were consolidated to form Siemens AG. The company now operates in 193 countries and employs 379,000 people worldwide.

Brief history

In 1847 Telegraphen-Bauanstalt Siemens & Halske (Siemens & Halske Telegraph Construction Enterprise) was established by Werner Siemens, Johann Siemens and Georg Halske. In 1848 Siemens & Halske began construction of the first long-distance telegraph line in Europe, stretching from Berlin to Frankfurt. This was completed in 1849. In 1853 the company began construction of the Russian state telegraph network and continued to expand its business throughout Europe. In 1918 it developed the long-distance radio transmitter. In 1934 the company built the first Moscow Metro (subway line) in the then Soviet Union and expanded into the heavy electrical engineering business throughout Europe.

In 1951 it developed semiconductor compounds; this marked the beginning of semiconductor engineering. In 1977 Siemens and Corning Glass established Siecor Optical Cable Inc. to manufacture and distribute fibre-optic cables. Corning Glass supplied optical fibres in the US, while Siemens provided the expertise necessary to install the fibres in the cables.

At the end of 1983 the company decided to continue with the production of memory chips and introduced a private communication system called Hicom. In 1984 the system met the world standard for ISDN (Integrated Services Digital Network) and the telecommunications network of the future. In addition to voice, the system can also transmit text, images and data over existing two-wire telephone lines. In 1985 this innovative communications technology was installed in Munich. During the period 1987–96 Siemens continued to make efforts to restructure and change its corporate culture, with the goal of achieving a stronger global presence and market share.

Innovation and significant contributions

To sustain growth over 150 years Siemens has invested heavily in R&D. As a result it has come up with many significant innovations in the fields of electronics and electrical engineering. According to the company, most of the world's state-of-the-art technologies in the area of electronics and electrical engineering have links of one form or another with Siemens. The company's technology was used to connect the first direct transatlantic cable from Ireland to the US (1874), in the first electric train (1879), the first electrified elevator (1880), the first electric street lighting (1888), the first-patented X-ray tube (1896), the first recording telegraph for transmission of images (1933), the first electron microscope (1939), the first real-time ultrasound diagnostic system (1965) and the first 256-megabit memory chip (1995). The 256-megabit memory chip was developed in collaboration with IBM and Toshiba.

Challenges and opportunities

In 1997 Siemens announced its mission to become one of the most competitive firms in the world in the field of electrical and electronics engineering. It seeks to accomplish this by increasing productivity, new product innovations and changing its corporate culture to become more adaptable to the changing business environment. The latter includes the recruitment and development of a cadre of internationally oriented management personnel and mobile employees, and the implementation of new promotion and compensation programmes. Major challenges include the need to increase the speed of its innovation and to respond more rapidly to the needs of the market. To meet these new challenges and take advantage of opportunities in the future, Siemens is now testing a programme called TOP (Time Optimized Process or Turn On Power), which is designed to optimize business processes to increase productivity, promote innovation and foster growth through cultural change. To maintain and increase its future competitiveness, Siemens must sustain innovation which accommodates ecological concerns.

Rosalie L. Tung and Mohi Ahmed
Simon Fraser University

Further reading

Feldenkirchen, W. (1992) *Werner von Siemens: Inventor and International Entrepreneur*, Columbus, Ohio: Ohio State University Press. (Gives a historical overview of the company.)

Spain, P.J. and Talbot, J.R. (eds) (1995) 'Siemens AG', *Hoover's Handbook of World Business 1995–96*, Austin: the Reference Press, Inc. (Gives a general overview of the company.)

Teresko, J. (1997) 'Managing innovation for 150 years', *Industry Week* 246(23), 15 December: 101–5. (Highlights how Siemens' management of innovation has contributed to the firm's success.)

Further resources

Siemens website
http://www.siemens.de/
http://www.siemens.com

Siemens' haunted history

Data Communications; New York;
August 1999; Marguerite Reardon

Abstract:

Siemens is coming to the US with a new name, new acquisitions, and a new strategy for the 21st century. It is also coming with some baggage from the 20th. Siemens is fighting class-action lawsuits filed by survivors of the forced labor camps it built during World War II. Siemens AG has never denied the use of forced labor in its factories. What it has denied are the charges that it used such workers willingly. It also points to reparations it has made over the years as proof of its willingness to accept its share of the blame. Survivors and their descendants only won the legal right to file claims against Siemens in 1997. That has given them the ability to seek the reparations they say are due – not just what Siemens deems appropriate. The publicity could not come at a worse time for Siemens, which is in an aggressive campaign to force its way into the US telecom market. Siemens has acquired 4 US telecom startups and will do business under the name Unisphere Solutions Inc.

As the company shapes its future, it's still forced to confront its past

Siemens is coming to the U.S. with a new name, new acquisitions, and a new strategy for the 21st century. It's also coming with some baggage from the 20th. Even as the company looks to make a fresh start in telecom, Siemens is fighting class-action lawsuits filed by survivors of the forced labor camps it built during World War II. Siemens AG (Munich) has never denied the use of forced labor in its factories. What it has denied are the charges that it used such workers willingly – claiming to this day it was forced to deploy them by the Nazi government. It also points to the reparations it's made over the years as proof of its willingness to accept its share of the blame. But survivors say Siemens is portraying itself as a victim only to avoid legal culpability. "Siemens' position is naive," says George Preston, who worked at the company's Bobrek plant, near Auschwitz, from November 1943 to January 1945. "The Nazis made slaves available and Siemens realized the profit." And DATA COMM has unearthed evidence indicating Siemens did in fact take a far more active role in procuring laborers than it contends.

Still, as Siemens mounts a defense and plaintiffs make their case, a question arises: Why now? The alleged crimes took place more than a half-century ago, and most of the individuals involved in Siemens' labor program have died. What's more, the passage of time is softening attitudes among the public – and members of the industry. In a recent DATA COMM poll, most readers said that the current Siemens leadership shouldn't be held accountable for the crimes of their predecessors. "Germany can't be an economic force if you're still going back to World War II," says Jorge L. Garcia, director for telecommunications at CPM Electronics Inc. (San Diego), a telecom networking integrator. "You have to be practical."

But there's a reason the issue is back in the spotlight: Survivors and their descendants only won the legal right to file claims against Siemens in 1997. That has given them the ability to seek the reparations they say they're due – not just what Siemens deems appropriate.

It's also helped illuminate the stories of survivors, accounts that sometimes point to the tangled nature of this particular situation. Preston says working in Siemens' factories saved him from all-but-certain death in Auschwitz. "If it had not been for Siemens, I probably wouldn't be talking to you today." But he states even more plainly that he will never be able to defend Siemens for what it did. "Siemens did not come to Auschwitz for humanitarian reasons or to save lives. They were there for financial reasons. They're not heroes by any means" (see "A Survivor's Story: George Preston").

Matters of publicity

The publicity couldn't come at a worse time for Siemens, which is in the middle of an aggressive campaign to force its way into the U.S. telecom market. Earlier this year the company announced its acquisition of four U.S. telecom startups: Accelerated Networks Inc. (Moorpark, Calif.), Argon Networks Inc. (Littleton, Mass.), Castle Networks Inc. (Westford, Mass.), and Redstone Communications Inc. (Westford). The total bill: $1 billion.

The newly restructured company also will henceforth do business under the name Unisphere Solutions Inc. (Burlington, Mass.). Some wonder how much the name change is an attempt by Siemens to distance itself from the bad PR. "They are presumably hoping to mask their identity," comments William Schechter, president of William Schechter Inc. (New York), a crisis management firm specializing in advising multinational companies on public relations. "It's not a strategy I would advise. People will still make the connection."

Siemens strongly denies that it was motivated by fear of bad publicity in choosing the name. It says it's trying to establish new brand equity in the U.S. for IP innovation. And even Thomas Rambold, a member of the board of Unisphere, admits that "many people see Siemens as a slowmoving dinosaur."

But the name issue might not be Siemens' only problem, according to Schechter, who also believes its decision to fight the lawsuits could backfire. "There's a vast difference between winning in court and winning in the court of public opinion," he says. "What companies like Siemens fail to realize is that a good reputation is earned over a long period of time, but can be dashed in a moment of bad publicity."

Willing participant?

The makeover comes exactly 60 years after Siemens is alleged to have begun its forced labor program. According to roughly half a dozen class-action lawsuits currently filed in U.S. courts, the company used almost 100,000 such workers between 1939 and 1945. Plaintiffs are seeking damages on behalf of those workers, whom they claim were subject to inhumane conditions (the mortality rate in one Siemens facility – Ravensbrueck – was believed to have been 80 percent).

Where did Siemens get its workforce? From among the prisoners of at least 20 death camps set up by the Nazis including Auschwitz, Flossenberg, and Gross Rosen. Siemens also is alleged to have used not only Jewish concentration camp prisoners, but also Jews and non-Jews from occupied territories like Poland and France, as well as gypsies, homosexuals, and prisoners of war.

Siemens does not dispute the basic contentions. But it is denying all legal responsibility – with the explanation that it used forced labor under duress. "The Nazi regime gave the companies concrete goals, and if they didn't have results, they provided laborers," says Eberhard Posner, head of Siemens corporate communications. "Siemens, like the other German industrial companies, couldn't say no to the Nazis."

But evidence on file at the U.S. Holocaust Memorial Museum (Washington, D.C.) and in the National Archives II (College Park, Md.) seems to undercut this claim. It includes sworn testimony from Rudolf Hess, commandant of Auschwitz, stating that German companies only received laborers if they made specific requests. There are also the affidavits of three key Nazi officials taken at the Nuremberg trials. Oswald Pohl (head of the WVHA, the main economic and administrative office for the Nazi government), Gerhard Maurer (chief of the WVHA department that allocated and processed applications for slave labor), and Karl Sommer (who worked for Maurer) all said high-ranking Siemens employees were actively involved in the development of the forced labor program. Sommer, for instance, named Fritz Lueschen, a member of the Siemens & Halske board and an SS major, as the person he dealt with regarding applications for use of forced laborers.

Other evidence indicates that Siemens not only was involved in setting up and running the forced labor program, but also played a key role in helping define Third Reich economic policy. Declassified documents from the U.S. OSS (Office of Strategic Services, the precursor to the Central Intelligence Agency) name Lueschen

as the head of the electrical engineering commission established to make decisions concerning war production. And a memorandum published by Siemens in the summer of 1945 acknowledges that Rudolf Bingel, the general director of Siemens, was a member of the Himmlerkreiss, a group of industrial and financial leaders who advised Heinrich Himmler, head of the SS.

Denials and damages

Of course, Siemens is not the only company in history to have sidled up to the party in power. But a report prepared on May 11, 1950, by the Office of Military Government for German (OMGUS) indicated that Siemens' business boomed during the reign of Hitler. "The effect of the war was to make Siemens even more of a monopoly than it was before," the report states. It goes on to say that Siemens managed in spite of allied bombing raids to retain 87 percent of its manufacturing capacity. AEG (Allgemeine Elektricitaets Gesellschaft, Frankfurt), its nearest competitor, emerged with only about 20 percent of its former production capacity.

This would perhaps not be so important an issue except that Siemens today is claiming something much different. The company says it suffered severe financial damage during the war, losing about 80 percent of its total assets.

Of less dispute are the payments Siemens has made to living labor camp survivors. In 1961, for instance, after years of negotiations, it agreed to pay $1.8 million to compensate 2,200 Jewish laborers (this payment did not include non-Jewish forced laborers or many of the Jewish survivors living in communist countries). Such companies as BMW AG (Munich) haven't paid any reparations to former forced laborers.

But it wasn't until 1998 that Siemens announced a relief fund for all former forced laborers, promising a total payout of about $11 million. So far, about 600 applications have been processed, with individual payouts amounting to about $5,450 per person. And in February 1999, the German government and 16 companies, including Siemens, agreed to establish a national humanitarian fund: Reports say it could be worth $1.7 billion. Organizers hope the fund will be ready September 1, the 60th anniversary of the invasion of Poland. Siemens estimates that as many as 700,000 people could make claims.

Still, there are strings attached. Companies involved in this fund insist the ability of victims to make claims should be contingent on their agreement to drop all pending and potential lawsuits. They also want to be absolved of any further legal responsibility. Lawyers involved in class-action suits are negotiating with the U.S. State Department, the German government, and the companies represented in the fund in an effort to resolve these issues.

The companies' demands have predictably sparked protests from survivors, who two years ago won the right to bring claims against German businesses for the use of forced labor in World War II. That's when a German court lifted the ban established by the London Debt Agreement of 1953, which was intended to prevent a repeat of the economic crisis that war reparations caused in Germany after World War I. Plaintiffs say they won't drop their lawsuits because the proposed payments don't amount to sufficient compensation. "They should be held responsible for what they did," says Tikva Slomovic, a former Siemens laborer and one of the few female survivors of Ravensbrueck – which with barracks that had no light, heat, or sewage facilities is acknowledged as one of the harshest in the Nazi system (see "A Survivor's Story: Tikva Slomovic").

Survivors aren't just angry at what Siemens did in the past. They're also upset by its current stance. Litigants want an apology from the company, something they say it has never offered. They also want it to drop its insistence that it never voluntarily used forced laborers.

New attitudes

But survivors aren't just fighting Siemens. They're also competing against the passage of time and the realities of economics. "Life goes on," says CPM's Garcia, noting that the alternative is to carry hate "across generations." "It happened so long ago that the people responsible aren't even in the company now," says Howard Rundy, IT director for the State Liquor Commission for New Hampshire (Concord, N.H.). "It's a terrible thing, but I wouldn't base a purchasing decision on it."

Nor, apparently, would the bulk of Rundy's corporate networking colleagues. Of 229 respondents to a DATA COMM poll on ethics, only 44 said that a vendor's past war crimes would affect purchasing decisions. And 160 respondents – about 70 percent of the total – would not hold a company responsible for using forced labor in World War II. But whether Siemens acted voluntarily or not might not change the essential nature of this story. On the cusp of a new millennium, those who lived through World War II – along with those born since – are still searching for ways to make sense of its darkest moments.

A survivor's story: Tikva Slomovic

[I] was 19 years old in 1944 when my family and I were taken by the Nazis from the ghetto in Sighet, Hungary, and transported to the death camp at Auschwitz. Everything we had owned was stolen or destroyed by the Nazis. When we arrived in Auschwitz they separated my sisters and me from our parents. My mother and father were sent to the crematorium. The guards took my sister's newborn baby from her arms. They were all killed.

My two sisters and I were among the 1,500 prisoners shipped to Ravensbrueck to work in the Siemens factory, where we built electrical switches for airplanes. Production was the only thing that mattered. Two shifts worked around the clock. For nearly six months, until we were liberated by the Russian army, we worked at least six days a week for 12 and 14 hours a day. We lived in fear of being punished. My younger sister had trouble finishing her work, and I used to work harder so that I could finish mine and help her. I was afraid for what the guards might do to her.

The living conditions were horrible. We didn't have light. We didn't have heat. We didn't have running water or toilets. There were six of us in one cot, and we were stacked in bunks. And the food…Once a day we were given a bowl of watery potato skin soup, and twice a week, a piece of bread. We had to walk from the barracks to the factory, and in the winter the soles of my shoes wore out. I had to wrap my feet in newspapers to cover the holes. Some people had to walk barefoot.

Even today it's painful to talk and think about. My husband needed a hearing aid, and the one that the doctor recommended was made by Siemens. Even if it's the best hearing aid available, I don't want him to have it. I don't buy anything that comes from Germany – and I certainly don't have to support a company that used me as a slave.

A survivor's story: George Preston

On August 8, 1942, I was arrested by the Nazis in Lille, France. I was 28 years old. I was put to work as a slave laborer – digging ditches, building railroads, and performing other manual labor. I was severely beaten by SS guards as well as civilian contractors. They seemed to take pleasure in beating us.

Then, in 1943, while I was a prisoner in Auschwitz, Siemens came to select skilled professionals to work in their plant manufacturing electrical components. I had earned a master's degree in electrical and mechanical engineering from the Polytechnique Institute in France, and I was a professional with 10 years of experience. Thousands of people claimed that they had technical experience, hoping to get away from the horrible smell and billowing smoke of the crematoria. I was given numerous tests and ultimately was selected as an engineer for Siemens. I was one of only six selected from Auschwitz to work in the plant at Bobrek, about 30 kilometers away.

Those of us working for Siemens were housed in Birkenau, which was a subcamp of the Auschwitz extermination camp. Birkenau was a horrible place. The man who ran it was a murderer named Bednarek. If prisoners were caught stealing a piece of bread he would make them take a cold shower and then stand outside in the freezing winter air. At one point I came down with typhus. If I hadn't been assigned to work for Siemens the SS probably would have sent me to the gas chamber. Instead, they sent me to a hospital.

Later, we were moved to a facility adjacent to the Siemens plant at Bobrek. The conditions in the Siemens camp were much more favorable. We still slept in bunks stacked on top of each other, but we had heat and enough food to survive.

As I have said before, I'm not glorifying Siemens for what it did. Siemens didn't come to Auschwitz to save Jews. If they were truly humanitarian they would have gotten us out of Auschwitz and put us somewhere where we could have lived and worked in normal conditions. I'm a professional with a master's degree in mechanical and electrical engineering. I worked 53 years for the DuPont company. I think my work was worth more than a piece of bread and a cup of soup.

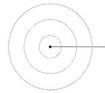

Company Profile 25
E.I. du Pont de Nemours and Company (DuPont)

Company overview

DuPont is one of the oldest industrial enterprises in the world. DuPont operates in approximately seventy countries and employs 97,000 people around the globe. About 35 per cent of DuPont's employees work outside the United States. In 1996 the company had revenues in excess of $39 billion. DuPont has 175 manufacturing and processing facilities worldwide – 140 chemicals and speciality plants, eight petroleum refineries and twenty-seven natural-gas processing plants. Its major products are chemicals, fibres, plastics, films, petroleum, healthcare products, biotechnology and composite materials.

Brief history

The company was established by a French immigrant to the US, Eleuthère Irenée du Pont de Nemours, in 1802 near Wilmington, Delaware. The company started its business in gunpowder production in 1804. In 1805 it exported its first products to Spain. Since the early 1900s DuPont has grown into a diversified chemical company specializing in synthetics. In the 1930s, with the invention and commercialization of nylon, DuPont expanded its range of products and business activities.

In 1958 DuPont began its major overseas expansion. During the 1950s and 1960s the company established subsidiaries in Europe, Latin America and the Asia-Pacific region. In the 1970s DuPont placed more emphasis on marketing and continued to grow through diversification. In 1981 DuPont purchased Conoco, a fully integrated oil, gas and coal company with operations around the world. Since the 1980s DuPont has continued its international expansion to serve local customers around the world. In 1993 DuPont acquired ICI's nylon business and ICI acquired DuPont's acrylic business. This transaction further strengthened DuPont's position in the global nylon business. In 1993–4, DuPont formed an alliance with Asahi of Japan to expand its nylon business in Asia.

Innovation and significant contributions

Starting with product innovation, DuPont has continued to create new products through R&D efforts. DuPont established the first industrial research laboratory in the United States. Its innovation in the area of synthetic materials has formed the basis of its global businesses. DuPont has made pioneering efforts to investigate the impact of chlorofluorocarbons (CFCs) on the atmosphere and introduced the first substitute compounds to replace CFC-based refrigerants. DuPont also played a leading role in establishing the Montreal Protocol to phase out CFC production. As a result, Charles J. Pedersen, a chemist at DuPont, was awarded the Nobel Prize in Chemistry.

DuPont considers its major strengths to lie in science and technology, commitment to safety, concern for people, a sense of community, an emphasis on personal and corporate integrity, a focus on the future and willingness to change. Every year DuPont spends over $1 billion on R&D. DuPont believes that the most important contributions can be made through collaboration with other companies. As a result, it has entered into collaborative R&D and joint-venture arrangements with several entities around the world, including Harvard University, Merck, Conoco and Asahi of Japan.

Challenges and opportunities

In the last decade of the twentieth century increasing attention has been paid to industrial ecology, which focuses on the interaction of industry and society with the global environment. To meet this challenge, companies have to reconsider their manufacturing strategies and come up with viable alternatives. DuPont, along with other large firms such as AT&T and General Motors, has made efforts to improve material and energy flows in its products and processes, and to implement sustainable manufacturing strategies to optimize the total materials cycle (i.e. from virgin material to finished material, product, waste products and disposals). While they pose challenges, such efforts can also create opportunities to develop new businesses, as the move towards industrial ecology fosters a cultural change within companies as well the communities they serve. According to DuPont, throughout the company's history many of its major contributions to the market have come through collaboration with other entities. DuPont will continue to collaborate on R&D efforts with other firms.

ROSALIE L. TUNG AND MOHI AHMED
SIMON FRASER UNIVERSITY

Further reading

Barnes, P. (1998) 'Industrial ecology', *Business and Economic Review* 44(2), January–March: 21–4. (Discusses industrial ecology issues and efforts undertaken by DuPont and other major companies in this regard.)

Cheape, C.W. (1995) *Strictly Business: Walter Carpenter at DuPont and General Motors*, Baltimore, MD: Johns Hopkins University Press. (A biographical account of Walter Carpenter, a former DuPont top executive.)

Colby, G. (1984) *DuPont Dynasty*, New Jersey: Lyle Stuart Inc. (Gives a detailed historical background of the company.)

Freeburn, C. (1997) 'DuPont keeps top spot', *Chemical Week* 159(48), 17 December: 20. (Discusses trends in the chemical industry.)

Kanter, R.M., Kao, J. and Wiersema, F. (eds) (1997) *Innovation: Breakthrough Thinking at 3M, DuPont, GE, Pfizer, and Rubbermaid*, New York: Harper Business. (Presents perspectives on innovations at several leading companies, including DuPont.)

Further resources

DuPont website
http://www.dupont.com

DuPont's punt

The Economist, 2 October 1999

Can the world's biggest chemicals firm embrace greenery and thrive at the same time?

TO GET a sense of the way safety is rooted in DuPont's culture, walk around the Brandywine valley in Wilmington. It was on these hills that E.I. du Pont de Nemours, a French immigrant, founded an explosives firm two centuries ago. At a time when rivals thought little about the well-being of workers, he invested heavily in safety. Factory walls were several feet thick in places, to absorb impact. Any workers found with matches were sacked on the spot. The firm used wooden railway tracks and tools, to prevent accidental sparks. The tradition of safety remains: DuPont's record is six times better than the industry average.

Chad Holliday, the current chairman of DuPont, is applying the same zeal to the environment. He no longer talks of delivering ever-bigger profits for shareholders, for example, but of "sustainable growth for stakeholders." Rather than banging the drum for increased sales volumes, he stresses the need to "reduce materials use dramatically".

In September Mr Holliday even attached numbers and dates to his environmental goals. The firm promises that fully a quarter of its revenues in 2010 will come from "non-depletable" inputs such as agricultural feedstocks – and, by implication, not from petroleum. The current share is less than 5%. The firm vows to reduce its emissions of greenhouse gases by 2010 to 65% below the levels in 1990, while keeping energy use flat. DuPont promises to do all this while maintaining returns on investors' capital in the high teens and lifting revenue growth to 6% a year, up from its recent annual average of 2%.

The energetic Mr Holliday (at 51, he is the youngest man without du Pont blood to run the firm) has already begun pursuing this greener and more profitable future. In only a year and a half at the helm, he has already hived off Conoco, the firm's oil division, and is about to complete a $10 billion takeover of Pioneer. The deal will transform DuPont into one of the world's biggest biotech firms.

This will inevitably attract protests from opponents of genetic engineering, but given that the aim is to use transgenic crops chiefly in polymers, rather than foods, Mr Holliday thinks such hostility will soon fade. Such a move will shift DuPont from dirty, depletable petroleum, the traditional bed-fellow of chemicals, toward the renewable resources of biotechnology. Indeed, DuPont prefers to call itself a "science" firm these days (it has just scrapped its pre-war motto, "Better things for better living through chemistry", for "The miracles of science").

Sceptics abound. Chemicals remain the heart of DuPont's operations – making them is still among the dirtiest of industrial processes. "I haven't seen a miracle except at Christmas," snorts one rival, "and that comes only once a year." She says her own firm thinks of voluntary environmental investment as a cost, and says it is naive to see it as a source of profits. One industry insider says "it will take a generation, not ten years, for renewables to replace a significant share of the current petrochemicals asset base."

Investors also have plenty of questions. DuPont's share price initially responded well to Mr Holliday's vision, but doubts then set in. James Wilbur of Salomon Smith Barney, an investment bank, does not really see the point of the green initiatives. He suspects that they are part of a broader strategy for DuPont to distinguish itself from its cyclical, low-growth peers so as to win a higher rating for its shares.

Mr Holliday says he understands the scepticism. He admits that his firm was for decades one of the "bad guys". Paul Tebo, its environmental boss, explains that it was a "regulations-plus kind of company": it would make only those investments in environmental quality that were required by law, along with others that led unambiguously to immediate profits. Now, say the firm's bosses, they see investment in the environment not as a burden, but as the core of a radically different way of defining growth.

Natural profits

This sort of view is usually championed by greens, not by bosses of a $25 billion chemicals firm. Amory Lovins, a well-known environmental activist, argues in "Natural Capitalism", a new book, that by promoting the efficient use of materials and insisting on clever, innovative design at every link in the value chain, firms can make more money even as they reduce their adverse environmental effects. He praises DuPont as a visionary firm that will change the behaviour of its competitors.

DuPont would be thrilled. One example of its new initiatives is its pledge to reduce what it calls the "environmental footprint" of all its businesses. To that end, the firm has changed the criteria on which managers are assessed, to include measures of green impacts. This has increased the efficiency of its use of raw materials. A decade ago, the firm's average materials yield was about 75% – ie, every pound of raw material yielded only three-quarters of a pound of goods. Now, the materials yield for products such as Lycra, a $2 billion business in its own right, is well above 90%. Mr Holliday wants to see that ratio climb across the firm, and he wants any waste that remains to be recycled. Inspired by the firm's commitment to "zero safety incidents", he says the goal is "zero waste and zero emissions."

As well as abolishing waste, the firm also wants to "dematerialise" its products. On the face of it there is something odd about a materials firm advocating less use of materials. Yet DuPont points to the example of its car-paints business: because it makes money by painting cars for car makers, it shares their incentive to sell less paint.

Mr Holliday explains the apparent paradox by pointing to the semiconductor industry: "Those firms make ever smaller products, but because they deliver more benefits they make bigger profits overall." Indeed, he sees Intel as a model of the "knowledge-based" firm that he wants DuPont to become. A good example is the polyester-films group, another billion-dollar business. Films have been getting thinner, but because they have been getting stronger and better, customers are willing to pay more for them. Whereas a film that is 0.9 microns thick sells for $170 a pound, for example, a 2 micron film fetches only $30 a pound.

Yet transforming DuPont into a green paragon will not be easy. One ingredient of success may lie on the estate where du Pont built his factory. The magnificent mansion that sits atop one of those hills is the founder's most telling commitment to safety. Du Pont was so sure that his factory would not blow up that he lived within a stone's throw of the works. If Mr Holliday wants to convince the world that DuPont is becoming green, perhaps he should consider living downwind from its dirtiest smokestack.

Company Profile 26
Corning Inc.

Company overview

Corning Incorporated (Corning) is one of the world's major manufacturers of diversified products and services. Its major products and services include optical fibre, cable, high-performance glass, components for television, electronic displays for communication and communication-related industries, advanced materials for the scientific, life sciences and environmental markets, and consumer products. The company values 'quality, integrity, performance, leadership, innovation, independence, and the individuals'. These values, in turn, contribute to the overall success of the company. Corning operates fifty affiliates in sixteen countries and employs about 20,000 people worldwide. The headquarters of the company is located in Corning, New York. The 1996 revenues of Corning exceeded $4 billion.

Brief history

The history of Corning began in 1851 when Armory Houghton started a business in Cambridge, Massachusetts. In 1854 he founded the Union Glass Company in Somerville, Massachusetts. Houghton later sold his interest in Union Glass and bought the Brooklyn, New York, based Flint Glass Company. In 1868 the company was relocated to Corning, New York, and renamed Corning Flint Glass Company. In 1875 the company was incorporated as Corning Glass Works. After its initial contact with the inventor Thomas Edison in 1880, the company began to produce the first blank (the glass part of a lightbulb) for incandescent lamps. From its beginning, the company has established a tradition of technological innovation. In 1989 the company changed its name to Corning Incorporated.

Innovation and significant contributions

In 1908 Corning established its first research laboratory, one of the earliest in the United States. In 1909 it began to produce heat-resistant glass for railway lanterns. Corning continued to innovate. Some of its major innovations are new glasses with X-radiation shielding and ultraviolet absorbing compositions (1916); the world's largest piece of glass, cast for the 200-inch telescope mirror on Palomer Mountain in California (1934); photochromatic spectacle lenses (1968); spacecraft windows, fibre optics, computer memories and integrated circuits

(1969); fibre for use in transmitting voice, video and data signals with laser beams (1971).

In 1984 a total quality management system was introduced and the Quality Institute was established. In 1991 Corning collaborated with Mitsubishi Electric Corporation of Tokyo to manufacture the world's largest mirror blank for Japan National Large Telescope on Mount Mauna Kea in Hawaii. In 1991 the company was selected as one of the major suppliers for Japan's Nippon Telephone and Telegraph's (NTT) Track III high-count optical-fibre cable development project in Japan. According to Corning, as a result of this project the company will install cabled fibre in every Japanese home and business by 2015. In 1993 Corning was selected by AT&T as the supplier of fibre-optic couplers for the next generation of undersea telecommunications system.

MCI Communications Corporation also collaborated with Corning to use dispersion-shifted optical fibre throughout the United States. Corning is the first optical-fibre manufacturer to sign a long-term supply agreement with several Russian cable manufacturers. In 1994 Corning was awarded the National Medal of Technology by the US President. The company's telecommunications products division won the Malcolm Baldridge National Quality Award in 1995.

Challenges and opportunities

Continuous improvement and better understanding and anticipation of customer needs are some of the major challenges for Corning. According to the company, to meet its challenges and to create new opportunities Corning has identified eight areas which it seeks to improve upon. The first five dimensions relate to how the company runs its businesses and the subsequent three pertain to how the company works. The areas are:

1   customer focus (anticipate and respond to customer needs);
2   result-oriented (customers keeps the company focused);
3   forward looking (perspectives on sustaining competitive advantage);
4   entrepreneurial (anticipate market need and promote ideas to market);
5   rigorous (clear communication and disciplined processes);
6   open (foster continuous learning);
7   engaging (involvement with customers for better solutions);
8   enabling (enable people to share information and involve the right people to make the correct decisions).

Rosalie L. Tung and Mohi Ahmed
Simon Fraser University

Further reading

Ackerman, R. (1997) 'After reengineering', *Executive Excellence* 14(5), May: 9. (Presents the views of Roger Ackerman, Corning's chairman, on why the company is successful.)

Hideo, F. (1992) 'History of optical fiber cable R&D in Japan', *Japan 21st*, 37(3), March: 53–6. (Discusses Japanese perspectives on R&D in optical-fibre communications systems and profiles key players in this sector, including Corning Inc.)

Hoover, G., Campbell, A. and Spain, P.J. (eds) (1995) 'Corning Incorporated', *Hoover's Handbook of American Business*, Austin: The Reference Press, Inc. (Gives a general overview of the company.)

LaPlante, A. and Alter, A.E. (1994) 'Corning Inc.: the stage-gate innovation process', *Computer World* 28(44), 31 October: 81. (Traces Corning's experiences in using the state-gate innovation decision method.)

Stoner, J. and Werner, F. (1994) *Managing Finance for Quality: Bottom-line Results from Top-level Commitment*, Milwaukee: ASQC Quality Press. (Discusses quality management at Corning, with a focus on finance.)

Further resources

Corning website
http://www.corning.com

The Dow Corning crisis: A benchmark

Public Relations Quarterly; Rhinebeck; Summer 1999; Katie LaPlant

Abstract:

The Dow Corning silicone breast implant crisis has become a benchmark of how not to handle a crisis. There are a number of valuable lessons learned from this particular crisis. Dow Corning's communications approach during the crisis is broken down into 3 time periods and examined. The communications strategies the company utilized during each stage are critiqued. In a crisis that involves public health and safety, the interest of the public should be the overriding concern. By denying fault, attacking their accusers and showing little sympathy to the alleged victims, Dow Corning did serious damage to its reputation and livelihood.

When you think of benchmark cases in crisis management, certain names come to mind immediately. Johnson & Johnson's handling of the Tylenol crisis is a superb example of crisis management and has become a benchmark of how to handle a crisis. The Dow Corning silicone breast implant crisis has become a benchmark of how not to handle a crisis. There are a number of valuable lessons learned from this particular crisis. Both crises dealt with public health and safety issues, but both were handled very differently. Because of this, Dow Corning's reputation and image suffered considerably.

As a result, Dow Corning is still suffering today from a crisis that began in the late 1980s. The company filed Chapter 11 bankruptcy in 1995 and is undergoing major corporate changes to recover from the crisis. Much of this irreparable damage began small and could have been contained. The very first lawsuit filed against Dow Corning for faulty implants was in 1977. This means company officials were aware that there would be problems over a decade before the actual crisis occurred. Issues management could have played a key role in detecting this problem.

Dow Corning is accused of manufacturing unsafe silicone implants and marketing them to the public, even though company officials knew they had potential to be dangerous to women's health. Thousands of women have filed claims against Dow Corning saying their ruptured silicone breast implants were the cause for very serious health problems. As of now, there is no conclusive scientific data that supports or denies this claim. "Upwards of 20 studies have failed to find a statistical correlation between silicone implants and the so-called auto-immune diseases they supposedly cause." With scientific evidence on their side, the company believed that its main defense of relying on that evidence was sound and rational. The public's perception during times of crisis is not rational, therefore; the public didn't accept the scientific evidence.

This crisis put Dow Corning's entire livelihood and reputation at stake. In fact, the mountain of lawsuits filed against the company forced it to leave the breast implant business. Dow Corning recently filed a bankruptcy reorganization plan and hopes to be able to recover by 1999.

The immediate impact of the crisis hit fast and hard. Highly publicized lawsuits and relentless negative media coverage casting Dow in an unfavorable light were overwhelming to the company, in spite of the fact that a crisis plan was in place. In a 1997 interview with The Public Relations Strategist, current CEO Dick Hazelton said, "The crisis plan, frankly, was overwhelmed by the facts and circumstances. The fundamental elements of the plan were to be open, state the scientific facts as we believed them to be, and to not hide anything. In theory, the plan was fine. But in practice, the crisis plan was inadequate for the intensity of what we saw in those early days."

This case study analyzes Dow Corning's communication approach during the crisis, broken down into three time periods. The communications strategies the company utilized during each stage will be critiqued.

Stage 1

In the first stage, July–September 1991, some of Dow Corning's most crucial mistakes were made. The onset of a crisis is when a company must appear the strongest and most in control to the public. Dow Corning's strategy was to rely on the scientific evidence and use that information as its only defense in its limited public statements. The company was not very open with the media, which fueled the crisis even more. When company statements were made, they were given by a variety of different spokespeople. During this time period, Dow Corning's publics needed 'one voice' from the company. The lack of sympathy in the company statements did nothing to improve its image either. This only added to the public perception of 'the huge company against sick and frightened women.' "Dow Corning has failed to be straightforward with its

publics, primarily with the FDA, plastic surgeons, and all silicone breast implant recipients."

Two of the biggest publics Dow Corning did not deal with properly were the media and the Food and Drug Administration (FDA). These two publics did the most damage to the company's public image and reputation. Dow Corning attacked the FDA in an effort to shift the public's attention away from the fact that it was demanding damaging internal documents to be released by the company. This did little to help Dow Corning's public image. By making the FDA struggle to get the internal documents, Dow Corning made a powerful adversary. "This stance accomplished little in restoring Corning's public image, but played a significant role in escalating the tensions between the company and the FDA." The company also treated the media in the same way. Refusal to release information and not making their executives available for questioning increased the negative media coverage.

Stage 2

During the second stage, September 1991–February 1992, Dow Corning continued to attack the FDA and deny accusations that its breast implants were unsafe. When the FDA put a moratorium on breast implants, Dow Corning agreed to do more testing on its product to assure the public of their safety. Several other actions were taken during this time period to improve its public image. First, CEO Lawrence Reed was replaced with Keith McKennon. Reed was not perceived as very media savvy and was creating more problems with the FDA and public. McKennon was a seasoned

Dow Chemical veteran who got the company through the Agent Orange crisis during the 1960s and 1970s. One of McKennon's first actions was to bring in an unbiased third party (former Attorney General Griffin Bell) to conduct an independent investigation of the silicone breast implants. Also, an implant hotline was set up during this time period for women concerned about breast implant safety. This effort backfired, however, when it was shut down by the FDA for giving out misleading information. Dow Corning reacted to the FDA shutting down the hotline with denial and attacks. The company claimed the FDA didn't understand what the hotline was trying to accomplish.

Stage 3

The final stage of the crisis, February 1992–present, was the most favorable for the company's public image. During this time period, Dow Corning accepted a certain amount of responsibility for the problems with the silicon implants and took corrective action. The company did not admit that the breast implants were unsafe. Internal documents questioning the safety of the implants were released to the public in an attempt to gain more credibility. The documents were accepted, but the company's failure to be more forthcoming earlier in the crisis didn't go unnoticed.

Dow Corning took two major steps during this stage; it left the breast implant business and eventually declared bankruptcy. "Their strategies did not accomplish the goal of re-framing the company's public portrait. Rather, they contributed to the decline of an image already crumbling under the weight of FDA and media attacks." Although these actions were perceived as "too little, too late," they did limit the amount of continued damage.

The Dow Corning crisis is a benchmark case that demonstrates valuable public relations lessons. "Early on, the company lost sight of the most basic crisis management tenet: In the pitched battle between perceptions and reality, perception usually wins." In a crisis that involves public health and safety, the interest of the public should be the overriding concern. By denying fault, attacking their accusers and showing little sympathy to the alleged victims, Dow Corning did serious damage to its reputation and livelihood.

© *Public Relations Quarterly* Summer 1999.